The TRIUMPH [...]

THE TRIUMPH TREE

Scotland's Earliest Poetry, 550-1350

🎜

edited by
THOMAS OWEN CLANCY

Translations and Notes by
Gilbert Márkus (Latin), Joseph P. Clancy (Welsh),
Thomas Owen Clancy (Gaelic, Old English)
Paul Bibire (Norse), Judith Jesch (Norse)

🎜

CANONGATE
CLASSICS
86

First published as a
Canongate Classic in 1998 by
Canongate Books, 14 High Street,
Edinburgh EH1 1TE.

Introduction copyright © Thomas Owen Clancy
and contributors 1998.

The publishers gratefully acknowledge subsidy
from the Scottish Arts Council towards the
publication of this volume.

Set in 10pt Plantin by Hewer Text Ltd, Edinburgh.
Printed by Clays Ltd, St Ives plc.

1

British Library Cataloguing-in-Publication Data
A catalogue record for this book is available
on request from the British Library.

ISBN 0 86241 787 2

CONTENTS

PREFACE

Over the past decade, the commitment and enthusiasm of scholars such as Kenneth Elliot and groups such as Capella Nova have begun to restore a sense of Scotland's early music to an appreciative public. Names such as that of Robert Carver, or the Inchcolm Antiphoner, once unknown to all but a few, now attract large and excited audiences to hear their works performed. We hope to restore in a similar way, if not one suited to the CD, a sense of Scotland's early poetry. The first eight centuries of the poetry of Scotland is not so much forgotten as unrecorded and uncollected. What is contained in this anthology is the first collection of the poetry composed by poets working in Scotland or working for Scottish patrons, or composed by poets of Scottish origin working for patrons elsewhere, in the period before 1350. It is an omnivorous collection, and by virtue of the period it covers, is in origin a multilingual and multicultural one. Although we present the poetry here only in English translations, it has been translated out of five different languages: Latin, Welsh, Gaelic, Old English and Norse.

Much of this poetry has long been known to scholars of the various medieval languages involved, but seldom has it been viewed in a Scottish context. We hope that assembling this poetry, as we have, in chronological order, mixing the various different poetic traditions, will allow a new sense of Scotland's unique and complex past to emerge, as well as providing a window on the thoughts and sensibilities, the imagery and ideals of earlier medieval Scotland.

The origins of the poetry, the reasons for its previous neglect, and our criteria for inclusion are set out in the introduction, alongside a fairly full treatment of the historical background, and notes on the various poetic traditions represented here. Real evaluation of the strength of some these traditions is still necessary – we hope this anthology may spur scholars to further research, and to provide editions, both new and initial, for some of this poetry. For those who want to follow the texts up further, we have included fairly full referencing to the sources used and further discussions.

This is also a period for which often our only or best historical source is poetry. The background to the long elegy series *The Gododdin* can only be inferred from the poem itself; Norse saga writers themselves drew heavily on the skaldic verse here translated to form their histories. As such, we also hope that this anthology may provide a convenient resource for these primary texts, and that reading them free of excessive historical commentary, not chopped into little sections, will allow scholars and students to come to terms with the texts in a new light. We also hope that the essential literary quality of these texts will thereby be better appreciated.

But most of all, this is an anthology for the general reader and the student, to allow a glimpse into the literary past of Scotland. Although no doubt much of the poetry here would benefit from more detailed commentary than we have been able to provide, we offer the collection to all who are willing to enter often different, sometimes strange worlds of image and allusion. Immersion is the best plan, though there is poetry here for dipping one's toes in also. To help readers find their way through the allusions to names and places, we have provided a fairly full glossary of place-names and personal names at the back, and have also provided a pronunciation guide for the Welsh and Gaelic names. We hope that this will allow readers to experience this poetry, translated though it is, as it is best experienced: read aloud.

As editor and instigator of the anthology, I owe some debts of gratitude. First, to Hugh Andrew of Canongate Books, whose ideas met happily with mine to generate the project, and whose patience with the backsliding tendencies of academics has been gracious indeed. Next, to many friends and colleagues who have been supportive throughout work on the project, most especially Roibeard Ó Maolalaigh, Dauvit Broun, Simon Taylor, Katherine Forsyth, Steve Driscoll, and Alex Woolf. I must thank Alex also for help with, and additional notes on, the historical background to some of the Norse poetry, and for his constant stream of stimulating ideas. William Gillies gave valuable advice at the infancy of this project, and I hope that what has resulted measures up at least partly to his standards. Donald Meek kindly allowed me a preview of his edition of the poem on Eoin mac Suibhne's voyage to Castle Sween, and allowed me use of it as the basis of my translation. Donald Watt, during a dinner in Aberdeen, along with Simon Taylor, dropped a casual remark which allowed us to include a whole range of poems which would otherwise have been omitted. On a more personal level, my wife, Anne Goldie, my in-laws, Jim and Joan Goldie, and my mother, Gertrude Clancy have given moral support even in the doldrums of the project.

But my greatest debt is without doubt to my fellow translators. The original idea was my own, its undoubted flaws are to be laid at my door, and the criteria for selection is largely my responsibility, and I must thank my four team members for their patience with what may have seemed eccentric choices as well as excess demands. Their translations are all models of the literal rendered poetic. Each demands a particular note of gratitude: Gilbert Márkus, for his unflagging friendship and encouragement; Judith Jesch, for heroically stepping in on some of the longer Norse poems and the Norse introduction to redeem a fractured timetable, producing elegant and exciting translations in record time; Paul Bibire, for his instant last-minute production of translations of poems which had escaped our net; and above all, my father, Joseph Clancy, for submitting himself to the curious experience of being edited by his much less competent son, and for inadvertently and obliquely, quite some time ago, starting the whole thing off.

THOMAS OWEN CLANCY
Glasgow
The Feast of St Dúnchad of Iona
25 May 1998

NOTES ON THE TRANSLATORS

Paul Bibire has taught and researched Old Norse at the University of St Andrews, and presently teaches at the University of Cambridge. He lives in Crail.

Joseph P. Clancy is a poet and has translated extensively from Welsh literature, most recently the stories of Kate Roberts, and the poems of Saunders Lewis and Alun Llywelyn Williams. Emeritus Professor of English Literature and Theatre Arts at Marymount Manhattan College in New York City, he now lives in Aberystwyth.

Thomas Owen Clancy is a poet and lecturer in the Department of Celtic at the University of Glasgow, author of articles on numerous aspects of early medieval Celtic studies, and co-author, with Gilbert Márkus, of *Iona: The Earliest Poetry of a Celtic Monastery*.

Judith Jesch is Reader in Viking Studies at the University of Nottingham, and author of *Women in the Viking Age* and numerous articles on skaldic poetry, sagas and runic inscriptions, and co-editor of *The Viking Age in Caithness, Orkney and the North Atlantic*.

Gilbert Márkus OP is Honorary Research Fellow in the Department of Celtic at the University of Glasgow, and Catholic Chaplain to the University of Strathclyde. He is author of numerous articles on early Gaelic Christianity, and most recently translator of *Adomnán's 'Law of the Innocents': Cáin Adomnáin*.

INTRODUCTION

THE ANTHOLOGY

This book has an ambitious aim. We wish to restore eight centuries of Scotland's literary heritage, lost or neglected by modern scholars and anthologists, and virtually unknown to the general public. Most anthologies of Scottish poetry, and indeed most discussions of Scottish literature, begin with the 14th century. They do this largely because the approach to our literary history has for long been Anglocentric, concentrating on the English-language tradition of Scotland, and that of its northern cousin, lowland Scots. Only in the 14th century, with the work of John Barbour and his contemporaries, does Scots begin to be recorded and used as a major literary language in Scotland. Coincidentally, that century really sees the firm establishment of something like a national consciousness about the kingdom of the Scots, and so it has seemed to most writers to be an appropriate place to begin to examine Scottish literature and history.

In beginning there, however, anthologists and critics are starting in the middle of the story, and have certainly been guilty of treating the centuries before as if they contained nothing of note. Of the major anthologies of Scottish poetry over the past century, only Hugh MacDiarmid's remarkable *Golden Treasury of Scottish Poetry* acknowledges the rich early medieval body of Gaelic verse, though it does not include translations of it. With that anthology alone does ours overlap, by one poem, the early Scots song on the death of Alexander III. MacDiarmid's collection was also notable in being the first to give due weight to Gaelic and Latin, alongside Scots and English. More recently, Roderick Watson's *The Poetry of Scotland, Gaelic, Scots and English* has given due place to Gaelic. *The Mercat Anthology of Early Scottish Poetry, 1375-1707*, has an inexplicable neglect of Gaelic and Latin verse, though it balances Scots and English in its chosen period more fairly.

All these anthologies share in their neglect of the period before 1350. As the existence and size of our collection hopefully suggests, this is not a small oversight. Although some critics have made nods in the direction of later Latin poets in Scotland, there is little excuse for the omission of well-known Latin poems of Scottish provenance, such as those by the early Iona poets, or the rousing Glaswegian *Song on the Death of Somerled*. Some critics

5

have acknowledged the existence of *The Gododdin* as a Welsh poem from early medieval Scotland (indeed, MacDiarmid wrote a long meditation on it), but have often treated it as a dead end. No one has really given proper due to the substantial remains of Gaelic and Norse poetry which survive from the early medieval period. We aim to redress this situation.

The collection

There are, it should be said, some very good reasons for the general neglect of the literature contained here. First, there is the problem of language. The Scots and English traditions from the 14th century onwards are relatively accessible to the modern speaker of either language, whereas before then we are dealing with a poetic legacy in five different and, in some cases, very difficult languages. The native peoples of southern Scotland, the northern Britons, were composing and evidently recording poetry in a language which we shall call Welsh (it is often, more accurately, called Cumbric or northern British), from the middle of the sixth century. This poetry provides our best evidence for the warfare against the incoming English of the east which gradually ate away at British territory and the strength of the Welsh language here. The colonising English, who established control over much of the eastern Borders and Lothian, as well as Dumfriesshire and Galloway, have left records of their poetry in both Old English and Latin, largely from the south-western region. It is their dialect of English which, combined with many other influences, would evolve into the Scots of the later medieval period and become one of Scotland's modern national literary languages.

Benorth the Forth, the native peoples whose language, Pictish, was fairly closely related to the Welsh spoken by the northern Britons, have left us no poetry in their own tongue. Indeed, they have left little of their language at all. Nonetheless, some poetry composed for Pictish kings survives. This poetry is in Gaelic, the language which expanded along with the growth in influence both of the rulers of the Gaelic region of Dál Riata (more or less the same as modern Argyll) and also of the Christian church, which was brought to the Picts largely by Gaelic speakers. We have poetry in Gaelic composed in a Scottish context going back to the very end of the sixth century. By the ninth century, Gaelic speakers had taken political control of the Pictish territories, and Gaelic began its steady expansion to become, by the 11th century, spoken nearly the length and breadth of what is now Scotland.

Nearly. Not in Orkney or Shetland, which had become during

6

the ninth century hubs of a colony established by Scandinavians, whose influence and whose language, Old Norse, at times extended right down the western seaboard of Scotland, to the Isle of Man and into Ireland. Not until 1266 would the western isles become politically part of the kingdom of Scots, and Orkney and Shetland remained outside it for the whole period this anthology covers. The mixing of Gaels and Norse speakers is evident in much of the later Gaelic poetry contained here, and gave Scottish Gaelic much of its distinctiveness. But Orkney for a time was a centre for the composition of fine, intricate court poetry.

Throughout the period of this anthology, poets were composing in Latin. The first and last poems in our collection are Latin ones, and we have Latin verse composed by native speakers of all the other languages discussed. Through the church, it was the common language of intellectual exchange and worship, here as throughout medieval Europe. Because of the diversity of the origins of the poets writing in Latin, and because Latin verse was used for some extremely common or garden purposes in the Middle Ages, it is harder to speak of a unified Latin poetry tradition here. Nonetheless, the continuing composition of liturgical, historical, narrative and instructive verse in Latin is an important part of the Scottish literary past.

Finally, we should note here a sixth poetic language for Scotland, Old French. The long verse narrative called *Fergus of Galloway* was almost certainly composed in Scotland, though its language is a northern French dialect. It reminds us that before Scots became a language of law and national expression in Scotland, French had supplanted Gaelic as the language of court for the later medieval Scottish kings. We have not included it here, both because of its length, and because a fine modern translation exists, that by D.D.R. Owen, published by Everyman.

This linguistic diversity is a formidable obstacle to the compilation of an anthology of poetry for the early period, partly because of the lack of knowledge even on the part of experts in one linguistic tradition about literature in the others. And so we have come together as a team of translators, each with our own linguistic speciality, to produce this volume. We hope thereby to have provided as wide a range of expertise and reference as possible. Although we have not included the originals, for reasons of space and the complexity of producing proper editions for the vast array of poetry contained here within a reasonable timespan, we hope that the fact that each translator has, by and large, been responsible for one linguistic tradition will give the poems in each language a consistent flavour beyond what is contained in the contents and structures of the poems themselves.

The array of different languages and poetic traditions presents other problems besides that of the translations themselves. Identifying the poetry contained here was in itself a hard task. That is because each of the poetic traditions is not exclusively Scottish, but shared with another country or countries. So, for instance, the early poetry of the northern British kingdoms, such as the long poem called *The Gododdin*, is central to the literary tradition and history of Welsh, and the poem belongs as much to Wales as to Scotland; the only manuscript of the poem is a Welsh one, which resides in Cardiff Free Library. To speak of it as a Scottish poem is not in any way to deny its equal importance as a Welsh one. So too the Old English poem *The Dream of the Rood*, earliest attested in stone on the Ruthwell Cross in Dumfriesshire. It is one of the masterpieces of Anglo-Saxon literature, and belongs in anthologies of that literature in many ways more than in this. Yet that can lead us to overlook the fact that it, and no doubt many now lost poems like it, were part of the literary heritage of southern Scotland.

This situation becomes even more confusing when we turn to the Gaelic and Norse material. For both of these traditions, the cultural centre, the place where poets were trained, the root and origin of their repertoire of allusions and history, was not Scotland, but the respective homelands of Ireland and Scandinavia. Poets travelled to and fro, poets from Scotland composed for Irish patrons, Irish poets composed for Scottish, or indeed Pictish, patrons. Skaldic verse was composed for rulers with territories in both Norway and the west, or by Icelanders for Orkney earls. In this context, sorting out poetry which can reasonably be considered to 'belong' in some sense to Scotland's literary past is extremely difficult. Take the case of the early poetry attributed to, and also addressed to, Columba. Much of this probably originates or was preserved in the prime Columban monastery of Iona, yet many of the monks of that monastery, and much of its patronage, came from Ireland. A poem addressed to Columba, unless it has some specific referent to locate it in Iona or Scotland, is as likely to be of Irish origin as Scottish. We have had to be cautious in approaching the vast catalogue of poetry concerning Columba, and have tried to include only ones which seemed strongly connected in one way or another with Scotland.

So marking out the criteria for what has been included in this collection was difficult, and it must be admitted that the exact

8

boundaries for admission remained somewhat permeable. We have included all the poetry we knew of from the period before 1350 which was written by poets from what is now Scotland, or resident in or working for patrons who lived in Scotland. Thus we have included the Scottish-born poet Gille-Brighde Albanach, although he wrote exclusively for Irish patrons, but we included also the Irish poet who sent a poem to the king of the Isles, Aenghus Mac Domhnaill, though he admits he never crossed the sea. In some cases we have also included poetry with a Scottish theme, such as the Gaelic poem on Arran, the provenance of which is completely obscure.

Our definition of 'Scotland' has been the territory of modern Scotland, rather than any more restricted medieval delineation. This is because we are interested in the literary heritage of all the regions of modern Scotland, not simply the core kingdom which later expanded to fill the modern boundaries. In two cases, however, we have strayed beyond Scotland's modern borders, and have included poetry pertaining to the Isle of Man and Cumbria. There are good reasons for doing so. In both cases, during certain periods, each place belonged to a greater whole which included much Scottish territory. So the Isle of Man was part of, indeed was the centre of, an extensive sea-kingdom which stretched as far north as Lewis. Cumbria, at least its northern part, was the centre of the British kingdom of Rheged, which extended into modern Scotland. The poetry of early Rheged is manifestly northward-looking, and was in at least some cases preserved in the kingdom of Dumbarton. In addition, both the Isle of Man and Cumbria belonged for significant periods in the central middle ages to the territory of the kings of Scots.

We have opted to be as inclusive as possible, even if on occasion we have brought a cuckoo or two into the nest. We are not, as has been stressed, laying exclusive Scottish claim to any of this poetry, and it often seemed best where a poem was relevant to Scotland or Scottish history to include it, even when its provenance might be somewhat doubtful. Part of our reason for this is that in many cases we are the first to treat these poems as part of the Scottish literary heritage – we are, in a sense, bringing the poetry to light. Some poems, indeed, have never been translated at all, and their significance has gone largely unremarked. Included in this list are some poems with clear historical significance, such as the short satirical poem on David, later king David I, and the poem on the destruction of the Columban federation c. 1210, *Columaba's Legacy*. The prayer to Columba, which prefaced a manuscript of his

9

Life, has never received an English translation; nor has Bishop Bjarni Kolbeinsson's poem on the Jomsvikings. So this anthology also acts as a resource, a first attempt to catalogue the poetic remains of early medieval Scotland and to make them accessible to an audience of general readers and professionals alike.

We have tried to justify where necessary our inclusion of poems. But we have excluded some fairly obviously Scottish material because it fell foul of our standards of poetic merit. There is a certain amount of verse – it rhymes, and only in that sense is it poetry – which we deemed too tedious for readers, and really only of interest as historical sources and not as literature. Into this category fell, for instance, the metrical list of the kings of Alba called *Duan Albanach*. So too we deemed *The Prophecy of Berchan*, the prophetic poem which also contains a list of the kings of Alba, but does contain some more juicy details about them, too long and in need of too much detailed explanation to be worth including. Earl Rogavald and the Icelander Hall Thorarinsson are jointly accredited with the composition of a long metrical teaching poem – this is fragmentary and too arcane for our collection. And although we have included many poems contained in the 15th-century Latin history of Scotland by Walter Bower, *The Scotichronicon*, we have excluded just as many, by virtue of their being mere annalistic doggerel, or because they were bad or boring. Some of these exclusions cause us regret, such as the verses on the Battle of Bannockburn, but we feel the collection is none the worse without them. Many of these excluded poems can be consulted in good modern editions and translations.

In one important sense, this poetry belongs to other countries than Scotland: very little of it was ultimately preserved here, in manuscripts of Scottish provenance. We can only speculate on the reasons for the appalling scarcity of early medieval Scottish manuscripts, though there are European regions in worse situations. Some of the poetry does come directly from Scottish contexts: the fragments of *The Dream of the Rood* preserved on the stone cross at Ruthwell, for instance, and the verse carved into the tomb at Maeshowe proclaim their provenance explicitly. The hymns and prayers to Columba from the *Inchcolm Antiphoner* come from a manuscript written on that island and now resident in Edinburgh. But the majority of poems were preserved outside Scotland, in manuscripts which ended up in Bamberg in Germany, Vercelli in Italy, Uppsala in Sweden and most of all from manuscripts copied by both Irish and Welsh scribes in the later Middle Ages and now housed in the major libraries of Ireland,

Wales and England. Only in a few instances, where good modern editions did not exist, have we gone back to the manuscripts of the poems themselves. For the most part, we have based our translations of these poems on earlier editions, and are indebted to the work of countless scholars of preceding generations and of the present one whose work has made the poetry available at least to the scholarly world, if not to wider audiences.

Some of this poetry has been frequently translated before, but it is hoped that the new translations provided here have merits that go beyond merely appearing alongside other Scottish material. Joseph Clancy's translation of *The Gododdin* supersedes his translation of 1970, and has the distinction of being the only translation thus far to present the poetry as it appears in the manuscript, rather than following a reconstructed edition based on scholarly theories of what the 'original' poem looked like. Gilbert Márkus's translation of *The Miracles of Bishop Nynia* presents the work for the first time as a poem, making much of its rhetorical nature more readily observable. Readers familiar with earlier translations of the poem on Arran, or Muireadhach Albanach's lament for his wife will find here, hopefully, translations which respect the poetry of the originals in form and feeling, while remaining as faithful as possible to the literal meaning.

That has been the standard we have tried to attain throughout: close compliance with original structure; some semblance of the poetry and tone of the originals; and faithfulness to meaning. We have no doubt frequently failed on some of these counts, and often had to weigh up the merits of sacrificing one for another. Nevertheless, we all are convinced that prose translations, while sometimes (though not always) conveying good strict literal sense, as often conceal as much as they reveal, and so we have tried to produce in our translations something that reads like poetry, something which you can enjoy reading out loud, or shouting in the shower, translations you can chew on. Something will always be lost in any case. We can only hope that some readers' enjoyment of this poetry will spur them to learn the languages in which they were composed, so that they can enjoy the originals in all their beauty and complexity. Meanwhile, we hope that all readers will be able to taste the flavour of the poems in what we have provided.

The historical context
Although this volume is called *Scotland's Earliest Poetry*, Scotland as a real concept hardly existed for much of the period it covers.

The poetry contained here belongs to a multicultural Scottish past, and one that may benefit from some historical scene-setting. There is obviously not the space here for a full-scale history of early medieval Scotland, and what we attempt to set out is an outline which makes the poetry more explicable.

To the Northumbrian monk and scholar Bede, writing around 731, Britain could be divided along political lines which corresponded closely to the four linguistic groups of the island. This was doubly true for northern Britain, and for the area which modern Scotland now occupies. Four linguistic and cultural zones jostled for power, overlapped, exchanged ideas and royal marriage partners, fought battles and wrote poetry. British kingdoms and Pictish kingdoms, made up of natives of Britain, filled the regions of the south and west, and the north and east respectively. In the north-west, Gaels were expanding from their base in Argyll into Pictish territory, and in the south-east the incoming English conquered ever more territory from the British.

Britain had been, before the Roman conquest of its southern half, a patchwork of tribes or kingdoms, apparently unified by language and broad cultural similarities. By the end of Roman rule, in the fifth century AD, those British peoples far outside Roman rule seem to have coalesced into a separate polity, with their own dialect of what must once have been a common tongue: these were the Picts with their Pictish language, still only poorly understood by modern scholars. From the Forth south, the tribes spoke British, and were at least influenced by Roman rule, identifying closely with their more Romanised southern neighbours. Both Pict and Briton shared certain ways of organising society, however. The fifth century saw the growth of small military aristocracies, partly in response to external threat, but also in response to the internal instability of Britain.

Some of the poetry from northern Britain which begins to be preserved from the sixth century on implies that the Picts and Britons shared the same political and cultural space. A poem attributed to Taliesin praises King Gwallawg by stating that his reputation stretches as far as Pictland (Prydyn):

> In Prydyn, in Eidyn, they confess,
> In Gafran, all about Brecheinawg,
> Embattled, in sturdy war-gear,
> Who's not seen Gwallawg won't have seen a man.

Much of Taliesin's poetry makes clear too the nature of the society which had succeeded Roman Britain, one based on raiding other kingdoms and redistributing the wealth among the retainers of the warleader. Poets like Taliesin lived by the spoils of war, and much of their praise is for their kingly patrons as great fighters, generous givers and strong leaders.

Some of his poetry, however, gives us glimpses of a new people on the scene in northern Britain, the English. They began to invade and settle in Britain from as early as the fourth century, growing probably out of a mixture of settled Germanic soldiers and mercenaries and raiding parties. These peoples, identified by the Romans and Britons as 'Saxons', are the people who lie historically behind England and the English language. We have good evidence for their establishment of settlements in the north by the sixth century. In time, kingdoms were created within the shells of earlier British territories, principally Deira in modern-day Yorkshire, and Bernicia, based on Bamburgh.

Taliesin, in poems like *The Battle of Argoed Llwyfain*, paints a vivid picture of warfare between incoming English armies and the native British, especially under his patron Urien of Rheged, and Urien's son Owain, called 'bane of the east' for his prowess in fighting the English. The poems which depict such battles seem to go beyond those which exult the king's raids against neighbouring British kingdoms. Although in many ways both English and British societies were similar, some things may well have set them strongly apart, particularly language and religion (the English were still pagan at this stage). Nothing else quite equals the gory, yet somehow beautiful, image of triumph in *The Lament for Owain son of Urien*, where Owain is praised for having mown down the army of the English (Lloegr) and their leader Fflamddwyn, the 'Fire-bringer':

> When Owain cut down Fflamddwyn,
> No more to it than sleeping:
> Asleep is Lloegr's broad war-band
> With light upon their eyes.

The most important work depicting the warfare between English and British kingdoms in the sixth century is undoubtedly Aneirin's long poem, or series of poems, called *The Gododdin*. It describes, by means of a circling concatenation of laments, the utter defeat of a raiding party of British warriors drawn mainly from the kingdom of the Gododdin, based on Edinburgh. The defeat happened at Catterick, in Yorkshire, but we do not know when, or much of the circumstances, outside of the poem's description of it. Still, it is a vivid realisation of the violence of the time, the masculine, warrior values of the kings, their courts and their poets. It is also an icon of the direction in which the struggle was going against the ever-expanding English kingdoms, soon to be joined together as Northumbria. It is an icon of defeat, of loss of territory, of the passing of an age for the British in the eastern lowlands of Scotland.

That said, it is pretty clear from a number of different traditions, including that recounted in the later poem cycle *The Fall of Rheged*, that the kingdom of Rheged, so rousingly praised by Taliesin, met its downfall not through English incursions but through internecine British rivalries. Gwallawg, king of an unidentified region in the north, and subject of two more Welsh poems attributed to Taliesin, was by tradition one of those who conspired in its king's death, and may have benefited from it. Nonetheless, the end of Rheged and Gododdin meant that by the middle of the seventh century much of what is now Cumbria and the south-eastern Borders of Scotland was within English power. That power continued to grow under a series of capable and expansionist kings, until by the 680s the kings of Northumbria held much of northern Britain, including some of the Pictish lands benorth the Forth, subject to them.

The battle that ended their northern hegemony in 685 is celebrated by yet another of the poems in the collection, *The Battle of Dunnichen*, by a cleric called Riagail of Bangor. It was a Pictish king, Bruide son of Bile (†693), probably a close relative of the Northumbrian king Ecgfrith, whom he killed in the battle, who finally reversed the balance of power in the north. From this point on, throughout the eighth century, without doubt the most powerful of the peoples of northern Britain was the Picts, whose kings exercised power over an increasingly efficient and centralised kingdom. Chief among these kings was Óengus, son of Fergus (†761), who rose to power in a four-sided contest in the 720s, and reigned for some forty years. He brought many of the neighbouring regions into submission to him, and so the poem which praises him probably has some justification in talking of him 'taking Britain':

> Good the day when Óengus took Alba,
>   hilly Alba, with its strong chiefs;

He brought battle to towns, with boards,
with feet and hands, and with broad shields.

The poems written in honour of both these Pictish kings, Bruide
son of Bile and Óengus son of Fergus were not written in the
kings' native tongue, Pictish. They are Gaelic poems, and remind
us of the most subtle but most far-reaching of the cultural changes
taking place in northern Britain in this part of the early Middle
Ages. The fourth linguistic group of Britain was that of the Gaels,
who principally occupied the region of modern-day Argyll, a
kingdom called Dál Riata. From the time our records become
reliable, Dál Riata appears as an expansionist kingdom, under
strong kings such as Aedán mac Gabráin (†c. 608). Alongside the
political expansion, we must place some untraceable popular or
linguistic expansion, such that by the eighth century the influence
of Gaelic on the politics and political geography of Pictland is
apparent. Partly, this is due to intermarriage between Pictish and
Gaelic royal families, and it was such intermarriage that allowed a
Gaelic leader to seize the Pictish kingship in the middle of the
ninth century, founding a dynasty which would continue to rule
the heartland of the Picts, and indeed the kingdom of Scotland,
for centuries. This leader was Cinaed mac Ailpín, known now
popularly as Kenneth MacAlpin, who on his death in 858 was
acclaimed as king of the Picts, but lamented in Gaelic:

That Cinaed with his hosts is no more
brings weeping to every home:
no king of his worth under heaven
is there, to the bounds of Rome.

His dynasty would change the name of the Pictish kingdom to
Alba, later Scotia in Latin, and lay the foundation for the
expanding and increasingly recognisable kingdom of Scotland,
a kingdom for which Gaelic would be the main language of court
and custom.

Part of the reason for the success of Gaelic in the Pictish lands of
the east was no doubt the influence of the Christian Church. In
the northern part of Scotland, the most influential centre was the
monastery of Iona, founded in 563 by Columba or Colum Cille,
an Irishman of royal extraction. Iona became, under his rule and
that of his successors, a centre of religion and great learning, and
from Iona came much of the impetus which converted those

regions of the Picts which were still pagan. In the late seventh century, Pictland could be described as lying under St Columba's patronage, and in 697 the king of the Picts was one of fifty kings who guaranteed a law protecting non-combatants from violence, a law devised by the ninth abbot of Iona, Adomnán. When Cinaed mac Ailpín took the Pictish kingship, his most significant act was to found a new church at Dunkeld and place there a portion of the relics of Columba, relics which would later be carried by Scottish armies into battle against Vikings in the tenth century, and against the English in 1314.

Unsurprisingly, much of the early religious poetry we have from Scotland is associated with Iona and Columba. Alongside Latin poems attributed to the saint himself must be placed a long line of poetry, mostly in Gaelic, in praise of him. Columba would continue to be a central saint for the burgeoning kingdom of Scotland, and he is invoked as its protector in Latin prayers from the beginning of the 12th century, and again in the 14th century, though these prayers originate from another island dedicated to the saint, in the heart of the eastern-oriented Scottish kingdom, the island of Inchcolm.

But the poetry of Columba and Iona is not the only religious verse of this early medieval period. One other powerful monastery, situated in the south, claims our attention as well, the monastery of Whithorn in Galloway. Founded probably in the sixth century, in a British territory from which there is a great deal of evidence for earlier Christian activity, the monastery is inextricably linked with the name of St Ninian. Nonethless, the earliest poem connected with Whithorn is attributed to a much more shadowy character, an abbot by the name of Mugint, who would appear to have flourished in the middle of the sixth century. His *Prayer for Protection* weaves biblical allusions into a powerful plea for salvation from plague. The poem is in Latin, but the poet's name is British, and certainly the earliest phase of religious activity at Whithorn belongs to a period when it was within Welsh-speaking territory.

This was not to last. During the years before 700, the English of Northumbria took over Dumfriesshire and Galloway, establishing a bishopric at Whithorn around 730. The English monks of Whithorn were great literary exponents of the cult of the Whithorn saint, Ninian, and the life of the saint, *The Miracles of St Nynia the Bishop*, as well as a hymn on the saint, travelled as far as the continent, where the only manuscript of these poems was preserved. One other major religious work belongs to the period

16

of English rule in the south-west of Scotland, *The Dream of the Rood*, written in Old English and partly inscribed in runes on the eighth-century sculptural masterpiece, the Ruthwell Cross in Dumfriesshire. Despite the brevity of English rule in the south-west, some two centuries, this poem is without doubt one of the greatest religious poems ever composed in English.

What spelled the end of English power in the south-west also lay behind many of the other great changes of the ninth and tenth centuries in Scotland: the arrival of a new set of peoples from Scandinavia, initially as raiders but in time as settlers, who brought with them a new culture and their language, Norse. Place-names of Norse derivation mark out their settlements, from Shetland to the Isle of Man, settlements which were a collection of autonomous polities owing allegiance at varying times to kings in Norway or in the Scandinavian trading-town of Dublin. The most important and long-lasting of the Norse settlements was in Orkney, where traditionally an earldom was founded late in the ninth century, from which a great deal of court poetry derives. This poetry reached its height, along with the power and prestige of the earldom, in the 12th century, symbolised by the poet-earl himself, Rognvald Kali (†1158).

However, further south, in the Hebrides, the Isle of Man, and Galloway, Norse settlers and Gaelic-speaking natives mixed to form a hybrid culture going by the name of the Gall-Gaidil, a name which lies behind that of Galloway, and the Gaelic name for the Hebrides, Innse Gall. Norse kings began to turn to Christianity, and patronise the older Gaelic centres of the church, such as Iona. The Norse king of Dublin, Olaf Cúarán, died on pilgrimage there in 980, the same year as a poet-abbot of Iona, Mugrón. By the 11th century, Norse poets were writing Christian themes into their skaldic verse, such as that by a sailor aboard a ship sailing west:

> I beg the monks' tester
> unmarring to direct my voyage;
> may the lord of the land's high hall
> hold his hawk's stall over me.

So too, by the middle of the 12th century the Orkney earldom would have its own strong saint's cult, one closely linked with the earls themselves, the cult of St Magnus. The fine 13th-century *Hymn to Saint Magnus* tells his story, and testifies to the strength of the church in later medieval Orkney, and its connections to the wider world. The fact that the hymn is in Latin also testifies to the advent of Latin scholarship and literature in Scotland's northernmost isles.

For nearly two centuries from the end of the 11th century, the territory that is now Scotland should be thought of as being divided into five parts, each with its own distinct character. At its centre lay the kingdom of Alba, the kingdom of the Scots, in the once Pictish heartlands of Strathearn, Fife, Angus and the Mearns, and radiating out into the highlands, to encompass such fractious regions as Moray. In the 11th century, the kings of Alba held control also over the second region, the separate lands of Cumbria and Lothian south of the Forth, which stretched in this period beyond the modern borders of Scotland, to include Carlisle and the lands as far as Penrith. The region south of the Forth became increasingly important in the 12th century, especially with the accession of David I, who had long held control, under the king, his brother, of the area. Although the kings of the Scots were still Gaelic speakers, and kings like Alexander I could still patronise the cult of St Columba (as witnessed by the prayer of Simeon the Cleric, which prefaces a copy of the *Life of Columba*), increasingly the Scottish kings were importing customs, personnel and linguistic affinities from further south, both French and English. David I was the chief pioneer of this and, even before he attained the kingship, new monasteries and burghs, populated largely by speakers of French and English dialects, had begun to pepper the lands south of the Forth. Though a short Gaelic poem satirises David for disturbing Scotland's equilibrium, it seems unlikely he would have been much bothered.

Fringing the kingdom of Alba and the regions of Cumbria and Lothian were territories which were a cultural mix of Norse and Gael. In the south-west, Galloway entered a period of renewed importance in the 12th century, under a mixed Gaelic and Norse dynasty. The long and highly comic Old French narrative poem *Fergus of Galloway*, not included here, was probably composed partly to satirise its kings, and also to entertain the Scottish court, to whom Galloway seemed a wild and rebellious region. A Latin poem, *The Song on the Death of Somerled*, makes clear that from the perspective of the settled lowlands, and of the new burghs like Glasgow and Renfrew, the western Highlands and islands seemed equally rebellious. The villain of that poem, Somerled mac Gille-

Brighde, was king of Argyll and of a series of islands in the southern Hebrides. He had fought his way to a division of western territory between himself and the king of Man and the Isles, and it was while attacking the Scottish mainland, at Renfrew, that he died in 1164. Somerled's descendants went on to become the dynasty which was first known as Kings of the Isles, and later as Lords of the Isles. Several of the poems in the collection are addressed to his descendants, such as the poem for Aenghus Mór of Islay, and the stern warning put in the mouth of St Columba, in the poem *Columba's Legacy*.

In *Fergus of Galloway* and *The Song on the Death of Somerled* it is possible to see the beginnings of the stereotyped image of the fierce, unlawful Gael which would later dominate Lowland perceptions of the Highlands. This should not lull us into a false sense that Gaelic had already disappeared from what we nowadays think of as Lowland Scotland. The best proof of this is the poetry of Muireadhach Albanach Ó Dálaigh, who, as an exile from Ireland, lived in the Lennox and composed poetry for the family of the earls of Lennox. That the earls, resident in Balloch, so close to modern Glasgow, were Gaelic-speaking nobles who were fond of their fictitious Irish origins, helps us to understand the internal linguistic complexity of Scotland in the later Middle Ages.

But Muireadhach, and his contemporary Scottish-born colleague Gille-Brighde Albanach, also remind us of the persistence of close relations between Ireland and Scotland, especially at the level of literary training. Both poets practised a type of poetry called *dán díreach*, strict-metre poetry which employed a language and metres codified in Ireland some time during the 12th century, termed Classical Irish. Both poets no doubt trained in bardic schools in Ireland, and both worked for similar Irish patrons, though because of his exile on account of murder, Muireadhach worked also in Scotland, fathering a learned family with a long and prestigious history. The later heart-rending lament by the father of Fearchar Ó Maíl Chiaráin, who died on a poetry tour of Ireland, also reminds us of the constant contact between the two islands on a literary level.

Muireadhach and Gille-Brighde also bring into focus Scotland's connections with the world at large. Both went as pilgrims together on the fifth crusade, and their homesick, somewhat weary poetry from the Mediterranean casts something of a shadow on their enthusiastic tonsuring poems before they set out. They were not the only poets from Scotland to participate in the crusades. An earlier lot of crusaders set out from Orkney, a group which included the earl himself, Rognvald Kali. They fought on the Mediterranean and were stationed at Acre, in addition to dallying in Spain and wooing, with some of the few love poems contained here, the widowed lady Ermengard of Narbonne. Most memorable of this period of Scottish poets in the south, perhaps, is the poet Armod's meditation while sailing on the Mediterranean:

> We keep, where the sea spills in
> over the stiff gunwale –
> this have we to do –
> watch on the prow-steed,
> while tonight beside the excellent,
> soft-skinned kerchief-tree
> the feeble wretch sleeps;
> I look over my shoulder to Crete.

These crusader-poets from Orkney bring us to the last of the five regions of Scotland in the later part of our period, the Northern Isles. Separate in language and culture from much of the rest of Scotland, Orkney and Shetland remained subject to the kings of Norway long after the treaty of Perth in 1266, which saw Norway cede their erstwhile rule over the Western Isles and the Isle of Man to the Scottish kings. Culturally, the Northern Isles looked north and east; much of the poetry of the court poets of the Orkney earls is preserved in Iceland and Norway, and much of what we know about the period results from histories and sagas written in Iceland. The islands, with their periodic Viking expeditions down the coasts of Scotland continuing into the 13th century, remained a potentially threatening region, and the Treaty of Perth also helped to secure better, more stable relations between Norway, the Orkney earldom and the Scottish kingdom.

One of the emblems of this better relationship was the marriage in 1281 of Margaret, daughter of the Scottish king, Alexander III, with Erik, king of Norway. This is celebrated in a marvellous epithalamium in Latin, for which we still have the music preserved, a rare glimpse into the sound as well as the tone of 13th-century Scottish court culture. This marriage was to prove briefly important, for when Alexander died accidentally in 1286, the daughter of Margaret and Erik, also called Margaret, was the king's only direct heir. She was an infant, yet the only clear solution to the problem of Scotland's imminent succession problem. That problem surfaced again in 1290 when the infant Margaret, the 'Maid of Norway', died at Orkney en route to assume the reign of Scotland.

Much, though not all, of the final lot of poetry in this collection pertains to the struggles of the next half-century, the wars of Scottish independence, in which something of a proper national identity was forged from the experience of warfare and political threat. One can already sense this in the mournful song that is one of the earliest pieces of Scots literature, as well as being the only piece in this collection in that language, which would become, in John Barbour's *Bruce* and Blind Harry's *Wallace*, the language par excellence of Scottish national identity. The song laments the state of Scotland in the wake of Alexander's death, though indeed it may date from somewhat later than his actual death:

> Qwhen Alexander our kynge was dede,
>   That Scotlande lede in lauche and le,
> Away was sons of alle and brede,
>   Off wyne and wax, of gamyn and gle.
> Our golde was changit in to lede.
>   Christ, borne in virgynyte,
> Succoure Scotlande, and ramede,
>   That stade is in perplexite.

We have, for reasons of space and the poor literary quality of the verses, omitted some poetry on the events of the wars, such as various accounts of the Battle of Bannockburn. But items like the marvellous lament on the death of King Robert Bruce, and the satirical anti-lament on the death of Edward I of England, certainly give a sense of the politics and personalities of the period, encapsulated in Latin verse. Perhaps the most vivid expression of the years of warfare comes in the prayers to St Columba which were composed in the early 14th century at the Augustinian priory on Inchcolm. That island in the Firth of Forth was more than once in the early 1300s subject to raids by English warships. This is the background to the pleas of the monks to their patron saint:

> Father Columba, splendour of our ways,
> receive your servants' offerings.
> Save the choir which sings your praise
> from the assaults of Englishmen
> and from the taunts of foes.

What is striking about the Inchcolm prayers, in addition, is the way in which they seem to bring the very beginnings of Scottish literature, in the sixth and seventh centuries, into contact with the period which ends this volume, the period which also sees the creation of a new Scottish identity and the beginnings of a new literature. Because, even in the 14th century, these Inchcolm poets drew on the imagery contained in the seventh-century *Life of Columba* by Adomnán, on centuries of devotional poetry to Columba and, no doubt, on their own traditions, and cast Columba in the role of patron to the nation:

> Mouth of the dumb,
> light of the blind,
> foot of the lame,
> to the fallen stretch out your hand.
> Strengthen the senseless,
> restore the mad.
> O Columba, hope of Scots,
> by your merits' mediation
> make us companions
> of the blessed angels.

The poetry

Above all, we would wish that readers will come to the poetry in this collection for the quality of the verse, which hopefully shines through even in translation, for the images, ideas and excitement of often quite alien visions of the world writ within the familiar context of this country. Granted that there is some verse here that never rises much beyond the serviceable, there are some literary masterpieces here of which Scotland can and should be proud, sharing the pride already taken in these poems by Wales, Ireland, Iceland or England. Among these we should count *The Dream of the Rood*, with its startling vision of a sentient cross, bound to Christ by masculine ties of lordship, and its heroic Christ climbing manfully upon it. Aneirin's *The Gododdin* is a problematic masterpiece, uncertain and perhaps unstable in its form, yet clear and bold in its statement of heroism and defeat, brilliant in its animalistic and bloody battle imagery. The later Welsh dramatic poetry cycle on *The Fall of Rheged* contains one of the most powerful images in Welsh literature, the speaker who carries his lord's head away from battle:

> It has twisted my arm; it has savaged my ribs;
> My heart it has broken:
> A head I nurse that nursed me.

Gruesome and poignant, the poem leaves unexplained the central mystery of who the speaker is, why he has cut off his lord's head, and what his role in the battle was.

Deft and dense, *The High Creator (Altus Prosator)* attributed to Columba creates a tapestry of creation and fall, which, if more warp than weft, is a feast for the senses. Several of the Gaelic laments here, especially the intensely personal, yet perfectly crafted and profoundly aristocratic elegies by the father of Fearchar Ó Maíl Chiaráin and that by Muireadhach Albanach Ó Dálaigh for his wife, are among the best in the Gaelic tradition. And the witty and intricate poetry of Rognvald Kali and his companions is justly seen as being redolent of a golden age of Norse court poetry.

For all that many of these poems are already celebrated, if not always widely known, there are some poets here who deserve celebration as well. Among these we may count the joyful, almost surreal imagery of Mugrón, abbot of Iona; the anonymous bombastic praise of the heavy-drinking Eithne; the rousing poems by William of Glasgow and Bishop Bjarni of Orkney; the battle incitement of Artúr Dall mac Gurcaigh; the wistful, anonymous lullaby *Dinogad's Coat*.

On the other hand, to many, perhaps most readers, there is much in this poetry that will seem difficult, unfamiliar, in style, imagery and references. The bulk of what is contained here is poetry of praise, predominantly written by professional poets, employed by royal or noble patrons. To the modern ear there may seem something false or cloying about such poetry, something redolent of speeches at party conferences or, in the case of the more bloodthirsty examples, of chants at football matches. There is no getting round the distance created by such poetry; it must be taken on its own terms. Some of the poets are brutally frank about their motivation. Taliesin always drops hints to his patron about his past generosity. Muireadhach Albanach's poem to Amhlaíbh, a Lennox nobleman, is nothing less than a statement of arrears, and the poem sent to Aenghus Mór of Islay is a bill of sale for a previous poem to the patron's father. It is clear also in that poem that the poet has never met the patron he so lavishly praises – how are we to understand such a world? Likewise Muireadhach's poem to Murchadh na nEach Ó Briain is nothing if not open about the fact that he does not know his subject, yet he goes on to compare him to all the great heroes of Gaelic tradition. This is more of a calling card, than a proper ode:

23

Guess who I am, oh Murchadh!
Good your claim to a fine cast:
    for discernment, your father
    surpassed the ranked battallions . . .

I've never seen you, round eyed one.
We've not made fast our union.
    Murchadh, diadem of eyes,
    we'll be friends when I return.

It is perhaps only in the laments of such praise poets that we are somewhat freed from the sense of ingratiation to fully appreciate the grandeur of the imagery of aristocratic praise, or warrior feats, or masculine virtue. Owain, son of Urien is praised, 'dawn's wing-tips his whetted spears'; one of the warriors of *The Gododdin* was 'Meat for wolves, before the marriage-feast, / Tid-bit for crows, before the altar.' Even here, though, the tone is only professionally tender. Outside some of the later, more personal, laments for wife or son, the poet rarely doffs his artistic cloak for a more emotional or soul-searching tone. To quote one of the translators of the poetry here, Joseph Clancy, in the introduction to *Medieval Welsh Lyrics*:

> The modern reader often brings to the poetry of other ages an attitude that is a barrier to his understanding and enjoyment. He is eager to find the 'individual' and impatient with the 'conventional'. But for the medieval Welsh bard, his essential task was not exploration but celebration, not the sensitive revelation of self at a single historical moment, but the enactment of permanently valid ritual. Within this, we can distinguish some quite individual voices, but it is wise to approach this poetry by attempting to understand its conventions and to cultivate a taste for ritual well performed. (Clancy 1965, 3)

The praise poetry is rewarding, and repays the effort of working with it. The praise poet was like a portait painter of more recent centuries, concerned to represent the patron with all the required attributes to display his superiority, his wealth, his landed status, and yet a good portrait painter may still be a good artist and craftsman. In most of the traditions represented here, what pleased was not outright originality, but the startling or striking combination of familiar imagery in unexpected ways, or simply extremely well-polished metre, combined with the intense craftsmanship and music of the prosody. A good example is perhaps this verse from Gille Brighde Albanach's poem in praise of Cathal Crobhdherg, which employs utterly traditional imagery to outstanding effect:

> His reign has put grain in the ground,
>   brought blossoms through branches' tips.
> The laws of that bright Greek candle
>   has brought acorns to the oaks.
>
> Banbha has recognised her king,
>   in one month, it's borne a quarter's growth.
> The wood which trembled with decay
>   has in his reign once more borne fruit.
>
> When autumn comes, the fruit will reach
>   Galway's lord of the swift mounts:
> cluster on cluster, ear on ear
>   will stretch from Ces Corrain to Cruach.

The other reason that understanding praise poetry is rewarding in the long term is that it lies behind much else that is here in the collection, from nature poetry to love poetry to religious verse. How else to understand the heroic Christ of *The Dream of the Rood*, other than alongside the brave, bloodstained warriors of *The Gododdin*? While praise of God is familiar from psalms and hymns, the poetry in praise of saints, such as those for Columba, draws strongly on the imagery and tone of secular Gaelic praise. And such verse can be as blunt about the desired outcome of praise for the holy patron as the professional poetry: the poet wants help in this life, heaven in the next, in return for his praise.

The nature poetry represented here, such as it is, draws heavily on the ideals of praise. Although in the poem *Columba's Island Paradise* the 12th-century author sees the natural world through the eyes of a fictitious and romantic Columba, his main object is celebration of the perfect location to carry out his religious calling. It is an unrealistically depicted island he wishes for, and an unrealistically set-out regime. Yet in this the poet draws on a stock type of poem known to professional praise poets in the Gaelic tradition, in which the poet would request a house from his patron, delineating its shape, size and accoutrements. Here, although never explicitly named, his patron is God, and we know, in a sense, through the conceit of the poet's use of Columba's voice, that he will be granted a wonderful island, that of Iona.

Arran is similar, in that we are treated to an ideal landscape, rather than one subject to the normal vicissitudes of bad weather. The island is treated much as a patron might be. The nature poetry also intersects with professional poetry in that both draw on close details of plant life and animal activity to depict the land in its optimal state, although in professional praise this is directed towards an evaluation of the righteousness of the ruler, and the glories of his place of residence. The lush, springtime atmosphere of the opening of the poem in praise of Ragnall, king of Man and the Isles is a good place to witness the landscape as being reflective of the lord's propriety.

> A fruitful place, the *sidh* of Emhain,
>> shapely the land where it's found;
> fair fort above all dwellings,
>> where bright apple-trees abound.

> Emain Ablach the freshest,
>> the summer hue it takes is sharpest,
> scarce a fort or hill is fairer
>> in its clear fresh green garment.

This is not to say that close observation and realistic depiction is entirely absent from these poems. The poem on Arran closes with the image of the longships sailing past it, and the poetry of the sea is very prominent in this collection. Beccán mac Luigdech, in his poems on St Columba, creates a heroic sailor saint from his subject, painting a vivid sense of the threat and toss of the sea. The elegy on the death of Conaing mac Áedáin personifies the sea as a wayward woman, tossing her hair at the young prince's frail wicker boat. And much of the poetry contained here from the eleventh century and later belongs to a world, both Norse and Gaelic, largely lived on the sea: the centrality of the ship in these poems is best realised in the battle-incitement poem addressed to Eoin MacSuibhne, in which his fleet is almost fantastically realised, and its journey across from Ireland to Scotland depicted in heroic detail.

There are, however, some types of poem that are very poorly represented here, though later they became central preoccupations of Scottish poetry. There is a selection of poems which play on the conventions of courtly love, but certainly never reach the heights of that literature as seen, for instance, in the Gaelic literature of

Scotland and Ireland in the 16th century. *The Blackthorn Brooch*, the sole Gaelic example, is only obliquely romantic, and instead uses the conventions of praise, directed here towards a woman. So too the poetry of Rognvald Kali and his companions for the Lady Ermengerd owe much to a fusion of skaldic and troubadour influences. Though the story of the Jomsvikings recounted by Bishop Bjarni of Orkney may be partly motivated by love, it is nevertheless primarily a straightforward tale of warrior heroism. Nonetheless, the author's infusion of the poem with his love-stricken voice is notable, and is perhaps the best locale for such sentiment here. On the other hand, the clearest expression of romantic love of a more genuine, less self-consciously literary kind is undoubtedly Muireadhach Albanach's lament for his wife. This is at once realistic – he details their life together, points to the deserted bed ('my long blanket, set a-swim') – and affecting.

> My body's gone from my grip
>   and has fallen to her share;
> my body's splintered in two,
>   since she's gone, soft, fine and fair.
>
> One of my feet she was, one side –
>   like the whitethorn was her face –
> our goods were never 'hers' and 'mine' –
>   one of my hands, one of my eyes.
>
> Half my body, that young candle –
>   it's harsh, what I've been dealt, Lord.
> I'm weary speaking of it:
>   she was half my very soul.

Alongside this, we should place the other great poetic genius of the 12th century, Rognvald Kali, in his kenning-strewn poem for his own sick wife:

> Yet I must often sit in my acre beside
> the sick goddess of the fishes of the
> island-watermeadows (red-faced for me
> is the table of the neck-ring),
> to accompany my falcon's land –
> so I, cunning, express hawk,
> seeking a seat
> for sorrow, on each day.

These are rare insights both into the emotions of professional poets and into the affection possible within marriage in a period which most people do not readily associate with marital love. There are a number of other striking, if more conventional and formal, depictions of marriage here: the biblically based epithalamium for Margaret of Scotland and King Eirik of Norway, and the intriguing tale of baby-swapping, *The Tale of Áedán mac Gabráin and Brandub mac Echach*.

Women are poorly represented, however, particularly as authors. This is odd since, in the 15th century, Gaelic literature would see the first in a long line of notable female poets who continued to play a strong role in the Gaelic mainstream until the 19th century. Presumably the reasons for the absence of women poets from this volume are the same ones that make praise poetry so prevalent: the dominance of an almost exclusively male professional poetic class in Norse, Gaelic and Welsh.

That said, this volume does contain what must be the oldest poem in a woman's voice in Britain or Ireland, a poem very likely to have been written by a woman. This is *Dinogad's Coat*, a lullaby of seventh-century Cumbria, tender and wistful. It was somehow picked up as one of the pieces of flotsam and jetsam which found their way into *The Gododdin* in the course of its earliest recording in the kingdom of Dumbarton.

Finally, a word should be said about narrative verse. From *The Bruce* to *Tam O'Shanter*, the tale told in verse was a staple of Scots poetry. It is well represented here in a variety of guises. There is straightforward narrative, such as *The Miracles of Bishop Nynia*, as well as more oblique stories told through dramatic monologue, such as *The Fall of Rheged* and *Krakumal*. Battle narratives predominate, from the pithy accounts of Taliesin, to the fantastic vision of William of Glasgow. The mix of the religious professions with the delight in a bloodthirsty tale well told is seen most evidently in William's poem on the death of Somerled, and in Bjarni, bishop of Orkney's near-pastiche poem on the Jomsvikings.

Because battle was so much a feature of the anthology, several of us wanted to call the book *The Corpse-Herring's Din*, a Norse kenning for battle, and a splendidly surreal one. *The Triumph Tree* is an appropriate title, and perhaps one which will turn fewer noses, if fewer heads. It describes the Cross of the Passion in *The Dream of the Rood* but, as an image, could stand for any one of a number of similar images from any of the poetic traditions. In the collection, lordly patrons are described as trees, sheltering, fruitful, sturdy; women are described as kerchief-trees, embroidery-trees, or Muireadhach's wife as 'the tall young long-fingered tree'; spears are trees; ships are trees; a saint is a 'leafy oak', and a harp is a music-tree. It is an image which both unifies and exemplifies the poetry contained here.

THE POETIC TRADITIONS

1. *The Latin Tradition* (Gilbert Márkus)

Before Latin writing and speech arrived here, there was no writing at all in these islands. Even Ogham (an early system of writing Gaelic on the corner of a stone in a pattern of notches and grooves) grew out of a Latin system of sound-representation, being invented either in Ireland or by Irishmen living in Britain. However, if literacy was first and foremost Latin literacy, Gaelic speakers and Britons quickly adapted their new-found skills to the writing of their own tongues, producing the first European vernacular literature. Indeed, it was the introduction of Latin literacy which made it possible for the great oral traditions of poetry, law, histories and genealogies to be recorded.

The area we now call Scotland marked the limit of the Roman Empire, and the Britons and Picts who lived here made their first acquaintance with Latin through contact with the empire's soldiers, officials and traders. Only gradually did this foreign language acquire an ecclesiastical dimension. However, after the withdrawal of Roman control from Britain in the early fifth century, the association of Latin with *imperium* became less significant, and the language became more closely associated with the churches and monasteries which continued to use it.

A second wave of Latin literacy came later with the arrival of Gaelic-speaking clerics and monks from Ireland, settling initially in Scotland's western seaboard in the territory of Dál Riata, before spreading east into Pictland, and south into northern England.

In this ecclesiastical culture, sacred scripture and the liturgy of the church were read in Latin, whose language – its sound and its rhythms as much as its vocabulary – soaked deep into the minds of Gaelic and British clerics and monks. The earliest Christian poets in Europe had followed the traditions of the declining classical world, their compositions based on elaborate rules of 'quantity'. Before long, however, they were producing a new poetry, and developing syllabic rhythmic features, and using more and more rhyme.

Latin poetry written in Scotland in the seventh and eighth centuries shows a great enthusiasm for these later features. The poets loved rhyme and alliteration, and brought forth ever more developed forms. An early poem, unreliably attributed to Colum Cille, has regular rhyming couplets and irregular alliteration of this sort. [Here rhymes are underlined, while alliterations are in bold type.]

> Noli Pater indulgere
> tonitrua cum fulgore
> ne frangamur formidine
> huius atque uridine.
>
> Te timemus terribilem
> nullum credentes similem
> te cuncta canunt carmina
> angelorum per agmina.

A hymn in praise of the Virgin, written in the early eighth century by Cú Chuimne, a monk of Iona, has fairly regular rhymes at some points (ending lines 2 and 4 of each stanza), while alliteration is more sporadic, as are other rhymes such as those binding the end of one line to the beginning of the next.

> Cantemus in omni die
> concinentes varie
> conclamantes Deo dignum
> ymnum sanctae Mariae.
>
> . . . Maria mater miranda
> patrem suum edidit
> per quem aqua late lotus
> totus mundus credidit.
>
> . . . Tunicam per totum textam
> Christi mater fecerat
> quae peracta Christi morte
> sorte statim steterat.

Some poets, however, shunned such ornament almost entirely. Here are the opening lines of the eighth-century poem on *The Miracles of Bishop Nynia*:

Rex Deus eternus, patris veneranda potestas,
tempore completo celi de culmine Christus
Venerat et castae matris de corpore carnem
Suscepit, ut nostrum quemquam salvaret ab ira.

It is important to remember that the milieu of this Latin poetry is originally ecclesiastical. It is part of a clerical and monastic culture, as is much of the Gaelic and Welsh poetry; we should not make the mistake of attempting to drive a wedge between two poetic cultures, one clerical and Latin, the other secular and vernacular. In fact the poetic traditions often cross over and influence each other. We have, indeed, Latin poetry written by poets who must have been native speakers of each of the other languages represented here. Indeed, some, such as William the Clerk who wrote the stirring Glaswegian poem on the *Death of Somerled* in 1164, could even have been from France.

The church origin of the Latin poetry explains why so much of it, especially in the early centuries, is devotional in content. The clergy later expanded their horizons somewhat, and wrote praise poetry, nationalist rants about Scotland's heroes and tales of battles, but the earlier material consists entirely of hymns to God, or in praise of saints or the Christian life. We should also bear in mind, reading these Latin poems, that the vast majority of them were written to be *sung*, though their exact musical arrangement is seldom known to us, except in the handful of cases where the later manuscripts contain musical notation. This small selection of poems for which the music is preserved (The *Hymn for St Magnus, The Wedding Song for Margaret of Scotland and Eirik, king of Norway*, and the various songs from the *Inchcolm Antiphoner*) must stand for all the others for which the music can only be inferred.

The bulk of the later Latin poetry contained here, especially the epitaphs on 13th-century rulers and poetry relating to the Wars of Independence, is extracted from one source. In the Augustinian abbey of Inchcolm, 'the Island of Columba', in the Firth of Forth, abbot Walter Bower wrote his great *Scotichronicon* in the 1440s. This history of the Scottish people was the culmination of a series of histories by Scotsmen seeking to give meaning to an independent nation's past. His work is marked by his quest for a sense of

Scottish identity, the need to celebrate and understand Scotland's struggle for independence. Scottish saints are given new importance, while his political perspective is often deeply anti-English. It is difficult really to know how much of the poetry Bower records is his own or has been edited or refashioned to his needs. Certainly, some is extracted from earlier sources, and we have given some representative examples here. The poetry from Bower needs, however, to be read with some caution when formulating a view of the Latin poetry of medieval Scotland.

2. *The Welsh Tradition* (Thomas Owen Clancy)

The peoples of the northern British kingdoms, known to later Welsh writers as *Gwyr y Gogledd*, the Men of the North, played an important part both in the history of southern Scotland and in the Welsh literary tradition. A ninth-century Latin text, written by a Welsh cleric, in describing the northern kingdoms and their struggles against the incoming English in the sixth century, mentions the skill of the northern poets:

> Then Talhaearn *Tad Awen* (Father of Poetic Inspiration) was famed in poetry; and Aneirin and Taliesin and Blwchfardd and Cian, known as *Gwenith Gwawd* (Wheat of Song), were all simultaneously famed in British verse.

Although we know nothing of three of these poets, the work of two, Aneirin and Taliesin, has survived in much later manuscripts, and alongside some anonymous fragments forms the earliest stratum of verse in the Welsh language. These poems in themselves are some of our best sources for the northern British kingdoms, and the kings and warriors addressed by these poets – Urien and Owain of Rheged, Gwallawg, Cynon Aeron, son of Clydno Eidyn – were important legendary characters in the later Welsh tradition, developing their own story cycles, and in some cases being absorbed into the mushrooming Arthurian legend.

Although the language these poets must have written in would now usually be called Cumbric, in the sixth century it would have been scarcely different from the other British languages spoken in Wales, Cornwall and the British colony of Brittany. Indeed, until the early seventh century, a Briton could walk from Land's End to Edinburgh and be constantly among people of the same language and culture. It was the encroachment of English overlordship and settlement on areas like Lancashire and Cumbria which split the kingdoms of the north from their Welsh neighbours, and the battles which, ultimately, led to the conquest by the English of the kingdoms of Gododdin and Rheged in southern Scotland are celebrated and lamented by turn in the poems of this period.

By around 700, independent British rule remained only in the kingdom ruled from *Al Clud*, the Rock of the Clyde, now Dumbarton Rock. In this kingdom, the substance of the Gododdin was preserved, and to some extent modified, collecting in the process poetic flotsam and jetsam like the lullaby from Cumbria, *Dinogad's Coat*, and the verses on *The Battle of Strathcarron* in 642. In this kingdom, too, some of the poetry of Taliesin may have been preserved, though this is less certain. The kingdom of Dumbarton remained strong and, indeed, in the period after 900, seems to have reconstituted itself and expanded back into former British territory. Its kings ruled as far south as Penrith, and their kingdom was now called Cumbria. It was perhaps in this context, contemplating the past of their regained territory, which had once been the kingdom of Rheged, that the group of more dramatic poems called *The Fall of Rheged* was composed.

How all this material was transmitted to Wales, and when, is extremely uncertain. But certainly the work of these early poets was known there before 1100, from which time Welsh court poets drew on their work to form the background of their own praise poetry, in vocabulary, imagery, metre and tone. These later poets gradually codified the metrical techniques of Welsh poetry, and it is through the lens of their much more systematic poetry that the shape of the early Welsh poetry of the northern British kingdoms is usually seen.

The praise poetry written by Taliesin is perhaps most readily described. Although there is some doubt over whether the system employed by Taliesin is fundamentally syllable- or accent-based, one can, fairly confidently, class the main type of praise poem as the *awdl*. By and large, this is a formal praise poem with groups of lines with clear end-rhymes, though the end-rhyme may vary, as may the number of syllables in each line.

The Battle of Argoed Llwyfain shows this metre, each line containing three stresses, with most lines containing either nine or ten syllables, ending on a strong rhyme. There is some use of alliteration, which would later be a major feature of Welsh verse, and some lines are further bound together by alliteration of the first sounds of each line. Here is how the beginning of it looks (alliteration in bold, rhyme underlined):

> Bore duw Sadwrn cad **f**awr a **fu**
> O'r pan ddwyre **h**aul **h**yd pan gyn**nu**.
> Dygryswys Fflamddwyn yn bedwar **llu**;
> Goddau a Rheged i ymddu**llu**,
> Dyfyn o **A**rgoed hyd **A**rfyn**ydd**,
> Ni cheffynt eirios hyd yr **un** d**ydd**.

Many of the Welsh poems translated here, however, resist easy classification. This is particularly true of *The Gododdin*, which displays a wide variety of poetic structure among its many verses. To some extent, it is more ornate than the poetry of Taliesin. Consider one of its most famous stanzas (§A.8). Here, in a series of lines of four stresses, and of between eight and ten syllables, alliteration is shown in bold, internal rhyme by italics, with end-rhyme underlined:

> **G**wyr a *aeth* **G**atr*aeth*, oedd ffr*aeth* eu **llu**,
> **G**lasfedd eu hanc*wyn* a **g**wen*wyn* **fu**,
> **T**rych*ant* **t**rwy beiri*ant* yn catá**u**,
> A **g**wedi *elwch*, taw*elwch* **fu**.
> Cyd elwynt lannau i benyd**u**,
> Dadl ddi*au* ang*au* i eu treidd**u**.

The other main form of poem translated here is quite different. This is the type found in the later, more story-based cycle of poems we have called *The Fall of Rheged*. This is written in a metre called *englyn*, which became likewise common in Wales for the composition of dramatic, tale-based poems, as well as gnomic, religious and informal verse. Unlike the *awdl*, it consists of stanzas, which in this early period contained three lines each (later the standard *englyn* would develop into a four-line stanza). In its simplest form, each stanza had around seven syllables, each ending on the same rhyme, although more complex forms with lines of variant length and internal rhyme between lines can be found in the *The Fall of Rheged*. These stanzas were linked mainly by 'incremental repetition', the continual or intermittent use of a short refrain to begin each stanza. The first two stanzas of the poem on *The Head of Urien* demonstrate this form:

Pen a borthaf ar fy nh<u>u</u>,
By cyrchynad rhwng deul<u>u</u>;
Mab Cyn*farch* b*alch* bieif<u>u</u>.

Pen a borthaf ar fy nh<u>u</u>.
Pen Urien llary, llywiai ll<u>u</u>,
Ac ar ei fron wen, frân dd<u>u</u>.

Welsh poetry continued to develop in Wales from these early
roots, but in the northern lands which were the birthing grounds
of this poetic tradition, *The Fall of Rheged* is the last poetry which
might legitimately be considered to have been composed there.
The northern British language Cumbric continued to be spoken
into the 11th century, but seems unlikely to have survived much
beyond 1100.

Background reading: Jarman and Hughes (1992); Clancy (1970);
Rowland (1990).

3. *The Gaelic Tradition* (Thomas Owen Clancy)

The Gaelic language traditionally arrived in Scotland with the
establishment of the colony of Dál Riata by Gaels in Argyll,
Kintyre and the southern Hebrides. The flitting of the ruling
dynasty of this colony to Scotland from Co. Antrim is tradition-
ally dated to c.500 AD, but Gaelic may have long been settled in
Argyll. From this base, the political influence of Gaels and the
cultural influence of Gaelic continued to grow until, by the mid-
ninth century, Gaelic-speaking rulers held sway over the eastern
kingdom of the Picts as well, and by the 11th century their
influence had extended south of the Forth and Clyde, into the
Welsh-speaking kingdom of Cumbria, and into the English-
speaking regions of Lothian. At the same time, the Scandinavian
settlers who had come to dominate the western seaboard of
Scotland gradually abandoned their Norse speech for that of
the natives, and Gaelic became once more the language of the
rulers of the Isle of Man and the southern Hebrides, and probably
through this route Gaelic came in force to Galloway.

Some of our earliest poems in Gaelic from Scotland are related
to the church, and in particular to the monastery of Iona. Gaelic is
notable for being one of the earliest vernacular languages to
develop a substantial literature, and this is at least partially due

to a strong and early rapprochement between the church and the native literary classes. This can be seen already in the elegy on the death of St Columba in 597, which straddles the world of secular praise poetry and religious ideals. Formally, too, the poem seems to partake of the older, inherited tradition of accentual verse, the poetry being bound together largely by means of alliteration and end-cadences, rather than rhyme.

However, the strong relationship between religious and native literary classes can be seen even more clearly in the evident effect that the verse forms of Latin hymns had on vernacular verse. From as early as the seventh century, Gaelic can be seen to have evolved a series of metres which are at least partially modelled on Latin hymnody, though betraying more traditional roots as well. It was in these new verse forms that the professional and learned poets of the early medieval period composed.

According to tradition, St Columba helped to save the poets from being banned at a great convention in 575. As a strong and restricted union, they had become too powerful and outlandish in their charges and abuse of privilege. Although this is no doubt legendary, it does give further insight into two other important aspects of the poetry of this period. It was written largely by professionals, who were either employed by secular rulers or, in this period, more often trained by and housed in monasteries. These professionals were highly status-conscious, acutely aware of ancient rights and origins, and dedicated to a rounded attainment of knowledge. The poet was responsible for knowing not just poetry but also genealogy, history, custom and story. We have a good sense of the poetic class of the early Middle Ages as scholarly, highly organised, stratified and self-important.

This impression is only sharpened by a reform in the poetic order which took place in the middle of the 12th century. We know too little about the circumstances of this reform, but its effects are plain to see. The long connection between monastery and poet was severed, and poets began to be trained in separate schools, run by families of respected poets. Poets were now almost exclusively in the employ of secular patrons and, while the earlier medieval period shows a great variety in types of composition, from around 1200 on we have some five centuries in which almost exclusively praise poetry has been preserved. The poetry from 1200 on is intensely conservative and uniform in style, metre and language. Indeed, this too is clearly an effect of the 12th-century poetic reform. Manuals of language and poetry, as well as the clear evidence of the poetry itself, demonstrate that the literary language of Gaelic had been standardised at this period (in Ireland, it should be noted, and to an Irish norm), as had the acceptable metrical conventions and forms.

In the period after 1200, Gaelic Scotland participated fairly fully in a standard literary Gaelic language, Classical Irish, although the spoken language here had no doubt been dialectically different since early times. One of the reasons for the consistency in literary language in Ireland and Scotland is the constant movement of poets for training, employment and touring. Many of our earliest poets appear to be churchmen, probably born in Ireland but working in monasteries like Iona, or in contact with eastern kings in Pictland. The Gaelic world was essentially one culture area, and so in many cases with the Gaelic poems it is difficult to have confidence that the poems we have published here are in any strong sense 'Scottish'. In the later period, the reformed poetic language and metres of the 12th century usually and properly referred to as Classical Irish may well have been introduced by poets such as Muireadhach Albanach, who was a son of the powerful Irish family of poets of Ó Dálaigh, and who sired Scotland's most prestigious poetic family, the MacMhuirichs; and by the likes of his companion on crusade Gille-Brigdhe Albanach, a native of Scotland but mostly employed in Ireland, and perhaps trained there.

The metres employed by the poems in this collection are fairly varied, but two of the most common can be demonstrated here. Both are metres based on stanzas of four lines each, bound together by patterns of end-rhyme and, at their most formal, by alliteration and internal rhyme also.

The first metre is called *rannaigecht*, which is characterised by end-rhyme between the second and fourth line of the quatrain, and internal rhyme between the end of the third line and the middle of the fourth. An early example is the *Elegy for Cinaed mac Ailpín*. Though it lacks the rhyme between the end of the third line and the middle of the fourth, there are other rhymes across the lines.

> Nad mair Cinaed co lín sc*or*,
>   fo déra *gol* i gach <u>taig</u>;
> óenrí a l*óga* fo nim
>   co bruinne R*óma* ní f<u>ail</u>.

From the later, Classical Irish, period of poetry, Muireadhach Albanach's *Lament for his Wife, Mael Medha*, demonstrates the form with elegance and perfection, including close rhyme between the words in the first and second lines, and between those in the third and fourth lines:

> M'*anam* do s*gar* r*iomsa* a-ra*oir*,
> c*alann* ghlan dob *ionnsa* i n-u*aigh*;
> rugadh br*uinne* m*aordha* m*ín*
> is *aonbhla lín* u*ime* u*ainn.*

The other major metre is called *deibide*, which in its main form consists of quatrains comprising two couplets, the rhyme between the lines of the couplets consisting of one stressed and one unstressed rhyme. The little verse on *Iona* ascribed to Adomnán represents this form:

> Má ro-m thoiccthi écc i ndh-Í,
> ba gabál di thrócar*i*.
> Nicon fettar fo nim gl*as*
> fóttán bad fherr fri tiugbá*s.*

Again, Muireadhach Albanach shows this metre in its classical perfection, in his poem *Returning from the Mediterranean, to Murchadh na nEach Ó Briain*: Here is the second stanza:

> Cá healadha fhoghnas d*amh*?
> tomhais, m*ása* thú M*urchadh*;
> *eirg* is i*arfaigh* d'Ú Dh*álaigh*,
> a dh*eirg* l*ianchair* leann*ánaigh.*

A number of the poems in this collection are fragments preserved in metrical tracts, and as such are often representative of unusual or innovative or elaborate metres. Such is the poem in 'Pictish metre' *On Gille Phátraic*. This poem, and a number of poems in Gaelic which praise Pictish kings, remind us that though we have no poetry, indeed, no literature in Pictish, we do have some literature in Gaelic which belongs, by way of patronage, to the parts of Scotland which were Pictish speaking up to c. 900.

If Pictish is the most poorly attested of early Scotland's literatures, Gaelic is one of the best, and with Gaelic as with no other tradition represented here do we have the sense that this anthology stops in mid-stream. This causes us some regret at our chosen cut-off date of c.1350, particularly since from the 15th century we have a good number and variety of very fine Gaelic poems, which have been poorly served by anthologies of Scottish poetry. Indeed, only Roderick Watson's *The Poetry of Scotland, Gaelic, Scots and English* gives even a representation of this verse, and the recent, poorly named *Mercat Anthology of Early Scottish Literature, 1375–1707* eschews Gaelic almost entirely. Nonetheless, we hope that the variety and splendour of the early Gaelic poetic tradition in Scotland will be noted for future anthologies.

Background reading: Williams and Ford (1992); Murphy (1961); Gillies (1987)

4. *Old English and Older Scots* (Thomas Owen Clancy)

It may seem strange that the language which would develop into Scotland's main literary language is so poorly represented here – only by two poems. For Old English this is less surprising, since its poetic corpus is in any case not very extensive.

English arrived with the settlement from assorted parts of the continent and Scandinavia of speakers of various Germanic dialects. These dialects evolved in time into the dialects of English, although coalescing into several more or less standard literary norms. The Old English represented here by one poem, *The Dream of the Rood*, preserved in part on a sculptured cross in Dumfriesshire, and *in extenso* in a manuscript from Vercelli in Italy, is, at least as far as the fragments on the cross are concerned, in the Northumbrian dialect. It spread into southern Scotland with the growing political and ecclesiastical hegemony of the kingdom of Northumbria, made up of a core of two fitfully united kingdoms, Bernicia and Deira.

Although English political power in this region was not long-lived – the rise of the Norse kingdom of York saw its downfall – still there is ample evidence that throughout the early middle ages, English was spoken in Lothian, the Borders, Dumfriesshire and Galloway, even if at times the population of English speakers may have dwindled, and certainly we should be imagining in any case bi- or trilingual populations in these areas.

In the 12th century, changes introduced by the Scottish kings allowed an influx of speakers of various languages, Flemish, French, German, but most of all English, into the newly established burghs. With the rise in the economic and political influence of English speakers in the burghs, in the court, and in the church, a northern, distinctively Scottish variety of English came to have ever greater importance, but only in the final century of this anthology, the 14th, did this language, which we would term Older Scots, come to have any apparent literary prestige.

As such, it is really only in that century that we can speak of an English or Scots poetic tradition beginning. Nonetheless, it may be useful briefly to describe the two poems we have included in the anthology. *The Dream of the Rood*, in Old English, participates in all the hallmarks of the Old English tradition of poetry. The exact poetic conventions used by Old English poets is still subject to much debate, but the opening of *The Dream of the Rood* demonstrates its basic building blocks. Old English poetry relies on strong rhythms and heavy alliteration. The lines here are composed of two halves across a caesura, linked by alliteration (shown in bold).

> Hwæt, ic **s**wefna cyst || **s**ecgan wille,
> hwæt **m**e gemætte || to **m**idre nihte
> si**þþ**an **r**eord-berend || **r**este wunodon.
> **þ**uhte me **þ**æt ic gesawe || **s**eldlicre treo
> on **l**yft **l**ædan || **l**eohte bewunden,
> **b**eama **b**eorhtost.

The Scots poem on the death of Alexander III is likewise invested with heavy alliteration, but here rhyme plays a crucial part, as it did in much English poetry by the end of the 13th century. Again, rhyme is underlined, alliteration in bold.

> Qwhen Alexander our kynge was d<u>ede</u>,
> That Scotlande l<u>ede</u> in **l**auche and **l**e,
> Away was sons of alle and br<u>ede</u>,
> Off **w**yne and **w**ax, of **g**amyn and **g**le.
> Our golde was changit in to l<u>ede</u>.
> Christ, borne in virgyny<u>te</u>.
> **S**uccoure **S**cotlande, and ram<u>ede</u>,
> That st<u>ade</u> is in perplexi<u>te</u>.

5. *The Norse Tradition* (Judith Jesch)

The Norse language came to Scotland around 800 AD when raids by Vikings, mainly from Norway, were followed by permanent settlement, predominantly in the Northern and Western Isles. The Northern Earldom (including Orkney, Shetland and, for part of the time, Caithness) remained a part of the Scandinavian world until the northern islands were handed over to the King of Scotland in 1468, and it was an important centre of Norse culture, especially in the 12th century. The Hebrides, Gaelicised by about the 13th century (the western islands were ceded to the King of Scotland in 1266), have left us fewer records from which to judge the nature of their culture in the Norse period.

The settlers no doubt brought with them the poetic forms of their Norwegian homeland, but the poetic tradition was nourished by continuing contact with Norway and, especially, with Iceland, where Viking settlers had also taken their poetic traditions, and where Norse poetry developed, thrived and was recorded for posterity. With the exception of the Maeshowe verse, all of the Norse items in this anthology were recorded in Icelandic manuscripts of the 13th century or later. The attribution of these items to poets active in the geographical area of Scotland depends on this Icelandic tradition, and both the poets and their poetry belong to the larger Scandinavian world of their time, rather than a specifically Scottish one. Indeed, the only poet represented here who was certainly born in Scotland is Bishop Bjarni Kolbeinsson and he, like Earl Rognvald Kali, had Norwegian origins.

Old Norse poetry is traditionally divided into two types, 'eddic' and 'skaldic'. The texts translated here are mostly skaldic, with only *Darradarljod* in the eddic style. As eddic poems are mostly anonymous, attempts to assign a Scottish origin to others in this genre can only be speculative. In skaldic verse, however, the poet's name is generally transmitted with the verse, giving us a better clue to date and place of composition. The genre had its origins at the courts of the Viking Age rulers of Scandinavia, perhaps in the ninth century, and the skalds were professional poets, their job to praise the king or chieftain and to entertain the court. In return, they received handsome financial rewards. The most common themes of such poems were the military exploits of the ruler at sea and on land. He was often also praised for his generosity, not only because this was a highly valued quality, but as a reminder by the poet of the fee he expected in return. As well as praising a living ruler, poets could be commissioned to compose a eulogy in memory of a dead one. In this anthology, Arnor, Earl's Skald, an Icelander who worked for kings of Norway as well as earls of Orkney in the 11th century, represents this genre most clearly.

However, skaldic poetry could encompass wider themes than just martial praise. Descriptions of seafaring provide some of the most effective skaldic verse which often transcends its rather dreary military context. Poems on mythological themes for the entertainment of the audience were also popular from an early stage. Later, skaldic forms could be used for verse on almost any subject and we have scurrilous verse, love poetry, dream visions and Christian praise poetry, especially from medieval Iceland, where the genre continued to be practised until well into the Middle Ages. Some of this extension of the themes of skaldic verse seems to have happened in Scandinavian Scotland. Poems such as *Krakumal* and Bjarni Kolbeinsson's *Jomsvikingadrapa* show the antiquarian interests of the Norse 12th-century renaissance (also evident in Rognvald Kali's metrical tour de force *Hattalykill*, now fragmentary and untranslatable), in which skaldic forms were harnessed to subjects from heroic antiquity rather than contemporary events. The most accomplished poet of Scandinavian Scotland, Rognvald Kali, Earl of Orkney, also extended skaldic forms in his witty travelogues, and comments on life and politics in the Northern Isles, in which, unusually for Norse poetry, we get a good sense of the poet's personality from his verse.

Skaldic poetry is stanzaic, and could consist of either a single stanza (known as a *lausavísa*, 'free-standing verse') or two or more stanzas strung together into a longer poem. Most of the Norse poems in this anthology are composed in either *dróttkvœtt* ('court metre') or in other forms that are a variant of, or derived from, this. In *dróttkvœtt*, the stanza has eight lines of six syllables each. Within this tight framework of 48 syllables, the poet had to juggle the metrical demands of alliteration and rhyme, and the stylistic demands of an elaborate poetic language. Each of the eight lines contains two rhyming syllables, with full rhyme in lines 2, 4, 6 and 8, but only half-rhyme ('consonance' in English parlance) in lines 1, 3, 5 and 7. Lines 1 and 2, 3 and 4, 5 and 6 and 7 and 8 were joined in couplets by alliteration, according to the standard practice of early Germanic poetry. Thus, two words in the odd-numbered lines and the first word in the even-numbered lines had to begin with the same sound, if a consonant (though all vowels and diphthongs alliterated with each other). The following stanza by Rognvald (verse 13) has been marked to demonstrate these rules – alliteration is marked in bold, half-rhyme by single underlining and full rhyme by double underlining:

Lætr of ǫxl, sá's útar
aldrœnn, stendr á tjaldi,
sig-Freyr, Svǫlnis Vára
slíðrvǫnd ofan ríða.
Eigi mun, þótt œgir
ǫrbeiðanda reiðisk,
blikruðr bǫðvar jǫkla
beinrangr framar ganga.

Not only did poets have to mind their syllables, they also made extensive use of an elaborate poetic language. Special poetic words were used for otherwise everyday things (known as *heiti*), as well as elaborate metaphorical constructions called 'kennings' that are familiar from poetry in other languages, but nowhere so consistently developed as in skaldic verse. The wide range of synonyms that *heiti* and kennings provided poets with made it easier for them to find words with the appropriate alliteration and rhyme to fit into their metrical jigsaw puzzles. Thus, in the stanza just quoted, Rognvald (describing a tapestry in his hall) combines mythological allusions and metaphors to make his point with elaborate circumlocutions: the god Odin is called 'Svolnir', his 'goddesses' are valkyries, the 'scabbard-wand' of valkyries is a 'sword'. Another term for 'sword' is 'battle-icicle' and the 'gleam-bush' of the 'battle-icicles' is a warrior, gleaming with his weapons. But a warrior can also be called a 'Freyr [god-name] of victory'.

Although Norn (the language derived from Norse) survived as a spoken language in Orkney and Shetland until the 18th century, Scots began to take over as the main spoken language from the middle of the 14th century, while our Icelandic sources do not preserve any evidence of Norse poetic composition in Scotland after the middle of the 13th century. The only surviving poetic work in Norn is an anonymous ballad of some 35 stanzas about the Earl of Orkney and the King of Norway's daughter Hildina, recorded on Foula, Shetland, in 1774.

Background reading: Barnes (1984); Barnes (1993); Barnes (1998); Bibire (1988); Jónas Kristjánsson (1988).

attributed to ST MUGINT (mid-sixth century)
Prayer for Protection (Parce Domine Latin)

This poem has an interesting preface in the *Irish Liber Hymnorum*, which
identifies its author as a certain Mugint. Little is known about him other than a
legend in the Preface to the hymn which takes place in *Futerna*, a Latin form of
the English *Hwiterne*, now Whithorn, in the sixth century. In the legend
Mugint makes an attempt on the life of Uinniau, or Finnian of Moville, while
he is at Whithorn – an attempt which rebounds on himself. In penance for his
sin, he recites this psalm-like prayer.

The whole piece reads as a cobbling together of bits of psalmody and other
biblical phrases with lines from the liturgy, many of which are still found in the
Roman liturgy. One may doubt the accuracy of the legend about Mugint's
homicidal conspiracy. Bernard and Atkinson (1898, vol. ii, 113) suggested that
it may have been composed as a prayer for protection from a plague, several of
which ravaged Scotland in the mid-sixth century and after.

Spare, O Lord! Spare your people
whom you, Christ, redeemed with your blood,
and do not be angry with us for ever.
We beseech you, Lord, in all your mercy,
turn aside your fury, your anger from this city
and from your holy dwelling.
For we have sinned, we have sinned against you, Lord,
and you are angry with us,
and there is no one who can escape your hand.
But we pray that your mercy may come upon us, Lord,
who in Nineveh spared those who called on the Lord.
Let us cry aloud: look upon your trampled and suffering people;
protect your holy temple, lest it be polluted by the wicked,
and show your measureless mercy to your afflicted city.
Let us all cry out to the Lord saying:
We have sinned, Lord, we have sinned.
Have mercy on us and deliver us
from the evils which daily rise against us.
Lord, forgive the sins of your people
according to the multitude of your mercy.
You were gracious to our fathers;
be gracious to us also, and your glory will fill all the earth.
Remember, Lord, and say to the angel destroying your people,
'Enough!' Hold back your hand, and let the slaughter cease
which proceeds among the people, lest you ruin every living soul.

ANEIRIN (sixth century)
The Gododdin Welsh

The poem or series of poems known as *Y Gododdin*, 'The Gododdin', has been in various contexts called 'the oldest Scottish poem', yet almost everything about it remains controversial. The setting of the poem is not in doubt: the action it describes belongs to the strife-ridden sixth century, and to the northern British kingdoms in a century which saw gradual loss of territory to English settlers, both through conquest and perhaps through assimilation. The kingdom at the heart of this literary work, speckled with vibrant heroic imagery, is that of the Gododdin, who occupied the territory of the Lothians, and had as their main fortress Din Eidyn (Edinburgh).

The basic facts about the venture it describes are taken for granted by the poem itself. Mynyddawg, ruler of Gododdin, assembled warriors from his own and other British realms at Din Eidyn, and after about a year of training and feasting the 300 or so rode south, engaging the English at Catraeth (present-day Catterick), an expedition that ended in the deaths of all but a few men. Whatever may have been the actual importance of this battle at the time, it became symbolic of the heroic attempt to halt the English conquest, not least because of Aneirin's poem.

There the straightforward description ends. *Hwn yw e gododin. aneirin ae cant.* 'This is The Gododdin: Aneirin sang it [i.e., composed it]'. The apparently simple statement at the beginning of the 13th-century manuscript known as *The Book of Aneirin* precedes two separate texts, each by a different scribe, each copying a different earlier text. Both texts are obviously incomplete, each contains material not in the other, and there are often considerable differences between the stanzas common to both. So the actual textual status of the work remains confusing; so too does its literary classification. While people unfamiliar with the poem are prone to describe it as an epic, that it certainly is not. It does not affect to tell a story, instead elegising and praising the dead warriors of a failed expedition, sometimes individually, sometimes in groups and sometimes as a body. It is thus unclear whether it was ever intended as a single poem, or whether it is instead a collection of poems based around the same event.

While a ninth-century text names Aneirin along with Taliesin as one of five outstanding poets in the British language (the ancestor of modern Welsh) of the sixth century, little is certain about him beyond what *The Gododdin* itself suggests: that he was a court poet at Din Eidyn, and a survivor of the military venture that is the subject of his poem. A traditional genealogy survives which connects him to other figures of the sixth century, making him son of Dunawd, ruler of a kingdom perhaps in the region of Dentdale in West Yorkshire, and brother of Deiniol, founder of the Welsh monastery of Bangor.

Nonetheless, persistent doubts remain about the language of the poem, since as it stands it does not seem to be Welsh in its sixth-century form. How did the text survive, how was it transmitted, how much was it changed in the course of transmission? While it seems certain that the poem was preserved in some form at an early date in the kingdom based around Dumbarton, the other questions are more difficult to answer.

specifies, not certain, but good representation (handwritten)

Nevertheless, in terms of its content and its general form and tone, the work does seem to represent a poem which is a remnant of the poetry of the Old North, and one of its masterpieces. Aneirin creates a loose weave of stanzas dealing with particular incidents in the battle, celebration of the heroism of the war-band in general, with bitter reflections on the folly of the campaign and the feasting that preceded it, and elegies of individual warriors, praising their past exploits as well as their deeds at Catraeth. Despite the incomplete survival of the work and the serious textual problems with some portions of it, *The Gododdin* has its own kind of unity, and in either text has a powerful cumulative effect that is absent if one reads only excerpts. We present here the entire poem, translated as it appears in the manuscript, allowing audiences to make their own judgment about what the poem is and what its context is.

The Gododdin (A-text)

1. Man's mettle, youth's years,
   Courage for combat:
   Swift thick-maned stallions
   Beneath a fine stripling's thighs,
   Broad lightweight shield
   On a trim charger's crupper,
   Gleaming blue blades,
   Gold-bordered garments.

   describe brilliant soldier (handwritten)

   Never will there be
   Bitterness between us:
   I do better by you,
   In song to praise you.
   The bloodsoaked field
   Before the marriage-feast,
   Foodstuff for crows
   Before the burial.
   A dear comrade, Owain;
   Wrong, his cover of crows.
   Sad wonder to me, in what land
   Marro's one son was slain.

2. Betorqued, to the fore wherever he'd charge,
   Shy of breath before a maid, he'd earn his mead.
   Rent the front of his shield, when he heard the war-cry,
      He'd spare none he pursued.
   He'd not turn from a fight till blood flowed;
   Like rushes he mowed men who'd not flee.
   The Gododdin tell, in the court's great hall,
   How before Madawg's tent when he'd return
   There would come but one man in a hundred.

3 Betorqued, a warrior, enemy's net,
Eagle's rush at river-mouths when roused.
His pledge was a purpose kept;
He bettered his intent: he was not turned back.
They fled before Gododdin's war-host,
Bold the pressure on Manawyd's land.
Neither mail-coat nor shield gave protection:
None could, on mead he was nourished,
Be kept from Cadfannan's stroke.

4 Betorqued, to the fore, a wolf in his fury,
The gold-collared warrior won beads of amber.
Gwefrfawr was worth much, for wine from a horn
He drove back the attack, blood on cheek.
Though Gwynedd and the northlands should come
    Through Ysgyrran's son's war-plan,
    Shattered shields.

5 Betorqued, to the fore, well-armed in combat,
Till his death a fearless man in a fray:
Champion charging at the head of war-hosts,
Five times fifty would fall before his blades.
There fall, of Deifr's and Brennych's men,
A hundred score to perdition in a single hour.
Meat for wolves, before the marriage-feast,
Tid-bit for crows, before the altar.
Before the burial, the bloodsoaked field.
For mead in the hall, among the hosts,
While there's a singer, Hyfaidd Hir will be praised.

6 Men went to Gododdin, laughing and chaffing,
Savage in battle, lances aligned.
A brief year in peace they stay quiet.
Bodgad's son, his hand-craft wrought slaughter.
Though they go to churches for shriving,
The old and the young, the bold and the meek,
True is the tale, death confronted them.

7 Men went to Gododdin, laughter-loving.
Assailants in a war-host, keen for combat,
They would slaughter with swords, in short order.
A pillar in combat, bountiful Rheithfyw.

8 Men went to Catraeth, in high spirits their war-band.
Pale mead their portion, it was poison.

48

Three hundred under orders to fight.
And after celebration, silence.
Though they go to churches for shriving,
True is the tale, death confronted them.

9 Men went to Catraeth, mead-nourished war-host,
Strong, vigorous – wrong should I not praise them –
With great dark-socketed crimson blades.
Close-ranked, stubborn, the warhounds fought.
Of Brennych's war-band I'd have thought it a burden:
Should I leave one in human form alive.
I lost a comrade, I was steadfast,
Ready man in combat, hard for me to leave him.
The hero sought no father-in-law's dowry,
Cian's young son from Maen Gwyngwn.

10 Men went to Catraeth at dawn:
Their fears had been left behind.
Three hundred clashed with ten thousand.
He stains spears ruddy with blood,
Most valiant bulwark in battle,
Before Mynyddawg Mwynfawr's war-band.

11 Men went to Catraeth at dawn:

Their mettle shortened their lives.
They drank mead, yellow, sweet, ensnaring;
Many a singer for a year was merry.
Crimson their swords, let their blades stay uncleansed,
   Lime-white shields and four-sided spearpoints,
Before Mynyddawg Mwynfawr's war-band.

12 A man went to Catraeth at daybreak:
He made mockeries of war-hosts.
They made certain biers were needed
With the most merciless blades in Christendom.
He fashioned, sooner than mention truce,
A bloodbath and death for one who faced him.
When he moved to the fore of Gododdin's war-host
Brave Neirthiad did what he boldly planned.

13 A man went to Catraeth at daybreak.
He guzzled mead-suppers at midnight.
Woeful, fellow-warrior's lament,
His campaign, hot-blooded killer.
   There hurried to Catraeth

[handwritten marginalia: a year of feasting / drinking in return for fighting for the king]

49

No great man with aims
  So expansive over mead;
None from Eidyn's fortress
  Would so completely
  Break up enemy ranks.
Tudfwlch Hir, from his land and homesteads,
Would slay Saxons at least once a week.
His valour will stay long-lasting,
Kept in mind by his splendid comrades.
When Tudfwlch came, people's sustainer,
Spearmen's post was a killing ground, Cilydd's son.

14 A man went to Catraeth at dawn,
Lordly face like a shield-wall.
Sharply they'd attack, they'd gather spoils,
Loud as thunder the crash of shields.
Ardent man, prudent man, singular man,
He'd rip and he'd pierce with spear-points.
Deep in blood he would strike with blades,
Hard-pressed, steel weapons on heads.
In the hall the hewer bowed humbly.
Facing Erthgi, war-hosts would groan.

15 It is told, of the region of Catraeth,
Men fall, long was the grief for them.
Through thick, through thin, they fought for the land,
The sons of Godebawg, a loyal people.
Long biers bore men drenched in blood.
Wretched was the lot, fate's strict demand,
Allotted to Tudfwlch and Cyfwlch Hir.
Though by candle's light we drank bright mead,
Though good was its taste, it was long detested.

16 First out of Eidyn's bright fort, he inspired
Faithful warriors who'd follow him.
Blaen, on down pillows, would pass around
The drinking-horn in his opulent hall.
The first brew of bragget was his.
Blaen took delight in gold and purple;
First pick of sleek steeds raced beneath him:
At sound of battle his high heart earned them.
First to raise the war-cry, gainful return,
Bear in the path, ever slow to retreat.

17 Force in the front line,
Sunlight on pasture:
Lord, where can be found
The isle of Britain's heaven?
Rough the ford before the warrior,
Shield as a shelter.
Splendid his drinking-horn
In Eidyn's great hall,
His grandeur a display.
His mead made one drunk;
He would drink strong wine.
In combat, a reaper,
He would drink sweet wine,
Battle-bold of mind,
Battle-leeks reaper.
Battle's bright arm,
They sang a battle-song.
Battle-armoured,
Battle-pinioned,
His shield was sheared thin
By warfare's spears.
Comrades fell
In warfare's strife:
Unfaltering his fighting,
Blameless he avenged them.
His rage was appeased
Before green turf covered
The grave of Gwrwelling Fras.

18 They revere what is right.
They stain three spear-shafts,
Fifty, and five hundred.
Three hounds with three hundred,
Three horsemen of war
From gold-smithied Eidyn,   3
Three mail-clad war-bands,
Three gold-torqued leaders,
Three furious horsemen,
Three peers in battle,
Three leaping as one,   Trinity
They routed foes savagely.
Three in hard fighting,
They slew foes easily,

Gold in close combat,
Three rulers of men
Who came from the Britons,
Cynri and Cynon,
Cynrain of Aeron.
The wily tribes
Of Deifr would ask:
Has there come from the Britons
A man better than Cynon,
Foe-stabbing serpent?

19 I drank wine and mead in the hall.
Numerous his spears
In the clash of men:
    He'd furnish food for eagles.
When Cydwal charged the battle-cry rose
With the green of dawn wherever he came.
He'd leave shields in splinters, shattered.
    Stiff spears the splitter
    Cut down in combat:
        He'd break the front rank.
The son of Sywno, a wise man knew it,
    Sold his life to purchase
    A famous name.
        He'd strike with sharpened blade.
He had cut down Athrwys and Affrai.
As pledged, he intended an onslaught:
    He would make corpses
    Of men brave in battle;
        He'd attack in Gwynedd's front line.

20 I drank wine and mead in the hall.
Since I drank, I attacked the border, mournful fate.
Not harmless, a reckless heart:
When all would fall back, you'd attack.
Glory come to you, for you would not sin;
World-renowned was reckless Breichior.

21 Men went to Catraeth, they were far-famed:
Wine and mead from gold cups was their drink
For a year, according to noble custom,
Three men and three score and three hundred, gold-torqued.
Of those who went forth after lavish drink
But three won free through battle prowess:

52

Aeron's two war-hounds and Cynon came back,
And I, soaked in blood, for my praise-song's sake.

22 My kinsman in carousal, no concern was ours,
Save what came of the feast, steel-hard warlord.
At court he was not kept short of mead.
He'd lay layer upon layer, with steady strokes,
Staunch in conflict, staunch in distress.
The Gododdin do not tell, after battle,
That any was keener than Llifiau.

23 Weapons scattered,
Column shattered, standing his ground,
Great the havoc,
The hero turned back the Lloegr-men's swarm.
He planted shafts,
In the front line, in the spear-clash.
He laid men low,
Made wives widows, before his death.
Graid ap Hoywgi,
Confronting spears, formed a rampart.

24 Hero, shield held below his freckled brow,
His stride a young stallion's.
There was battle-hill din, there was fire,
There were swift spears, there was sunlight,
There was crows' food, a crow's tid-bit.
And before he was left at the ford,
As the dew fell, graceful eagle,
Beside the wave's spray, near the slope,
The world's poets pronounce him great of heart.
His war-plans cost him what by rights was his;
Wiped out, his picked warriors by foemen.
And before his burial below Eleirch Fre
    There was valour in his breast,
His blood had washed over his war-gear.
Undaunted, Buddfan ap Bleiddfan.

25 Wrong to leave him unremembered, large his achievement:
He'd not leave a breach out of cowardice.
He did not leave his court, reward of song,
On New Year's Day, of his own will.
Though his land be desert, it was not for ploughing.
Too bitter the conflict, generous warlord,

53

Lord drenched in blood, after the wine-feast,
Gwenabwy ap Gwen, the battle of Catraeth.

26 It was true, as Cadlew declared:
No man's horses could overtake Marchlew.
He would plant spears in a conflict
From a leaping, wide-ranging steed.
Though not reared for burdens, for hardship,
Fierce his sword-stroke at his station.
He would plant ashen spears from his hand's clutch
　　Atop his steaming trim roan.
The lord much-loved would share his lavish wine;
He would slash with furious bloodstained blade:
As a reaper hacks in turning weather,
So Marchlew made the blood gush forth.

27 Isag, much-esteemed man from the south,
Like the flow of the sea his ways,
　　Congenial and generous,
　　And well-mannered drinking mead.
Where his weapons delve, they call it quits,
Not wishy-washy, no shilly-shally.
His sword rang in the heads of mothers.
Warfare's wall, Gwyddnau's son was renowned.

28 Ceredig, cherished his fame,
He would seize, would preserve renown.
Pet cub, at peace before his death-day came,
　　Supreme his courtesy.
May one who loved songs come, in due time,
To heaven's land, recognition's home.

29 Ceredig, beloved leader,
Ferocious champion in battle,
Battlefield's gold-fretted shield,
Spears broken to bits, splintered,
Sword-stroke furious, not feeble,
Like a man he'd hold the spearmen's post.
Before earth's grief, before suffering,
Firm in purpose he'd stand his ground.
May welcome be his among the host
With the Trinity, in total unity.

30 When Caradawg would charge into battle,
Like a wild boar, three war-hounds' slayer,

54

Bull of the war-host, hewer in combat,
He'd provide wolves food with his hand.
My witness is Ywain ab Eulad,
And Gwrien and Gwyn and Gwriad,
From Catraeth, from the carnage,
From Bryn Hyddwn, before they were taken.
After bright mead held in hand,
Not a one saw his father.

31 Men launched the assault, leapt forwards as one.
Short-lived, drunk above clarified mead,
Mynyddawg's war-band, renowned in battle:
For their feast of mead, their lives were payment,
Caradawg and Madawg, Pyll and Ieuan,
Gwgon and Gwion, Gwyn and Cynfan,
Steel-weaponed Peredur, Gwawrddur and Aeddan,
Attackers in a battle of shattered shields.
And though they were being slain, they slew.
None to their own regions returned. *much destruction*

32 Men launched the assault, nourished as one
For a year over mead, grand their design.
How sad their tale, insatiable longing,
Bitter their dwelling, no mother's son cherished them.
How long the grief for them and the yearning
For ardent men of wine-nourished lands.
Gwlgawd of Gododdin, for lively men
He provided renowned Mynyddawg's feast,
And its price, the battleground of Catraeth.

33 Men went to Catraeth in force, in full cry,
Swift steeds and dark-blue war-gear and shields,
Spear-shafts held high and spear-points sharp-edged,
And glittering mail-coats and swords.
He'd take the lead, he'd bore through war-hosts:
Five times fifty would fall before his blades.
Rhufon Hir, he'd give gold to the altar,
And rewards and rich gifts to the singer.

34 Never was built a hall so acclaimed,
So great, so mighty for slaughter.
You'd prove worthy of mead, firebrand Morien.
He'd not say, Cynon, that he'd make no corpses,
Armour-clad, loud-shouting spearman:
His sword sounded atop the rampart.

No more than a broad-based rock will budge
Would he be budged, Gwid ap Peithan.

35 Never was built a hall so renowned,
Save for Morien, heir of Caradawg,
There came from combat, lordly his ways,
No fiercer fighter than Fferog's son.
Firm his hand, he'd inflame a runaway horseman,
Bold warrior, refuge for a frightened war-band.
Before the war-host of Gododdin his shield was shattered:
    Hard-pressed, he was steadfast.
On the day of battle he was quick to act, bitter the
                                        recompense:
Mynyddawg's man would prove worthy of mead-horns.

36 Never was built a hall so faultless)
    [. . .]
Than kind-hearted Cynon, jewel-decked lord.
Rightly he'd sit in the place of honour.
Whoever he'd strike was not struck again.
Sharp-pointed his spears,
Shield in pieces, he'd bore through war-hosts,
Speedy his steeds, front-runners.
On the day of battle his blades were deadly
When Cynon would charge in the green of dawn.

37 Never was built a hall so flawless,
    [. . .]
So generous, lion's rage, wide-ranging,
As kind-hearted Cynon, lord most fair.
Refuge in combat, on the far wing,
Door, war-host's anchor, noblest of blessings.
Of those I have seen, and I see, in the world
Wielding weapons, the bravest in battle.
He would slash the foe with sharpest blade:
Like rushes they'd fall before his hand.
Son of Clydno, long-praised, I will sing to you, lord,
    Praise unstinted, unstilled.

38 He attacked full force, at the forefront:
He drove out the foe, he drew the line.
Spear-thrusting lord, laughing in combat,
He displays his valour, like Elffin,
Far-famed Eithinyn, wall of war, bull of battle.

56

alliteration

39 He attacked full force, at the forefront,
For mead in the hall and drinks of wine.
He planted his blades between two war-hosts,
Superb horseman before the Gododdin,
Far-famed Eithinyn, wall of war, bull of battle.

40 He attacked full force for eastern herds.
The war-band rose, shields shredded.
Shield rent before Beli's bellowing cattle,
Lord deep in blood, border's fleet defender,
He sustains us, grey-haired, on a charger,
Prancing steed, stubborn ox, gold torqued warrior.
The boar made a pact before the line, cunning man,
Deserving of his due, a cry of resistance:
'Let him that calls us to heaven protect us in battle.'
    He brandishes his war-spears.
Cadfannan gained plunder, great his praise:
No dispute that a war-band lay prostrate before him.

41 For the feast, most sad, disastrous,
For settled, for desolate land,
For the falling of hair from the head,
Among warriors, an eagle, Gwyddien.
Fiercely he defended them with his spear,
A planner, a tiller, its owner.
Morien defended
Myrddin's praise-song, and placed the chieftain
In earth, our strength, our support.
Worth three men, for a maid's favour, Bradwen;
Worth twelve, Gwenabwy fab Gwen.

42 For the feast, most sad, disastrous,
Hard worked, the shields in the fighting,
In the fury of swordstrokes on heads.
In Lloegr, torn flesh before three hundred lords.
Who would seize a wolf's mane without sword in hand
    Needs a bold heart under his cloak.
From the clash of rage and destruction
Bradwen perished, he did not escape.

43 Gold on fortress wall,
Battle's onslaught
    [. . .]
    [. . .]
    [. . .]

[. . .]
The living will tell
Of a leader's doings,
Of [. . .]
The living will not say that in the hour of slaughter
Cynhafal would not lend his support.

44 When you were a far-famed warrior
Fighting for enemies' fertile land,
Of right we were called outstanding, noteworthy men.
He was a firm door, firm fort of refuge;
He was gracious to earnest suppliants;
He was fortress for a war-host that trusted him:
Call for Gwynfyd, and there he'd be.

45 I'm no wearied lord.
I'll avenge no affront.
I'll laugh no laughter
Under crawlers' feet.
Outstretched my knee
In an earthen dwelling,
A chain of iron
Around my two knees.
Of mead from drinking-horn,
Of Catraeth's men,
I, not I, Aneirin,
(Taliesin knows it,
Skilled in word-craft),
Sang The Gododdin
Before next day dawned.

46 The north's valour, a man enacted it,
Kind-hearted, bountiful lord by nature.
Does not walk the earth, mother has not borne,
One so comely and strong, iron-clad.
By his bright sword's strength he saved me,
From earth's harsh prison he brought me,
From a place of death, from a hostile land,
Cenau ap Llywarch, bold, undaunted.

47 The court of Senyllt, its cups brimming with mead,
     Would not be disgraced.
He'd set his sword against wrong-doing;
He'd set his strides to warfare;
He'd bear bloodstained men in his arms

Before Deifr's and Brennych's war-host.
Constant in his hall, swift horses,
Bloodied spears, and dark-blue war-gear,
A long brown spear in his hand,
And rushing about in his wrath,
Smile giving way to frown,
Bad-tempered and good in turn.
No sight of his men's feet in flight,
Heilyn, raider of every border.

48 Standing stone in cleared ground
On Gododdin's border
[. . .]
[. . .]
[. . .]
[. . .]
Season of storm,
Storm season,
[. . .] before the war-host.
From Din Dywyd
Came to us, came upon us
[. . .]
They strike harshly; they harrow the war-band.
Grugyn's shield, before battle's bull, its front was shredded.

49 His foe trembles before his blade,
Savage eagle, laughing in battle.
Sharp his stag-horns around Bancarw;
Speckled fingers, they crush a head.
Varied in mood: tranquil, turbulent;
Varied in mood: thoughtful, mirthful.
Briskly Rhys charges, furiously,
Not like those whose assault will falter.
Whoever he overtakes will not escape.

50 Unluckily the shield was pierced
Of kind-hearted Cynwal;
Unluckily he set his thighs
On a trim long-legged grey.
Dark his brown spear-shaft,
Darker his saddle.
The hero in his hut
Chews on the leg

Of a buck, his cell's wealth.
May he suffer this seldom.

51 Good fortune, Addonwy, you'd vowed to me:
What Bradwen did, you'd do; you'd slash, you'd burn;
You would do no worse than Morien.
You held neither far wing nor front line:
Bold eye, unblinking,
You did not see the great surge of horsemen.
They cut down, they did not spare Saxons.

52 Ready warriors rose for combat.
A strong land will be heard in pursuit.
A wave is beating, bright wayfarer,
Where the lively, the noblest are.
Of stockade, not a stick can you see.
A worthy lord brooks no provoking;
Morial will bear no reproach in pursuit,
Savage sword-blade ready for bloodshed.

53 Ready warriors rose for combat.
A strong land will be heard in pursuit.
He slaughtered with cudgel and blade
And ferocious hooves men in battle.

54 Warriors rose for combat, formed ranks:
With a single mind they assaulted.
Short their lives, long their kinsmen long for them.
Seven times their sum of Lloegr-men they slew.
Their fighting turned wives into widows;
Many a mother with tear-filled eyelids.

55 After wine-feast and mead-feast
They furnished slaughter.
    Manly youth, highly praised,
He made a stand
Before Buddugre's slope:
    Crows arose, cloud-climbing.
Warriors falling
Like a fresh swarm on him:
    Not a move towards fleeing.
Far-sighted, swift-moving,
From grey steeds a sword-edge,
    From the mound a sword-stroke.

Foremost at a feast, sleepless;
No sleeplessness today:
    Rheiddun's son, lord of warfare.

56 After wine-feast and mead-feast they left us,
Mail-clad men, I know death's sadness.
Before hair turned grey came their slaughter.
Before Catraeth, brisk was their war-band.
Of Mynyddawg's men, great the grief,
Of three hundred, but one man returned.

57 After wine-feast and mead-feast they charged,
Men renowned in battle, reckless of life
Bright ranks round the wine-bowl, they dined together;
Wine and mead and bragget, they made them theirs.
Of Mynyddawg's men, I am woeful,
Too many I lost of my true kinsmen.
Of three hundred champions who charged on Catraeth,
Alas, save one man, none returned.

58 As he'd always be when they rose for battle,
    Like a bouncing ball,
So he'd be until they returned.
So did the Gododdin
Take wine and mead in Eidyn,
    Unyielding in close combat.
And beneath Cadfannan a stud of red steeds,
Wild horseman, in the morning.

59 Anchor, Deifr-router,
Serpent with fearsome sting,
He'd trample dark-blue armour
    In the war-band's vanguard.
Terrifying bear;
Furious defender,
He'd trample spears
In the day of battle
    On a wall of alder.
Lord Neddig's heir,
Through rage he furnished
A feast for birds
    From battle's din.
Rightly are you called, for your loyal deeds,
Foremost leader, wall of a war-band,
Merin ap Madiain, blessed was your birth.

60 Song befitting a war-band is found:
   Soldiers were embroiled around Catraeth;
   Bloodstained garments, trod on, were trampled;
      Battle's branches were trampled.
      Mead payment in mead-horn,
         It was made good by corpses.
   Cibno will not say, after battle's furor,
   Though he took communion, that he had his due.

61 Song befitting a noble war-band;
   Roar of fire and thunder and flood-tide.
   Superb courage, strife-embroiled horseman,
   Red reaper, he hungered for war.
   Tireless fighter, he would hasten to battle
      In whatever land he might hear it.
   With his shield on his shoulder he'd lift a spear
      Like a glass of sparkling wine.
   Silver held his mead, gold was his due.
   Wine-fed was Gwaednerth ap Llywri.

62 Song befitting glittering battle-bands:
   And after it's risen, a river will flood.
   He sated grey eagles' grasping beaks;
      He furnished food for scavengers.
   Of gold-torqued men who went to Catraeth
   On Mynyddawg, ruler of men's, campaign,
   There came blameless from among Gododdin's Britons
      No man much better than Cynon.

63 Song befitting a well-trained war-band.
   World's cheerful small corner, he was spendthrift;
   He would have, world-wide, singers' acclaim
   For gold and great steeds and mead-drunk men.
   But when he came from battle they'd praise
   Cynddilig of Aeron, bloodstained men.

64 Song befitting glittering battle-bands;
   On Mynyddawg, ruler of men's, campaign,
   With the steeds of Eudaf Hir, Gwanannon's affliction,
   Was one who wore purple, land of broken men.

65 Cowards could not bear the hall's clamour
   Like a roaring fire when kindled.
   Tuesday, they donned their dark war-gear;
   Wednesday, their shields were made ready;

Thursday, certain their devastation;
Friday, carcasses were carried off;
Saturday, fluent their working as one;
Sunday, their crimson blades were wielded;
Monday, men seen hip deep in bloodshed.
The Gododdin say that after hard labour
Before Madawg's tent on their return
There would come but one man in a hundred.

66 Up early in the morning,
Fighting before the front line.
A breach, a blazing breakthrough:
Like a boar you charged uphill.
He was mannerly, was stern,
Was dark-hued war-hawks' blood-bath.

67 Up early, at dawning,
For hot work before the border.
In the lead, leading, pursuing,
Before a hundred he charged to the fore.
Fiercely you'd fashion a blood-bath
Like quaffing mead while laughing;
Easily you'd cut down corpses,
Fleet-footed man's bold sword-stroke.
    So eagerly was it
    He'd kill an enemy,
        Gwrhafal, in the war-host.

68 He fell into the depths, headlong.
The ready lord will not do as he designed.
Loss of honour, his slaying with spear.
Ywain's way was to mount the rampart,
Plying, before burial, the best spear,
Pursuing disaster, loss of songs.
Grey death, his gauntlet's office,
He dealt with his mailcoat-stripping hand.
    The lord will deal out reward
    From his earthen casket,
Chill, sad, the praise, pallid cheeks.
Shy when a maid would sit in judgment,
Owner of horses and war-gear and ice-bright shields,
Comrade in combat, mounting, falling.

69 Battle-leader, he led to war:
The land's war-band loved the bold reaper.

Greensward bloodsoaked around the fresh grave.
Armour covered his crimson garments,
Trampler on armour, armour-trampler.
Weariness came down like death.
Spears splintered as battle begins,
A clear path was the aim of his spear-thrust.

70 I sang a splendid song of your dwelling's ruin
And the hall that once was there.
It merited sweet ensnaring mead,
The champion's assault at dawn,
Fine tribute to Lloegr-men's war-bands.
Too great penance while they're let live.
Gwynedd's man, his glory will be heard;
Gwanannon will be his grave.
Steadfast, Cadafwy of Gwynedd,
War-band's bull, fierce clash of rulers,
Before a bed of earth, before burial.
Gododdin's border will be his grave.

71 A war-host accustomed to battle,
A lord, war-band's harsh-handed leader.
He was wise and refined and proud;
He was not rude to fellow-drinkers.
White horses whinnied under his protection:
It did Pobddelw's land no good.
We are called the wing and the vanguard in battle;
In the clash of spears, spears equally matched.
Honed blades' defense, champion in the fray,
Forceful man, flaming steel against the foe.

72 His war-steeds bore bloodstained war-gear,
      A red herd at Catraeth.
Blaenwydd fosters a fearless war-host,
War-hound charging a hill on the day of battle,
And renown, bright fame, will be ours.
From Hedyn's hand, a planting of iron.

73 A lord of Gododdin will be praised in song;
A lordly patron will be lamented.
Before Eidyn, fierce flame, he will not return.
He set his picked men in the vanguard;
He set a stronghold at the front.
In full force he attacked a fierce foe.
Since he feasted, he bore great hardship.

Of Mynyddawg's war-band none escaped
Save one, blade-brandishing, dreadful.

74 With Moried's loss, there was no shield:
They bore, they exalted the champion.
He carried blue blades in his hand;
Weighty spears threatened threatener's head.
From a dapple-grey steed, arching its neck,
Heavy the carnage before his blades.
When he triumphed in combat, not one to flee,
He earned our praise, sweet ensnaring mead.

75 Lucky victor, light-hearted, fearful folks' backbone,
With his blue blade that forced back a foreign foe,
Mighty stalwart, massive his hand,
Stout-hearted, clever, they press him hard.
    His way, to attack
    Before nine champions,
    Between friend and foe,
        And hurl defiance.
I love the victor, his was a seat of honour,
Cynddilig of Aeron, praiseworthy lion.

76 I loved his front-line attack at Catraeth
In return for mead in the hall and wine.
I loved it that he did not scorn a spear
Before he was slain, far from green Uffin.
I loved the heir of renown, he furnished bloodshed;
He laid on with his sword in fury.
The valiant will not say before the Gododdin
That renowned Ceidio's son was not a champion.

77 Grief to me, after the hard struggle,
The bearing of death's agony in anguish,
And worse, heavy grief to me, the sight
Of our warriors falling headlong.
And long the moaning and the mourning
For the home soil's stalwart men,
Rhufon and Gwgon, Gwion and Gwlyged,
Boldest men at their posts, staunch under stress.
May their souls be, after the battle,
Made welcome in heaven's land, home of plenty.

78 He drove back the press across a pool of blood;
He cut down, boldly, rows that would not retreat.

Tafloyw, with a flourish, would toss off a glass of mead;
   Before monarchs he'd toss a war-host.
His counsel was sought where many will not speak;
   Were he crude, he'd not have been heard.
Before the charge of axe-strokes and sharp-edged swords,
   A feast is held, his voice is called for.

79 War-host's haven,
His blade a haven,
With the war-band's vanguard
On the front line
In the day of battle,
In the clash of weapons.
They were heedless
After being drunk
With drinking mead.
There was no escape from
Our joyous charge
On the destined day.
   When the tale is told
The assault was broken
Of steeds and warriors,
   Sworn men's fate.

80 When a crowd of cares
Comes on me, I brood on my fear.
Breath failing
As in running, at once I weep.
The dear one I mourn,
The dear one I'd loved, noble stag.
With Argoed's men,
Alas, he always took his place.
Well did he press
Against war-hosts, for rulers' good,
Against rough wood,
Against grief's flood, for the feasts.
He escorted us to a blazing fire
And to white fleece and sparkling wine.
Geraint from the south, the war-cry was raised,
Gleaming white, fair the look of his shield.
Gracious lord of the spear, praiseworthy lord,
The sea's benevolence, I know its nature,
I know Geraint: you were a bountiful prince.

66

81 Ungrudging his praise, his renown,
Unbudging anchor in combat,
Unconquerable eagle of wrathful men.
Bent on battle, Eiddef was comely,
His swift horses were foremost in conflict,
    Cub fostered on wine from the cup.
Before a green grave, his cheek turning pale,
A reveller he was, above clear mead from the cup.

82 Ruin to all low ground, a flood:
His fetter, the same fullness.
    Rent the front of his shield,
    Hating hindrance, enraged,
        Rhufoniawg's defender.
They were called on again, each side of the Aled,
In the battle of horses and bloodstained war-gear.
    Immovable war-host,
    Mighty men in battle,
    Red the parish ground
        When they are aroused.
In hard fighting he'd slash with his blade;
He'd bear a harsh warning of battle.
He would furnish song for New Year's.
There could come before the son of Erfai,
There could come before the proud boar,
Any lady and maiden and noble.
And when he was son of a rightful ruler,
Among the men of Gwynedd, Clyd the merciful's blood,
    Before earth covered his cheek,
    Bountiful, prudent, undaunted.
        After praise and favour, sad
The grave of Garthwys Hir from Rhufoniog's land.

83 A loss has come to me, unlooked-for.
There comes, there will come, none heavier.
Was not nourished in hall one bolder than he
    Or more steadfast in battle.
And at Rhyd Benclwyd, foremost his horses,
Far-reaching his fame, riddled his shield.
And before Gwair Hir was hid under turf
He'd earn mead-horns, Fferfarch's only son.

The Gododdin (B-text)

1 Standing stone on cleared ground [. . .]
Fair play before Gododdin's border [. . .]
  He brought the luxury
  Of wine tents for the land's good.
  Season of storm,
  Foreign ships, foreign war-band,
  Treacherous war-band,
Splendid ranks, swift before a champion.
  From Din Dywyd
  It came upon us, came to us.
Grugyn's shield, facing battlefields its front was shredded.

2 Ruin to all low ground, a flood:
His like, the same fullness.
  Rent the front of his shield,
  Hating hindrance, reckless,
    Rhufoniawg's defender.
They were seen again, on each side of the Aled,
His war-steeds and his bloodstained war-gear.
  They must be steadfast,
  Greatly gifted,
  Valiant men
    When they are aroused.
In hard fighting he'd slash with his blade:
A hundred bore a bitter warning from battle.
  He would furnish song for New Year's.
There could come before the son of Urfai,
There could come before the proud boar
Any lady and maiden and noble.
And since he was son of a rightful king,
Lord of Gwynedd's men, of Cilydd the merciful's blood,
  Before earth covered his cheek,
  Bountiful, prudent, sought out for
  His gifts and fame, and sad
Is the grave of Gorthyn Hir from Rhufuniog's border.

3 For the feast, most sad, disastrous,
For settled, for desolate land,
Three boars primed for combat at cock-crow
[. . .] Morien with his spear,
[. . .]

68

Against pagans and Gaels and Picts.
Very dear, the stiff red corpse of Bradwen,
Right hand of Gwenabwy fab Gwen.

4 For the feast, most sad, disastrous,
Heavy, grievous, most desolate land,
The battle-leader,
The bearded warrior [. . .]
[. . .] beholding Eidyn and its land.
His gauntlet was raised
Against pagans and Gaels and Picts.
Who tugs a wolf's mane without spear in hand
  Needs a brave heart under his cloak.
I will sing so that Morien should not die,
Right hand of Gwenabwy ap Gwen.

5 Good fortune, Addonwy, you'd vowed to me:
What Bradwen did, you'd do; you'd slash, you'd burn.
You held neither far wing nor front line.
Bold eye [. . .]
I have not seen from sea to sea
A horseman who'd be worse than [. . .]

6 Three hundred, gold-torqued, launched the assault,
Defending the land: there was slaughter.
Although they were being slain, they slew,
And till the world's end, they'll be honoured.
And of all those who went, companions,
Alas, save one man, none escaped.

7 Three hundred, gold-torqued,
Aggressive, accomplished;
Three hundred proud men,
Of one mind, well-armed;
Three hundred fierce horses
Bore them into battle.
Three hounds and three hundred:
Alas, they did not come back.

8 Savage in battle, stubborn under stress,
There was no truce he'd make in combat.
In the day of wrath he would not shun strife:
A raging boar was Bleiddig ap Eli.

He guzzled wine from brimming glasses.
And on the day of conflict he'd perform a feat
On a white stallion before he died:
He'd leave crimsoned corpses behind him.

9 Hard-pressed before the ford, he'd stiffen his troops,
War-band's firm spear.
Splendid his assault, mind bent on glory.
Skilful charge
His joyous charge, I heard his war-cry.
He'd make men lie low
And wives widows, before his death.
The right of Bleiddgi's son:
Confronting spears, to form a rampart.

10 Splendid your conduct [. . .]
[. . .] spears from him [. . .] you'd put to flight.
When all would turn back, you'd attack.
Were it wine, the blood of all those you struck dead,
You'd have plenty for three years and four:
You'd make short work of it for your steward.
Heaven's home be yours, because you would not flee.
World-famed was unshakable Breichiawl.

11 When he'd raid in the borderland, great was his fame;
He would earn his wine, gold-torqued warrior.
He'd give gleaming array to the brave;
He'd defend a hundred men, lordly hero,
Noble by nature, foreign horseman,
Cian's only son, from beyond Bannawg.
The Gododdin will not say on the field of battle
There was anyone fiercer than Llif.

12 Anchor, Deifr-router,
Serpent with fearsome sting,
Unbudgeable rock
  In the war-host's front line,
Power in readiness,
Violence under stress,
Overpayment
  Of spears' pressure:
Rightly are you called, for your loyal deeds,
Foremost leader, wall of all your countrymen,
Tudfwlch, forceful in battle, barred fortress.

13 Anchor, Deifr-router,
   Serpent with fearsome sting
      In the war-host's front line.
   Rightly are you called, for your loyal deeds,
   Foremost leader, wall of every people,
   Merin ap Madiain, blessed was your birth.

14 Anchor, Deifr-router,
   Unbudgeable rock
      In the war-host's front line.
   Many were crimsoned,
   Both horses and men,
      Before the Gododdin.
   Fleet the baying hounds,
   The war-band's rising,
   Full cover of mist,
      Before Merin's stronghold.

15 Shield hammered hard, he'd yield to no one:
      He nursed his thirst for honour.
   Heedless of war-gear and horses in the van of battle,
      They'd plant bloodied spears of holly.
   When my comrade was struck, he'd strike others:
      He would bear no affront.
   Firm in guarding the ford, he was proud
   When his was the prize portion in the hall.

16 True what Tudlew told you,
   That no man's horses overtook Marchlew.
   Though not reared for hurdles, for hardship,
   Strong was his sword-stroke at his station.
   He'd scatter ashen spears from his hand's clutch
      Atop his steaming trim bay.

17 Heaven's haven, longed-for land's home:
   Woe is ours from yearning and ceaseless sorrow.
   When noblemen came from Din Eidyn, a band
      Of picked men from each provident region,
   In strife with Lloegr's mingled war-hosts,
   Nine-score to one on each mail-clad man,
   Piled-up horses and war-gear and silken garments,
   Gwaednerth held his own in battle.

18 Of Mynyddawg's band, when they launched the assault,
Bright ranks round the wine-bowl, they'd dined together:
For Mynyddawg's feast, my mind is woeful,
Too many have I lost of my true kinsmen.
Of three hundred, gold-torqued, who charged on Catraeth,
Alas, save one man, they did not escape.

19 Gododdin's picked men on shaggy mounts,
Swan-white steeds, war-harness drawn tight,
And in the vanguard attacking the war-host,
Fighting for Eidyn's forests and mead.
      Through Mynyddawg's war-plan
      Shields went spinning,
      Blades descended
          On pallid cheeks.
They loved [. . .] attacking;
They bore no disgrace, men who would not flee.

20 I drank deeply of mead in my turn,
Wine-fed before Catraeth, at a single gulp.
When he slashed with his blades, unbudging in battle,
      He was no sorry sight.
He was no ugly spectre, providing protection,
Baneful shield-bearer, Madawg of Elfed.

21 When he came to a conflict
No thought of survival.
Aeron's avenger,
He would charge, gold-adorned,
Britons' defender.
High-spirited, Cynon's horses.

22 Standing stone on cleared ground, on cleared ground a hill
On Gododdin's border [. . .]
      Foreign ship, foreign war-band
      [. . .]
      [. . .] motley war-band
      From Din Dywyd
          Came upon us.
Grugyn's shield, before battle's bull its front was shredded.

23 Gold on fortress wall,
Ardent assault,

Sinful not to be roused for battle.
One [. . .] Saxon
Rewarded the birds.
[. . .]
[. . .]
The living will tell
Of a leader's doings,
Of one like a lightning-bolt.
The living will not say
That on the day of slaughter
Cynhafal did not lend his support.

24 Who'll become heir
With Heinif gone?
One above the throng,
Of the noblest name,
He slew a great host
To gain renown.
He slew, son of Nwython,
Of gold-torqued warriors
A hundred princes
That he might be praised.
He was better when he went
With the men to Catraeth:
Wine-nourished man,
Generous-hearted,
A man brisk in battle,
Mail-coat router,
He was rough, he was reckless,
On his stallion's back.
There armed for battle,
Brisk his spear and his shield
And his sword and his dagger,
Than Heinif ap Nwython
No better man.

change in conjugation

25 From beyond Merin Iddew, valiant in battle,
Thrice as fierce as a fierce lion,
Bubon wrought with mighty wrath.

26 Natural – on a charger to defend Gododdin;
    In the vanguard, swift his grey steed;
Natural – that he should be fleet as a stag;

Natural – before Deifr's picked men he'd attack;
Natural – what he said, Golystan's son, would be heard,
  Though his father was no high lord;
Natural – on Mynyddawg's behalf, shattered shields;
Natural – a crimson spear before Eidyn's lord, Urfai.

27 Stewards could not bear the hall's clamour.
From the war-band, an outburst of fighting
Like a roaring fire when kindled.
Tuesday, they donned their comely war-gear;
Wednesday, their common cause was savage;
Thursday, envoys were pledged;
Friday, carcasses were calculated;
Saturday, unhindered their working as one;
Sunday, crimson blades were shared by all;
Monday, men seen hip deep in bloodshed.
The Gododdin say that after long hard labour
Before Madawg's tent on their return
[There would come but one man in a hundred.]

28 He attacked in full force for eastern herds.
Like a lion, I honour him:
At Gwanannon, for mead the greatest valour.
And a lucky warrior, splendid leader,
Renowned Eithinyn ap Boddw Adaf.

29 Superb men, they have left us.
They were wine-fed and mead-fed.
    For Mynyddawg's banquet
    I am grief-stricken,
        For a stern warrior's loss.
    Like peals of thunder
    Shields would resound
        Before Eithinyn's onslaught.

30 Early rising, at dawning,
When warriors attack in a war-host,
In the lead, leading, pursuing,
Before a hundred he charged in front.
He was as greedy for corpses
As for quaffing mead or wine,
    So eagerly was it
    He'd strike an enemy,
Ithael, fierce in assault.

74

31 Early rising, in the morning,
  In conflict with a chief before the border,
      He was a bitter fighter
      In the van of battle,
      A beloved friend
          Where he chose to be.
  He was mannerly, he was stern;
  He was a dark-garbed spear-lord.

32 His blades were seen in the war-band,
  Contending with a stubborn foe.
  Before his shield's clamour they'd cower:
  They'd flee before Eidyn's hill, countless men.
  Those his hand grasped would not leave him.
      There were candles for him, and chanting.
  Stubborn, shield shredded, when hard pressed he'd press on;
      He'd not strike twice: he'd strike when struck.
  Frequent after the feast was his gift to the enemy;
      Bitterly was he dealt with.
  And before he was covered with clods of earth
  Edar earned the right to drink his mead.

33 Boldest man in a fortress,
  Splendid supporter,
  Bright [. . .]
  Fierce [. . .]
  [. . .]
  [. . .] his purpose.
  The Gododdin will not say, in the day of slaughter,
  That Cynhafal did not lend his support.

34 Crimsoned blades
  Covering the ground,
      Hero ruddied in his rage,
  Champion, slayer,
  He would be joyful,
      Wolvish at his post, war-host's wolf.
  War-band's herb-garden,
  Champion slaying,
      Before he was blinded, no weakling.
  Rightly are you called, for your loyal deeds,
  Foremost helmsman, wall of all your countrymen,
  Tudfwlch, forceful in battle, barred fortress.

35 He encountered a bitter foe,
    Wrathful slayer of a raider band.
    He was not hid from sight and outlawed;
    Erf was no bitter-sweet fellow-drinker.
    Grey horses snorted under his protection;
    It did Pobddelw's land no good.
    He withdrew, battle's bull, not an acre,
    Stubborn in purpose, true leader.

36 He thrust beyond three hundred of the boldest;
    He would mow down centre and wing.
    He was worthy, in the van of the most bountiful war-band;
    He'd bestow horses from his herd in winter.
    He would sate black crows on the fortress wall
        Though he was not Arthur.
    He did mighty deeds in combat,
    A rampart in the front line, Gwawrddur.

37 Song most fit for a skilful war-band.
    And before the loss of Aeron's door-bolt
    The beaks of grey eagles gave praise to his hand;
        Enraged he furnished food for scavengers.
    For the sake of Mynyddawg, ruler of men,
    He set his side against enemy spears.
    Before Catraeth the gold-torqued were brisk:
    They struck, they cut down those who stood firm.
    They were far from their land, whelps of war.
    Seldom in battle from among Gododdin's Britons
        Was there one much better than Cynon.

38 Song most fit for a war-band is found:
    Soldiers were embroiled around Catraeth;
    Bloodstained garments, trod on, were trampled;
        Battle's branches were trampled.
        Retribution for mead-payment,
            It was made good by corpses.
    Cibno will not say, after battle's furor,
    Though he took communion, that he had his due.

39 His hand provided food for birds.
    I revere him, mighty war-lord,
    Savage warrior and slasher.
        He was garbed in gold

In the front line,
    In war-lords's fierce contention.
Battle's speckled wine-steward,
Third Fearsome One,
War-cry's pursuer,
    Ferocious bear in attack,
War-host's arouser,
Talk of the war-band,
    Comely was Cibno mab Gwengad.

40 Song most fitting a well-trained war-band.
    World's cheerful small corner, he was spendthri

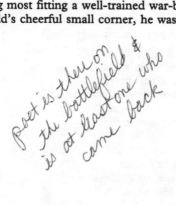
poet is there on the battlefield & is at least one who came back

Prologue(s) to *The Gododdin* (c. 650?)

Both the texts of *The Gododdin* contain what appear to be versions of a prologue, designed to be declaimed by later poets reciting the poem. These verses invoke the Gododdin, and revere the memory of Aneirin, the poet. In the B-text, it is the second stanza, coming after the stanza on the battle of Strathcarron. In the A-text, a similar stanza occurs as the 55th indicating that the scribe did not recognise its nature. The parallels in the texts suggest an original single source; the differences suggest that reciters varied this prologue to suit particular occasions.

B

Gododdin, I make claims on your behalf,
In the host's presence, boldly, in the hall.
And the song of Dwywai's stout-hearted son,
Wherever made known, it will prevail.
Since a gracious man, battle's wall, was pierced,
Since earth came down on Aneirin,
Now song and Gododdin are parted.

A

Gododdin, I beseech your favour,
In valleys beyond Drum Esyd's ridges,
Youth eager for silver, blameless.
From the lore of Dwywai's son, your valour.
He was not weak or base before a blazing fire.
From daylight to daylight, pinewood alight,
Door alight for a wayfarer in purple.
Gracious man slain, courteous man pierced, battle's wall,
Unparted were his song and Aneirin.

TALIESIN (late sixth century) Welsh

Much of the early poetry addressed to patrons in the northern British king-doms is attributed to the poet Taliesin. Little can be said about him historically. He is one of five poets mentioned as 'famed in British verse' at a period we may date roughly to the late sixth century. Most of the poems we may attribute to him are addressed to Urien ap Cynfarch, king of Rheged, a territory which certainly included modern-day Cumbria, but also perhaps some of southern Scotland. Urien is also represented in one poem as an overlord in Ayrshire. These poems end with a distinctive coda, something of a signature, proclaiming his devotion as poet to his patron, Urien. There is also an elegy for Urien's son, Owain. The poems are set against a backdrop of constant battle, both between the native British and Anglo-Saxon settlers and among the British kingdoms themselves.

In the later Welsh tradition, Taliesin became the subject of legend and his own poetry was mixed with both saga poems and prophetic verse in the 13th-century manuscript known as *The Book of Taliesin*. In a late prose romance he is represented as a magician as well as poet, with a mysterious birth, transformations into animal forms and the power to rescue his ruler, Elphin, by poetic spells. *The Book of Taliesin*, however, contains an early core of some 12 poems which may indeed be Taliesin's, and certainly seem to belong historically to the late sixth century.

The Battle of Gwen Ystrad

Catraeth's men set out at daybreak
Round a battle-winning lord, cattle-raider.
Urien he, renowned chieftain,
Constrains rulers and cuts them down,
Eager for war, true leader of Christendom.
Prydain's men, they came in war-bands:
Gwen Ystrad your base, battle-honer.
Neither field nor forest shielded,
Land's protector, your foe when he came.
Like waves roaring harsh over land
I saw savage men in war-bands.
And after morning's fray, torn flesh.
I saw hordes of invaders dead;
Joyous, wrathful, the shout one heard.
Defending Gwen Ystrad one saw
A thin rampart and lone weary men.
At the ford I saw men stained with blood
Down arms before a grey-haired lord.

They wish peace, for they found the way barred,
Hands crossed, on the strand, cheeks pallid.
Their lords marvel at Idon's lavish wine;
Waves wash the tails of their horses.
I saw pillaging men disheartened,
And blood spattered on garments,
And quick groupings, ranks closed, for battle.
Battle's cloak, he'd no mind to flee,
Rheged's lord, I marvel, when challenged.
I saw splendid men around Urien
When he fought his foes at Llech Wen.
Routing foes in fury delights him.
Carry, warriors, shields at the ready;
Battle's the lot of those who serve Urien.

And until I die, old,
By death's strict demand,
I shall not be joyful
Unless I praise Urien.

In Praise of Urien

Urien of Yrechwydd,
Most bountiful of Christians,
Much you bestow
On the men of this land.
As you gather in,
So you give away.
Joyful Christendom's poets
As long as you live.
Greater is the joy
To have such a hero,
Greater is the glory
Of Urien and his offspring,
Since he is chieftain,
Ruler supreme,
Wayfarers' refuge,
Powerful champion.

Lloegr-men know him
As they will report:
Death's what they get

And pain a-plenty,
Their dwellings ablaze
And their garments seized,
And heavy losses
And grievous hardship,
Getting no deliverance
From Urien of Rheged.

Urien is ruthless

Rheged's defender,
Renowned lord, land's anchor,
I delight in you
From all that's reported:
Savage your spear-thrust
When battle is sounded.
When you charge into battle
You wreak a slaughter,
Houses fired before daybreak
By Yrechwydd's lord.

Most fair, Yrechwydd,
And most bountiful its men.
No safeguard for Angles:
Round the bravest ruler,
The bravest offspring.
You yourself are best:
Was not nor will be
Ever your equal.
When one beholds him
Great is the terror.
Ever joy around him,
Round a spirited monarch,
Around him rejoicing
And abundant riches,
Golden king of the north,
High lord of monarch.
And until I die, old,
By death's strict demand,
I shall not be joyful
Unless I praise Urien.

The Court of Urien

My place of ease,
With Rheged's men:
Respect and welcome
And mead in plenty,
Plenty of mead
For celebration,
And splendid lands
For me in abundance,
Great possessions
And gold and wealth,
Wealth and gold,
And high honour,
High honour
And fulfilled desire,
Desire fulfilled
To do me good.

He slays, he hangs,
Supplies, provides,
Provides, supplies,
In the lead, he slays.
He gives great honour
To the world's poets.
The world for certain
Submits to you.
At your will,
God, for your sake,
Has made lords groan
Fearing destruction.
Rouser of battle,
Defender of the land,
Land's defender,
Battle's rouser,
Constant around you
Hooves stamping,
Stamping of hooves
And drinking of beer.
Beer for the drinking
And a splendid dwelling,
And a splendid garment
Was handed to me.

82

Llwyfenydd's people
All entreat you
With a single voice,
The great and the small.
Taliesin's praise-song
Will entertain them.
You are the best
Whose qualities ever
I have heard of,
And I will praise
All that you do.

glorification

as though he is a god

And until I die, old,
By death's strict demand,
I shall not be joyful
Unless I praise Urien.

The War-Band's Return

Throughout one year
One steady outflow:
Wine, bragget, mead,
Valour's reward.
A host of singers,
A throng around spits,
Torques round their heads,
Their places honoured.
Each went on campaign
Eager for combat,
His steed beneath him,
Making for Manaw
And greater gain,
Profit in plenty,
Eight score, the same colour,
Of calves and cattle,
Milch cows and oxen,
And each of them comely.

eager for combat

first person

I could not be joyful
Were Urien slain,
Much loved before he left
For spears' clashing contention,

With white hair soaked
And a bier his fate,
With cheek bloodstained,
Besmeared with blood.
Proud steadfast man,
His wife made widow,
My true sovereign,
My true reliance,
My lot, my bulwark, my chief,
Before savage strife.

Go, fellow, to the door,
See what's causing commotion.
Is it earth shaking?
Is it sea rushing in?
The chant grows louder
From marching men:
Be there foe on hill,
Urien will shake him;
Be there foe on hill,
Urien will strike him;
Be there foe on mountain,
Urien conquers him;
Be there foe on hillside,
Urien shatters him;
Be there foe in ditch,
Urien smites him.
Foe on path, foe on peak,
Foe at every bend,
Not one sneeze or two
Will shield him from death.

There would be no famine:
Herds of cattle surround him.
Battle-keen conqueror,
Well-armed, weapons gleaming,
Like death his spear
Mows down his foes.

And until I die, old,
By death's strict demand,
I shall not be joyful
Unless I praise Urien.

84

The Battle of Argoed Llwyfain

There was a great battle, Saturday morning,
From the time the sun rose till it set.
Fflamddwyn came on, in four war-bands.
Goddau and Rheged were mustering,
Summoned men, from Argoed to Arfynydd:
They were given not one day's delay.
Fflamddwyn shouted, big at boasting:
'Have my hostages come? Are they ready?'
Answered Owain, bane of the East:
'They've not come, are not here, are not ready,
And a cub of Coel's line must be pressed
Hard before he'd render one hostage.'
Shouted Urien, lord of Yrechwydd:
'If a meeting for peace-talk's to come,
Let our shield-wall rise on the mountain,
And let our faces lift over the rim,
And let our spears, men, be raised high,
And let us make for Fflamddwyn amidst his war-bands,
And let us slay him and his comrades.'
  Before Argoed Llwyfain
  There was many a dead man.
    Crows grew crimsoned from warriors.
And the war-band charged with its chieftain:
For a year I'll shape song to their triumph.

  And until I die, old,
  By death's strict demand,
  I shall not be joyful
  Unless I praise Urien.

In Praise of Rheged

Rise, Rheged, well-furnished with lords:
I have cherished you, though I be not yours.
They moan facing sword-blades and spears;
Men moan underneath round shields.
Greedy the white gulls' cries in Mathreu.
Not well fought, a lie does a lord no good.
A ruler's braced for adversities.
He'll send peace-seekers no message,

Fine swift horseman, fame of Gwrion.
Leader feckless, Idon was abandoned:
Till Ulph came, stern hand on his foes,
Till Urien came in his day to Aeron,
There was no warrior, was no welcome.
Noble-browed Urien, against Powys:
Not keen, the keen stock of Cyrrwys.
Bold against Gododdin, bright leader,
Strong in endurance, with a wild beast's nature,
Unblemished bearer of Gwyddien's blood-line.
Llwyfenydd saw lords tremble
In public defences at Mehyn.
A battle at Rhyd Alclud, battle for a crown,
A battle at Brewyn's cells, battle long to be honoured,
A battle at Prysg Catleu, a battle at Aber.
He fought with resounding steel.
The great battle of Cludfein, the fight at Pencoed,
A ravenous wolf-pack glutted with blood
Falling, men fierce in alliance.
Angles are bent on resistance,
Bloodstained venture, with Ulph in the ford.

*   *   *

I moaned in my breast with pride:
Spears on shoulder, shield in hand,
Goddau and Rheged making ready for battle.
I saw a man fashion a rampart,
Fair-famed chieftain, renowned trampler.
I know war is in the offing
And those I may lose will be lost.
I too was made drunk by mead-drink
From a dauntless bold man, fierce in pursuit.
I too proclaimed a shelter in battle:
My lord shares joyful blessings.
Worthless the best land compared to Urien.

    And until I die, old,
    By death's strict demand,
    I shall not be joyful
    Unless I praise Urien.

The Spoils of Taliesin

My courage asks, sorely troubled,
May I say what truly I see?
I saw before my lord, who saw not me,
All those dear to him, bold their requests.
I saw plants on display at Easter,
I saw leaves as accustomed break forth,
I saw a branch, all alike its blossoms,
I saw a lord, most gracious his ways.
I saw the ruler of Catraeth beyond the plains.
Let him be my lord, fellow-lords will not love him:
For my song, great will be his gifts.

The chief of warriors my choice, plentiful the spoils:
A spear of ash is my muse,
A shield before a chief, my bright smile.
Splendid chief, the boldest, is Urien:
He'll not withstand me, raucous cattle-raider,
Battle-ready, brightly armed, blue steel glinting.
Far and wide all these sing his praises.
A coward's tread's timid in court,
Fearsome lord, where he pleases to go.

Yellow gold's splendour in the hall,
Rich the defender of Aeron,
Great his passion for songsters and stags,
Great, ferocious, his wrath against foes,
Great his might on the side of the Britons.
Like a flaming wheel crossing the world,
Like a wave, rightful lord of Llwyfenydd,
Like a song, fit for prayer and battle,
Like a treasure-rich sea is Urien.

Delightful the dawn's abundant shoots,
Delightful is a lord, leader in battle.
Delightful are war-bands' swift steeds
At the start of May, war-hosts in Powys.
Delightful in Defwy, when he visits his people,
A highland eagle sauntering by.
I joined, on a fleet-footed steed,
A singular tribe, for the spoils of Taliesin.
Delightful the assault of steed and champion,

Delightful a nobleman, gift to a lord,
Delightful a herd of deer in hiding,
Delightful a wolf, broom-hidden, ravenous,
Delightful are the landsmen of Eginyr's son,
Of one blood and one voice, warriors at war,
One in voice their wicked war-whoop
With the sons of Nudd Hael, wide his realm.
And if I am brimming with joy
I will make the world's poets merry,
Before they are dead, the sons of Gwyddien,
War-leader of Urien's fair land.

Plea for Reconciliation

A ruler most valiant
I'll not abandon:
It is Urien I seek,
To him will I sing.
When my warrant comes
I will find a welcome
In the best of regions
Beneath the best of rulers.

No great matter to me,
Those princes I see:
I'll not go to them;
With them I'll not be:
I'll make for the north
To mighty monarchs:
Though for high stakes
I should lay a wager,
No need to boast,
Urien will not spurn me.

Llwyfenydd's land,
Mine are their riches,
Mine is their good will,
Mine their generosity,
Mine are their garments
And their luxuries,
Mead from drinking-horns,
And no end of good things
88

From the best of kings,
Most generous I've heard of.

Kings of every tribe,
All to you are bound.
Before you, they complain,
One must give way.
Though once I was willing
To mock an old man,
None better I loved
Before I knew him.
Now it is I see
How much I possess:
Save to God on high
I will not surrender him.
Your regal sons,
Most generous of men,
They will make their spears sing
In enemy lands.

And until I die, old,
By death's strict demand,
I shall not be joyful
Unless I praise Urien.

Elegy for Owain ab Urien

Soul of Owain ab Urien,
    May his Lord attend to its needs.
Rheged's lord, a green burden hides him,
    It was no light thing to praise him.
Locked below, a famed song-praised man,
    Dawn's wing-tips his whetted spears,
For there is found no equal
    To splendid Llwyfenydd's lord,
Reaper of foes, grasper,
    Of father and grandfather's make.
When Owain cut down Fflamddwyn,
    No more to it than sleeping:
Asleep is Lloegr's broad war-band
    With light upon their eyes.
And those who fled but little,

They were bolder than was need:
Owain punished them fiercely
  Like a wolf savaging sheep.
Splendid man, clad in pied war-gear,
  He'd grant steeds to suppliants:
Though he'd store up like a miser,
  It was shared, for his soul's sake.
Soul of Owain ab Urien,
  May his Lord attend to its needs.

attributed to TALIESIN (sixth century) Welsh

A further two poems, usually attributed to Taliesin, are addressed to Gwallawg ap Lleenawg, a king whose territory is as yet uncertain. It has often been placed in Elmet (Welsh *Elfed*), a kingdom not far from Leeds, still marked by place-names such as Sherburn-in-Elmet. Internal evidence of the poems, however, especially the proposed sites of the battles mentioned, suggest a more northerly location, such as southern Scotland.

In Praise of Gwallawg

In the name of Heaven's Lord, a rich retinue
   Is his, their sustainer.
Keen their lordly spears,
Savage war-loving lords.
He defended splendid Llan Lleenawg,
Conquers Unhwch's war-band, protector.
They meet the demand from Prydyn,
   From Perth Manaw and Eidyn.
They brook no opposition,
Clydwyn's company's companions.
He supplied enough spear-shafts
For a fleet, by ferocious fighting,
Timber for all in his rage,
Made war-hosts helpless, Gwallawg,
   Preferred carnage to playing games.
A battle by the tide, song-incited,
   He caused quite a stir in Efrawg;
A battle near Bre Trwyn, much heated,
   His fury's a mighty fire;
A battle before splendid ramparts,
   A hundred war-bands trembled in Aeron;
A battle in Arddunyon and Aeron Eiddyned,
   A grief to young men;
A battle in Coed Beidd at daybreak,
   You thought little of your foes;
A battle before Gwyddawl and Mabon,
None spared to speak till doomsday;
A battle at Gwensteri, Saxons submitting,
   Spearman [. . .];
A battle on Rhos Terra at dawn,
Mighty the man's war-cry in combat.

A beginning, my praise in verse
Of lords faultless in warfare:
Men who fill byres with cattle,
Haearddur and Hyfaidd and Gwallawg,
And Owain of Mon, true to Maelgwn's line,
Who lays marauders low.
    At Pen Coed, daggers:
    Once more rotting corpses
    And crows scavenging.
In Prydyn, in Eidyn, they confess,
In Gafran, all about Brecheinawg,
Embattled, in sturdy war-gear,
Who's not seen Gwallawg won't have seen a man.

Elegy for Gwallawg

In the name of Heaven's Lord, the war-hosts sing:
    They lament for a chieftain.
He drove back enemies' attack, the war-bands
    Of Rhun and Nudd and Nwython.
I will praise with the song of the Britons' poets
A nobleman's wealth of wisemen, single-voiced,
    Songful songster.
I will weave words, I will sing for a ruler:
He was dreaded in his land.
He'll do me, I'll do him no harm.
Hard the letting go, riches will not fail
    The ruler who never begrudges.
To the onlooker, heavy-hearted are kings
While they live, wealth's not theirs in the grave:
They can take no pride in their way of life;
Harder the torment to which they may go.
The earthly throng over Prydain, over-anxious,
The pompous will not away, let them rot,
Will be terrified, will be judged.
All will judge the man who is judged,
Who was honoured as judge over Elmet.
To no feckless man, his tribute,
Hot-headed lad with headlong courage.
Swift was Gwallawg in a war-band;
Slow was Gwallawg in retreat.

He asks none what a lord may do;
  A lord says not 'No' or 'Be gone.'

*　　*　　*

His war-band won't conquer by stealth,
Not slow to pin an enemy down.
Shield-heads are piercing horse-heads,
  From horsemen a valiant uproar.
A fierce royal war-band loves you.
They pledge sureties, the wealthy.
From Caer Glud to Caer Garadawg,
Pen-prys' land as well, Oh Gwallawg,
The rulers are silent, peaceful.

DINOGAD'S COAT (c. 650?) Welsh

This poem is the penultimate stanza in the A-text of *The Gododdin*, to which it clearly does not belong. The presumption is that the scribe found it in the margin of his manuscript and copied it unthinkingly. It is usually thought of as a 'cradle song', or a mother's song to her little boy in what was plainly a wealthy household, but the tense of the verbs gives it something of an elegiac tone. There is no good reason to assume it was not composed by, as well as being in the voice of, a woman, and thus may be the earliest poem by a woman to have been preserved in Britain.

Specked, specked, Dinogad's coat,
I fashioned it of pelts of stoat.
Twit, twit, a twittering,
I sang, and so eight slaves would sing.
When your daddy went off to hunt,
Spear on his shoulder, club in his hand,
He'd call the hounds so swift of foot:
'Giff, Gaff – seek 'im, seek 'im; fetch, fetch.'
He'd strike fish from a coracle
As a lion strikes a small animal.
When to the mountain your daddy would go,
He'd bring back a stag, a boar, a roe,
A speckled mountain grouse,
A fish from Derwennydd Falls.
Of those your daddy reached with his lance,
Whether a boar or a fox or a lynx,
None could escape unless it had wings.

onomatopea

attributed to St Columba (†597)
The High Creator (Altus Prosator) Latin

Though this is one of two poems attributed to Columba of Iona by a preface in the *Irish Liber Hymnorum*, it may in fact be a slightly later composition of the seventh century. Its author draws on a wide range of biblical data to paint an awesome picture of the divine creation, the fall of angels and of our first parents, and the judgment, with the possibility of salvation for a few people only making a brief appearance at the very end.

The Latin original is an 'abecedarian' poem, a new letter of the alphabet beginning each stanza in order. The poet delights in using obscure words, words with pagan associations, Greek and even Hebrew roots. He is concerned to display his learning as well as to move the hearer to fear of God.

In performance it is likely that the poem was sung with the disturbing response after each stanza, 'Who can please God at the end of time?'.

A

The High Creator, the Unbegotten Ancient of Days,
limitless, without origin of beginning he was,
he is and he will be for endless ages of ages,
with whom is the only-begotten Christ, and the Holy Spirit,
co-eternal in divinity's everlasting glory.
Three gods we do not confess, but say one God,
saving our faith in the three most glorious Persons.

B

Good angels he created, archangels and the orders
of Principalities and Thrones, of Powers and Virtues,
so that the goodness and majesty of the Trinity
might reveal itself in every work of bounty,
have heavenly beings in which he might greatly
show forth his favours by a word of power.

C

From the Kingdom of Heaven's summit, where angels stand,
from his own radiant brightness and the loveliness of his form,
through pride Lucifer fell, whom he had formed,
and the apostate angels also, by the same sad fall
of the author of vainglory and obstinate envy,
while the rest continued in their dominions.

D

The great Dragon, most loathsome, terrible and ancient,

the slippery serpent, more cunning than all the beasts
and than all the fiercer living things of earth,
dragged down with him a third of the stars into the pit
of infernal places and sundry prisons,
fugitives from the true light, hurled down by the Parasite.

E
The Most High, planning the frame and harmony of the world,
had made heaven and earth, fashioned sea and waters,
and also shoots of grass, the little trees of the woods,
the sun, the moon and stars, fire and necessary things,
birds, fish and cattle, beasts and living creatures,
and finally the first-formed man, to rule with prophecy.

F
At once when the stars were made, lights of the firmament,
the angels praised, for his wonderful creating,
the Lord of this immense mass, the Craftsman of the Heavens.
With a praiseworthy proclamation, fitting and unchanging,
in an excellent symphony they gave thanks to the Lord,
not by any endowment of nature, but out of love and choice.

G
Our first two parents having been assailed and led astray,
the devil falls a second time, together with his retinue,
by the horror of whose faces and the sound of whose flying
frail men might be dismayed, stricken with fear,
unable to gaze with their bodily eyes on those
now bound in bundles in the bonds of their prisons.

H
Driven from the midst and thrust down by the Lord,
the space of air was choked by a wild mass
of his treacherous attendants, invisible, lest
tainted by their wicked examples and their crimes
– no fences or walls ever concealing them—
folk should sin openly, before the eyes of all.

I
Clouds bear wintry floods from Ocean's fountains,
from the three deeper floods of the sea,
to the expanses of sky, in azure whirlwinds,
to do good to the cornfields, the vines and the shoots,

driven by winds emerging from their treasuries
and drying up the sea's receding pools.

K

The momentary glory of the kings of the present world,
fleeting and tyrannical, is cast down at God's whim.
See, giants are shown to groan beneath the waters
in great affliction, scorched by fire, in torment,
and stifled by the swelling whirlpools of Cocytus,
covered with rocks, destroyed by billows and sharp stones.

L

The waters bound in clouds the Lord releases frequently,
lest all at once they should break out, their barriers broken.
From their most plentiful streams, as if from breasts,
slowly flowing across the tracts of this earth,
freezing and warming at different times,
the rivers flow everywhere, never failing.

M

By the divine powers of the great God is hung
earth's globe, the circle of the great deep placed about it,
held up by the strong hand of almighty God,
with columns like bars supporting it,
promontories and rocks as their solid foundations,
firmly fixed as if on sure immovable bases.

N

No one can doubt that there is a hell below
where there are darkness, worms and dreadful beasts,
where there is sulphurous fire burning with voracious flames,
the screaming of men, weeping and gnashing of teeth,
where there is the groaning of Gehenna, terrible and ancient,
the horrible fiery burning of thirst and hunger.

O

There are those, as we read, who dwell beneath the earth,
whose knee bends often in prayer to the Lord,
but who could not open the written book
sealed with seven seals according to Christ's warnings,
which he himself unsealed after he had arisen as victor,
fulfilling what the prophets had foretold of his Coming.

P

Paradise was planted from the beginning by the Lord,
as we read in the most noble opening of Genesis,
and from its fountain-spring four rivers flow,
in whose flowery midst there stands the Tree of Life
whose leaves, bearing healing for the nations, do not fall;
whose delights are abundant, indescribable.

Q

Who has climbed Sinai, the appointed mountain of the Lord?
Who has heard the immeasurable thunders sound,
the echoing clamour of the mighty trumpet of war?
Who has also seen the lightning flashing all around,
the flashes and thunderbolts and the crashing of rocks,
but Moses alone, the people of Israel's judge?

R

The day of the Lord, most righteous King of Kings, is at hand:
a day of anger and vindication, of darkness and of cloud,
a day of wonderful mighty thunders,
a day also of distress, of sorrow and sadness,
in which the love and desire of women will cease
and the striving of men and the desire of this world.

S

We shall stand trembling before the Lord's judgment seat,
and we shall render account of all our deeds,
as we see our crimes placed before our gaze
and the books of conscience thrown open before us.
We will break out into most bitter weeping and sobbing,
the possibility of repentance being taken away.

T

At the First Archangel's wonderful trumpet blast,
the strongest vaults and tombs shall break apart,
the chill of the men of the present world melts away,
their bones gather to their joints from every place
while their ethereal souls go to meet them,
returning once more to their accustomed dwellings.

U

Orion wanders from his turning point at heaven's hinge –
the Pleiades being left behind, most splendid of the stars –

across the boundaries of the sea, of its unknown eastern rim.
Wheeling in fixed circuits, returning by its former paths,
after two years Vesper rises in the evening.
These things are seen as figures, understood as signs.

X

When Christ, the most high Lord, comes down from heaven,
the brightest sign and standard of the Cross will shine forth.
The two principal lights being obscured,
like the fruit of a fig-tree the stars will fall to earth,
the world's face will be like the fire of a furnace
and armies hide themselves in mountain caves.

Y

By the singing of hymns eagerly ringing out,
by thousands of angels rejoicing in holy dances,
and by the four living creatures full of eyes,
with the twenty-four joyful elders
casting their crowns under the feet of the Lamb of God,
the Trinity is praised in eternal three-fold exchanges.

Z

The raging anger of fire will devour the adversaries
who will not believe Christ came from God the Father.
But we shall surely fly off to meet him straight away,
and thus we shall be with him in several ranks of dignities
according to the eternal merits of our rewards,
to abide in glory from age to age.

[Response]
    Who can please God at the end of time,
    the noble ordinances of truth being changed,
    but those who despise this present world?

Helper of Workers (Adiutor Laborantium) Latin

Together with the foregoing *Altus Prosator*, this work is attributed to Columba in the preface in the *Irish Liber Hymnorum*. Though they are similar in their abecedarian character, this one is quite different in style with its short exclamatory lines of almost litanic quality. Its tone is also different, being one of prayer and trust in God's help.

O helper of workers,
ruler of all the good,
guardian on the ramparts
defender of believers,
you who raise the lowly,
you who crush the proud,
ruler of the faithful,
enemy of the impenitent,
judge of all judges,
who punish those who err,
pure life of the living,
light and Father of lights
shining with great light,
denying to none who ask
your strength and help,
I pray as I am, a little man
trembling and most wretched,
rowing through the infinite
storm of this age,
that Christ may draw me after him
to life's lofty lovely haven
          . . . an unending
holy hymn for ever.
From my enemies' envy lead me
into the joy of paradise.
        Through you, Christ Jesus,
        who live and reign . . .

Prayer for Protection from Lightning (Noli Pater) Latin

This poem is attributed to Columba in a preface in the *Irish Liber Hymnorum*, but it is unlikely to be his. The first six lines are probably from an original work, to which were added at a later date the verses concerning John the Baptist, which are partly from the Roman liturgy, but here we offer the entire amalgamation as it appears in the manuscripts.

It is a prayer for protection, one of a genre of prayers in which the power of God or of a saint is invoked against the threat of the natural world, in this case lightning. Though the story is told of Columba using this prayer to prevent fire, he normally specialised in sea-rescue miracles. There are, however, a number of aspects of the cult of John the Baptist that connect him with fire.

Father, do not allow thunder and lightning,
lest we be shattered by its fear and its fire.

We fear you, the terrible one, believing there is none like you.
All songs praise you throughout the hosts of angels.

Let heaven's heights, too, praise you with roaming lightning,
O most loving Jesus, O righteous King of Kings.

Blessed for ever, ruling in right government,
is John before the Lord, till now in his mother's womb,
filled with God's grace in place of wine or strong drink.

Elizabeth of Zechariah begot a great man:
John the Baptist, the forerunner of the Lord.

The flame of God's love dwells in my heart
as a jewel of silver is placed in a silver dish.

DALLÁN FORGAILL (fl. 597)
Elegy for Colum Cille Gaelic

This poem, traditionally composed by a secular poet called Dallán Forgaill upon the death of St Columba, is by that token one of the earliest pieces of poetry in Gaelic. Although there is still some lingering uncertainty about the date of the poem, the material within it certainly attests to an early set of traditions about Columba, and attitudes towards the saint which are not represented in later texts. It is a highly wrought, often difficult poem, which was preserved in later years almost as a piece of scripture, glossed and commented on. The poet divides his elegy into ten main sections, each reflecting on different aspects of the saint. Important aspects to be noted are his attention to Columba as a scholar, mentioning his use of patristic authors, such as Basil the Great and John Cassian; the imagery of light which pervades much of the poem; and the blend of secular praise (emphasis on the saint's ancestry, the use of epithets appropriate to warriors) and Christian ideals.

God, God, may I beg of Him
before I go to face Him
through the chariots of battle.
God of heaven, may He not leave me
in the path where there's screaming
from the weight of oppression.

Great God, protect me
from the fiery wall,
the long trench of tears.
Just God, truly near,
who hears my wailing
from cloudy heaven.

I

Not newsless is Níall's land.
No slight sigh from one plain,
but great woe, great outcry.
Unbearable the tale this verse tells:
Colum, lifeless, churchless.
How will a fool describe it – even Neire –
the prophet has settled at God's right hand in Sion.
Now he is not, nothing is left to us,
no relief for a soul, our sage.

For he has died to us, the leader of nations who guarded
the living,
he has died to us, who was our chief of the needy,
he has died to us, who was our messenger of the Lord;
for we do not have the seer who used to keep fears from us,
for he does not return to us, he who would explain the true Word,
for we do not have the teacher who would teach the tribes of
the Tay.
The whole world, it was his:
It is a harp without a key,
it is a church without an abbot.

II
By the grace of God Colum rose to exalted companionship;
awaiting bright signs, he kept watch while he lived.
His lifetime was short,
scant portions filled him.
He was learning's pillar in every stronghold,
he was foremost at the book of complex Law.
The northern land shone,
the western people blazed,
he lit up the east
with chaste clerics.
Good the legacy of God's angel
when he glorified him.

III
He reached the apostles, with hosts, with archangels;
he reached the land where night is not seen,
he reached the land where we expect Moses,
he reached the plain where they know the custom of music,
where sages do not die.
The King has cast off His priests' troubles.

IV
He suffered briefly until he triumphed:
He was a terror to the devil,
to whom Mass was a noose.
By his mighty skill,
he kept the law firm.
Rome was known, order was known,
knowledge of the Godhead was granted to him.

Truly blessed in death,
he was wise about apostles, about angels.
He applied the judgments of Basil,
who forbids acts of boasting by great hosts.

V

He ran the course which runs past hatred to right action.
The teacher wove the word.
By his wisdom he made glosses clear.
He fixed the Psalms,
he made the books of Law known,
those books Cassian loved.
He won battles with gluttony.
The books of Solomon, he followed them.
Seasons and calculations he set in motion.
He separated the elements according to figures among the
                                        books of the Law.
He read mysteries and distributed the Scriptures among
                                        the schools,
and he put together the harmony concerning the course of
                                        the moon,
the course which it ran with the rayed sun,
and the course of the sea.
He could number the stars of heaven, the one who could tell
                                        all the rest
which we have heard from Colum Cille.

VI

Who was, who will be alive who was as wonderful as he,
the very restrained one from the northwestern lands?
He knew the Laws from Old to New, he who knew no falsehood.
His work poured out saints
towards ladders for the City.
He climbs to the depth
for the sake of the God of humanity.
By longings he is stretched,
he sold his eye's desire.
A sound, austere sage of Christ:
no fog of drink nor fog of delights –
he avoided the fill of his mouth.
He was holy, he was chaste,
    he was charitable, a famous stone in victory.
He was a full light.

He was an ample fort for guests.
He was obedient, he was noble,
  his death was dignified.
He was pleasant, he was a physician
  in every sage's heart.
Our hero used to speak with the apostle.
It was restraint for which he died.
It was sweet, it was unique,
  his skill at priestly matters.
To people, inscrutable:
he was a shelter to the naked,
he was a teat to the poor.
Fresh was each bitter blast he suffered.
From Colum, the restraint of nations.
A great honour we reckon his heavenly food.
Christ will take him to serve among the just,
through the long days he has gone with them.

VII

Discerning the sage who reached the path of the four.
He went with two songs to heaven after his cross.
The guardian of a hundred churches, a wave which accomplishes
                                        the sacrifice.

A mighty hero, no idolator,
he did not assemble a crooked company
who scattered under instruction.
He accepted neither indifference nor heresy.
He would do no fast which was not the Lord's law,
that he might not die an eternal death.
Living his name, living his soul,
  from the crowds he prepared under the holy Law.
He averted his side's softness.
His body's desire, he destroyed it.
He destroyed his meanness:
truly the boy is a son of Conn's offspring.
He destroyed the darkness of envy,
He destroyed the darkness of jealousy.
You find his grave good in its virtue,
appointed for every trouble of weather.
From among an idolatrous people,
he abandoned possessions,
for clerics, chariots.
He fought a long and noble battle against flesh,

so that he will not go to the King's son under God's
dual judgment
in the second saying, the second verse.
He was buried before age, before weakness,
in Britain for fear of Hell.

VIII

Áed pledged it for all people:
a solid song when the hero went to heaven.
Not worthless, not slight, not contentious,
not a hero unvigorous towards Conall's covenant.
His blessing turned them, the mouths of the fierce ones
who lived on the Tay, to the will of the King.
From the dark journeys of man
he sat down with God.
In place of pomp, in place of splendour, he bestowed,
the pure descendant of Conall ruled in his monastery.
A fair sage at his death,
and master of a community,
he spoke with an angel;
he studied Greek grammar.
A freeman outwith the tribe, thus I declare,
the son of Fedelmid, he fought the tribe, he knew his end.
He did not suffer for the world:
he was constant to the memory of the cross.
What he conceived keeping vigil,
by action he ascertained.
A splendid birth was born of Art's offspring
– they have not Níall's strength—
one who commits no wrong from which he dies.

IX

Grief broke Conn's Part for the going to rest of such a good one.
The son of the Cross his name:
to him his due – behold, heaven – I will truly tell.
In the otherworld, they find it sweet to meet the pure one anew.
Until death, how may I describe
in flesh his path to heaven?
His choice poured out joy, quiet peace;
he attained them, the famous man of wisdom.
Surely for him,
not the wail of one house,
not the wail of one string;

heavily does the word wound the people.
He deserved the Lord God's light,
   which was quenched, which has blazed again.

X

This is the elegy of the king who rules me.
He will protect us in Sion.
He will urge me past torments.
May it be easily dark defects go from me.
He will come to me without delay,
the descendant of Cathair's offspring, Coirpre, with dignity.
Vast the variations of the poem, vast the splendid sun of heaven,
I have no time.

BECCÁN MAC LUIGDECH OF RUM (†677) Gaelic

These two early poems on Columba show the development of his cult into one in which the saint became important to his followers as a guide in this life and the next, and as a spiritual patron of poetry. Beccán mac Luigdech, to whom the poems are attributed, is probably the same as the Beccán the hermit active in Iona's administration in the 630s, and also the same as Beccán of Rum, who died on 17 March, 677.

In Praise of Colum Cille

Bound to Colum, while I speak,
    may the bright one guard me in the seven heavens;
when I go to the road of fear,
    I'm not lordless: I have strength.

It was not on cushioned beds
    he bent to his complex prayers:
he crucified – not for crimes –
    his body on the grey waves.

He staked the marvellous claim
    when Mo Chummae set down in Iona.
It's more than anyone can grasp,
    what the King did for his sake.

Though it was known near and far
    who Colum was, he was unique.
His name glistened like the sun;
    he was a light before all.

The one best thing of all things:
    he has freed his monks from wealth,
a great beacon, after his death,
    the name that's nobler than men's.

The shield of a few, a crowd's shield,
    a fort where all unsafe are safe;
he is a tight fort – fair prize,
    to be in Colum Cille's care.

No slight refuge after penance,
    for one who'd not thin down his tale:
he parted with true sayings,
    with fair news in his mouth for kings.

Singly triumphant over lust,
  the northern folk raised a flame.
Well-known, well-born, greatly blessed
  the pure mother who screamed for him.

To heaven's King he was known,
  towards each threat He lit his mind;
greatly blessed in every plight
  he who'd praise Colum úa Néill.

Not scant the thanks the birds give,
  acclaim along Connacht's roads.
His brilliant fame – just in speech –
  he was the spearcast, lies were slain.

Godly love – a post its strength –
  he took to, often travelling:
after his time, when all was done,
  he was the Christian God loved.

He left Ireland, entered a pact,
  he crossed in ships the whales' shrine.
He shattered lusts – it shone on him –
  a bold man over the sea's ridge.

He fought wise battles with the flesh,
  indeed, he read pure learning.
He stitched, he hoisted sail tops,
  a sage across seas, his prize a kingdom.

Prosperous, numerous, safely,
  a storm blew them in boats over brine.
Colum Cille, Níall's candle:
  not found in a body his like.

Brave the host which has his hardness,
  an order with true angels' acts:
though they were deaf, they had hearing;
  though they were lame, they had strength.

At the waves' glen they took rest,
  Colum's crew, a famous band.
Bold number, they had a foot
  with Colum, they had a hand.

Great treasure in every place,
  Colum Cille, of all Níall's folk:

not chiefless, they have a lord,
  on darkness' path, they have sense.

Colum within on each mouth,
  Colum outside, common speech,
Colum Cille, he sloughed softness,
  strangers swear by him, friends cheer.

He served with a blessed band,
  he often spent nights withdrawn;
silence, too, thinness of side;
  Britain's beacon, his mouth's wisdom.

Holy Colum's blessing on me,
  that he may be my daily trail;
the High-king's blessing be on me,
  that I be spared the risk of pain.

May he save me from fire – common fight –
  Colum Cille, noble candle,
his tryst well-famed – he was bright –
  may he bear me to the King who ends evil.

Colum Cille, while I live,
  will be my chant, till the grave's tryst;
in every risk I'll call him,
  when I'll praise him with my full strength.

No 'cry to wastelands' what's on my lips,
  I'll beg of my God my hero's prize;
may he bear me past the king of fire,
  then my protection is his.

Royal kin of triumphant kings,
  lord full of grace, thus may he guard us.
I'll take off the devils' noose:
  his bards' prayer perhaps may save us.

May mercy come to me before death,
  may it be penance that I seek.
May I be in my mind and my sense,
  bound to Colum while I speak.

Last Verses in Praise of Colum Cille

He brings northward to meet the Lord a bright crowd
        of chancels –
Colum Cille, kirks for hundreds, widespread candle.

Wonderful news: a realm with God after the race,
a grand kingdom, since He's set out my life's progress.

He broke passions, brought to ruin secure prisons;
Colum Cille overcame them with bright actions.

Connacht's candle, Britain's candle, splendid ruler;
in scores of curraghs with an army of wrteches he
        crossed the long-haired sea.

He crossed the wave-strewn wild region, foam-flecked, seal-filled,
savage, bounding, seething, white-tipped, pleasing, doleful.

Wisdom's champion all round Ireland, he was exalted;
excellent name: Europe is nursed, Britain's sated.

Stout post, milk of meditation, with broad actions,
Colum Cille, perfect customs, fairer than trappings.

On the loud sea he cried to the King who rules thousands,
who rules the plain above cleared fields, kings and countries.

In the Trinity's care he sought a ship – good his leaving –
on high with God, who always watched him, morning, evening.

Shepherd of monks, judge of clerics, finer than things,
than kingly gates, than sounds of plagues, than battalions.

Colum Cille, candle brightening legal theory;
the race he ran pierced the midnight of Erc's region.

The skies' kind one, he tends the clouds of harsh heaven;
my soul's shelter, my poetry's fort, Conal's descendant.

Fame with virtues, a good life, his: barque of treasure,
sea of knowledge, Conal's offspring, people's counsellor.

Leafy oak-tree, soul's protection, rock of safety,
the sun of monks, mighty ruler, Colum Cille.

Beloved of God, he lived against a stringent rock,
a rough struggle, the place one could find Colum's bed.

He crucified his body, left behind sleek sides;
he chose learning, embraced stone slabs, gave up bedding.

He gave up beds, abandoned sleep, finest actions;
conquered angers, was ecstatic, sleeping little.

He possessed books, renounced fully claims of kinship:
for love of learning he gave up wars, gave up strongholds.

He left chariots, he loved ships, foe to falsehood;
sun-like exile, sailing, he left fame's steel bindings.

Colum Cille, Colum who was, Colum who will be,
constant Colum, not he a protector to be lamented.

Colum, we sing, until death's tryst, after, before,
by poetry's rules, which gives welcome to him we serve.

I pray a great prayer to Eithne's son – better than treasure –
my soul to his right hand, to heaven, before the world's people.

He worked for God, kingly prayer, within church ramparts,
with angels' will, Conal's household's child, in vestments.

Triumphant plea: adoring God, nightly, daily,
with hands outstretched, with splendid alms, with right actions.

Fine his body, Colum Cille, heaven's cleric –
a widowed crowd – well-spoken just one, tongue triumphant.

GAELIC ELEGIAC VERSES

These short fragments have been preserved in Irish annals and in technical tracts on versecraft. They both mourn the sons of famous kings who died tragically young in the seventh century, though the poems may be from a somewhat later period.

1. On the drowning of Conaing son of Áedhán (†622)
The sea's great clear waves,
   the sand-beds which they cover:
in his fragile wicker boat,
   they've conspired against Conaing.

That woman's tossed her white mane,
in his boat, against Conaing;
   crookedly she's grinned today
   at the great-tree of Tortan.

2. On the death of Mongán son of Fiachna (†625)
Cold is the wind across Islay.
Kintyre's warriors draw near;
   thence they will do a dreadful deed,
   they will slay Mongán, son of Fiachna.

VERSES ON THE CHILDREN OF BELI SON OF NWYTHON

Nothing testifies more to the interconnectedness of the ruling families of the different kingdoms of seventh-century Scotland than the two brothers Owain and Bridei (Bruide) son of Beli (Bile). Both were apparently sons of Beli, king of Dumbarton, and grandsons of Nwython (Nechtan), who may have been king of the Picts. Both also won crucial victories in battles in the seventh century. The first, Owain, was apparently king of Dumbarton, and victor of the battle of Strathcarron in 642, where he defeated the king of Dál Riata, presumably ending a period of British subjugation to Dál Riata. The second brother, Bridei (in Gaelic, Bruide), was king of the Picts, and victor of the watershed battle of Linn Garan, or Dunnichen, near Forfar in Angus, in 685, which saw the eclipse of Northumbrian domination of Northern Britain. Bruide's mother may well have been English, for he is described by Bede as the cousin of Ecgfrith, the Northumbrian king he killed in 685, and lamented in the second poem as Oswiu's son.

That the poetry in praise of them was composed in two different languages is significant also of the linguistic mix in Scotland at this period. It is notable that the two poems on Bruide were composed by Gaelic-speaking churchmen.

The Battle of Strathcarron (c. 642?) Welsh

This stanza celebrates the victory of Ywain, ruler of the Britons of Dumbarton, against the ruler of the Scottish Gaelic kingdom of Dál Riata, Dyfnwal Frych (Domhnall Brecc), in a battle at Strathcarron in 642. It was preserved in the manuscript of *The Gododdin*, where the stanza is the first in the B-text, the 79th in the A-text. That the stanza was incorporated with it has been a basis for proposing that *The Gododdin* was transcribed in the kingdom of Dumbarton before the texts were transmitted to Wales. The stanza is likely to be a fragment from a longer work.

A

I saw a war-band, they came from Pentir,
And splendidly they descended around the beacon.
I saw in due time they pressed hard on the homestead,
And the men of Nwython's grandson were roused.
I saw battle-ready men, they came with a war-cry,
And crows picked at the head of Dyfnwal Frych.

B

I saw a war-band, they came from Pentir,
And splendidly they bore themselves around the beacon.
I saw a second, they came down from their homestead:
They had risen at the word of Nwython's grandson.
I saw stalwart men, they came at dawn,
And crows picked at the head of Dyfnwal Frych.

Riagail of Bangor
The Battle of Dunnichen (c. 685) Gaelic

Today Bruide gives battle
  over his grandfather's land,
unless it is the command
  of God's Son that it be restored.

Today Oswiu's son was slain
  in battle against iron swords,
even though he did penance,
  it was a penance too late.

Today Oswiu's son was slain,
  who used to have dark drinks:
Christ has heard our prayer
  that Bruide would save Breo.

attributed to ADOMNÁN OF IONA (†704)
Elegy for Bruide Son of Bile
(Bridei Son of Beli †693) Gaelic

The source of this short poem is a tenth-century *Life of St Adomnán,* and there
it is placed in a fabulous tale of Bruide's death. The source of the tale is Iona,
and the poem may well be early, but it is not clear whether as it stands it can be
as early as Adomnán's time. It is the unique witness to the fact that Bruide was
the son of Beli of Dumbarton.

Great the wonders he performs,
  the King who is born of Mary:
the life of little sheaves in Mull,
  death for Bruide mac Bili.

It is strange,
  after ruling a kingdom:
a small ruined hollow of oak
  about the son of Dumbarton's king.

ADOMNÁN OF IONA (†704)
Prayer to Colum Cille Gaelic

May Colum Cille
commend me to God
when I go – may I not go soon –
(after great good fortune,
it is mine, my prophecy)
to the place of the angel host
(the name of Níall's famous descendant,
not small its protection)
to the archangels of God in Sion,
in the strongholds of God the Father,
among the ranks of the twenty-four fair justified elders
who praise the heaven of the mysterious, splendid King;
lamentation has not reached them, does not touch them –
it is mine by right, my Christ,
of my powerful sins.

attributed to ADOMNÁN
Iona (eighth–ninth century?) Gaelic

Like the poem on Bruide above, this poem derives from the tenth-century *Life of Adomnán*. The tradition is an Iona one, but it may be doubted that this poem is much older than the text which contains it.

If death in Iona be my fate,
merciful would be that taking.
  I know not beneath blue heaven
  a better little spot for death.

CÚ CHUIMNE OF IONA (†747)

Cú Chuimne, 'the Hound of Memory', was an Iona monk. His death is recorded in AD 747, where he is 'Cú Chuimne the Wise'. To him is ascribed the editorship of the important collection of church precepts called the *Collectio Canonum Hibernensis*, along with another Irish monk. He therefore had widespread learning in law and theology, reflected in some of the poetry here. The little poem on Cú Chuimne suggests a few skeletons in his closet – his poem on the Meath chieftain Garbán suggests too a period of patronage by secular rulers. Nonetheless, his poem on Mary is one of the earliest Marian hymns we know, and is a vibrant testimony to his skill as poet and theologian.

Anonymous
On Cú Chuimne Gaelic

Cú Chuimne
read the doctors halfway through.
 The other half of his fosterage fee,
 he gave up for the sake of women.

That which Cú Chuimne had,
he gave up, till he turned a sage:
 he has left the women there,
 he has read the other half.

On Garbán Mide Gaelic

Unless it should honour evil,
 an enthroned prince is not unsafe:
for me to be on a calfskin rug
 in Garbán's house is lovely.

Hymn for the Virgin Mary
(Cantemus in Omne Die) Latin

The words of this Marian hymn themselves may suggest its original mode of performance, one choir against another, in alternating verses. Mary's role in the Gospel is stressed here in a series of paired images: the Father's bosom from which Christ's divinity flows is twinned with the Virgin's womb, from where his humanity is drawn. As Eve's disobedience resulted in the Fall, so Mary's obedience brought salvation into the world. As death came through the tree in the garden of Eden, so life came through the cross of Mary's son.

Let us sing every day,
harmonising in turns,
together proclaiming to God
a hymn worthy of holy Mary.

In two-fold choir, from side to side,
let us praise Mary,
so that the voice strikes every ear
with alternating praise.

Mary of the Tribe of Judah,
Mother of the Most High Lord,
fitting care she gave
to languishing mankind.

Gabriel first brought the Word
from the Father's bosom
which was conceived and received
in the Mother's womb.

She is the most high, she the holy
venerable Virgin
who by faith did not draw back,
but stood forth firmly.

None has been found, before or since,
like this mother,
not one of all the descendants
of the human race.

By a woman and a tree
the world first perished;

by the power of a woman
it has returned to salvation.

Mary, amazing mother,
gave birth to her Father,
through whom the whole wide world,
washed by water, has believed.

She conceived the pearl
– they are not empty dreams –
for which sensible Christians
have sold all they have.

The mother of Christ had made
a tunic of seamless weave;
Christ's death accomplished,
it remained thus by casting of lots.

Let us put on the armour of light,
the breastplate and the helmet,
that we might be perfected by God,
taken up by Mary.

Truly, truly, we implore,
by the merits of the Child-bearer,
that the flame of the dread fire
be not able to ensnare us.

Let us call on the name of Christ,
angels our witnesses here below,
that we may delight and be inscribed
in letters in the heavens.

On Almsgiving Latin

The following poetic sequence is preserved in a place where one might not normally look for poetry: in a collection of church canons, compiled in the early eighth century, probably on Iona. Though we cannot be certain that the poem was composed on Iona, since most of the surrounding material is from Ireland, continental church councils and mainstream patristic authors, it may be a verse that was collected by the editors of the *Collectio*, Cú Chuimne of Iona and Ruben of Dair-Inis in Co. Waterford, or it may be an original composition by one of them. We have included it here tentatively, partly because it is so beautiful.

Its almost litanic form, typical of the period in Gaelic clerical circles (see the *Helper of Workers*, attributed to Columba, and *The Litany of the Trinity*, by Mugrón, abbot of Iona), string together a long list of the spiritual benefits of almsgiving, many of which are drawn directly from scripture.

[Augustine said]
Almsgiving is a holy thing;
enriching in the present life,
it takes away our sins.
Our years of life it multiplies,
lends nobility to the mind;
widening our boundaries,
it washes away all sin.
Freeing us from punishment,
it joins us to the angels,
and keeps us far from demons.
An invincible wall around the soul.
It drives out devils
and brings the angels close.

[Jerome said]
Almsgiving pierces heaven,
goes before the giver
and knocks on the kingdom's door,
summons angels to meet it,
and calls God to its aid,
a wonderful trumpet, yet soundless.

[The Lord said through Isaiah]
Mercy I want, not sacrifice.
As water puts out fire,
so do alms extinguish sin.

THE DREAM OF THE ROOD (c. 700) Old English

One of the most famous of all Anglo-Saxon poems is first represented carved in runes on a splendidly sculpted free-standing cross at Ruthwell in Dumfriesshire. On the cross, the poem is fragmentary, and seems to consist of quotes from a longer poem, which we have in a later manuscript version. The full poem tells of a vision of the cross which appears to the poet, the cross itself speaking to him of the events of the Crucifixion and the fate that befell the cross afterwards. The poem interweaves images of death and glory, and identifies the suffering cross with the suffering Christ, while sewing together the twin speakers, cross and dreamer, in a singular statement of Christian faith. Both sculpted cross and original poem probably date from the early eighth century, a time when Northumbrian power had stretched into Dumfriesshire and Galloway, and when the cult of the Holy Cross had come to the British Isles from the Mediterranean, attended by some excitement.

The Ruthwell Cross Crucifixion Poem

I
God almighty stripped himself,
  when he wished to climb the cross
 bold before all men.
 to bow [I dared not,
 but had to stand firm.]

II
 I held high the great King,
 heaven's Lord. I dared not bend.
Men mocked us both together. I was slick with blood
 spr[ung from the Man's side . . .]

III
 Christ was on the cross.
 But then quick ones came from afar,
 nobles, all together. I beheld it all.
I was hard hit with grief; I bowed [to warrior's hands.]

IV
Wounded with spears,
they laid him, limb-weary. At his body's head they stood.
There they looked to [heaven's Lord . . .]

The Dream of the Rood

Listen! The best of dream I will describe,
which I dreamed at midnight,
when living men lay asleep.
It seemed I saw a splendid tree
soaring aloft, wound round with light,
the brightest of boughs. That beacon was all
girded with gold: gems stood
fair at its foot and five also were
on the cross-beam above. All God's angels kept it,
fair through their creation: truly no criminal's cross,
but holy souls beheld it there,
men upon earth, and all this great making.
Wondrous was that triumph-tree, and I tainted with sin,
wounded with wrongness. I saw the tree of glory
adorned with vestments, vividly shining,
got out with gold; gems had
worthily wreathed the Ruler's tree.
Still through that gold I could sense
the former pains of wretches, for it first began
to bleed on its right side. I was all beset with sorrows,
I was afraid at this fair sight. I saw that flickering beacon
changing cloths and colours: now it was soaked in wetness,
drenched with dripping blood; now, adorned with jewels.
Yet, lying there a long while
I sadly gazed at the Saviour's tree,
until I heard that it held forth;
the best of woods began to speak words:

'That was years ago – I mind it yet –
when I was felled at the forest's edge,
taken from my trunk. Strong foes took me,
made me a spectacle, bade me hold felons high.
Men then hauled me on shoulders, until I was set on a hill;
many foes then fastened me. I saw mankind's Lord
rush with great courage to climb upon me.
Then I dared not, against the Lord's word,
bow or break, when I saw trembling
the earth's surface. All those enemies
I might have felled: yet I stood fast.
Then the young Hero stripped himself – that was God almighty –
strong and steadfast. Bold in the sight of many
122

he mounted the cross, since he would ransom mankind.
I trembled when the Man embraced me;
                    I dared not bow to earth,
fall to earth's surface: I had to stand firm.
  I was hoisted, a cross. I held high the great King,
  heaven's Lord. I dared not bend.
They drove me through with dark nails –
                    on me those deep wounds were clear,
open hate-made holes – I dared hurt none of them.
They mocked us both together. I was slick with blood
sprung from the Man's side when he sent his spirit forth.

  'On that hill I have borne many
  grievous fates: I saw the God of hosts
  sorely outstretched. Shadows had
  covered with clouds the Lord's corpse,
  that shining splendour. Shadow went forth,
  dark under the clouds. All creation wept,
  keening the King's death: Christ was on the cross.

  'But then quick ones, came from afar
  to the Ruler's Heir. I beheld it all.
I was hard hit with grief, yet I bowed to warriors' hands,
meekly, with great eagerness. They took then God almighty,
they lifted him from torment's load. The warriors left me
standing swathed in wetness; I was all wounded with spears.
Then they laid him, limb-weary; at his body's head they stood;
they looked to heaven's Lord, and he then lay awhile resting,
spent after those great struggles. They started to shape a tomb
within his slayer's sight; men carved it from bright stone.
Therein they set triumph's Lord.
                    They began to sing sorrowful songs,
woe-filled at evening. Then they went away
sad, from the great Lord: small was the crowd where he rested.
  Yet we there, weeping a good while,
  stood at the spot; the sound of warriors
  had gone quiet. The corpse grew cold,
  the fair life-house. Then men began to fell us
  all to earth. That was an awful fate.
Men dug us a deep pit. But the Lord's men then
and his friends found me. [. . .]
  They girded me with gold and silver.

'Now you may hear, my beloved man,
how I have suffered, the work of evil sinners,
wretched torments. Now the time is come
when they honour me far and wide,
men upon earth and all this great making
pray to this sign. On me the Son of God
suffered awhile. Wherefore now, resplendent,
I rise up under heaven, and I can heal
everyone who holds me in awe.
Long ago I became the cruellest of tortures,
to people most hateful, until I opened to them
the way of life, rightly to all the living.
Listen! Glory's Lord exalted me
over the trees of the wood, Ward of heaven,
just as he also, Almighty God, for all men,
exalted over all womankind
his own mother, Mary herself.

'Now I bid you, my beloved man,
to describe this dream to men,
reveal in words that it is the heaven-tree
which Almighty God suffered on
for mankind's many sins
and Adam's act of old.
Death he tasted there; but the Ruler rose again
with his great might to save men.
He ascended to heaven. Hither he will come
again to this middle-earth to seek mankind
on the day of doom, the Lord himself,
Almighty God amid his angels,
that he might then judge (he who has judgment's power)
each one as he earlier
earned here in this ephemeral life.

'No one then may be unafraid
awaiting the words the Ruler will say.
He will ask before many where the man is
who for the Lord's name would taste
cruel death, as he did once upon the cross.
Then they will be fearful and have few thoughts
concerning what they could say to Christ.
But none need be frightened
who bears on his breast this best of signs.

And through the cross each will seek a kingdom
far from earth's paths, every soul
who may long to live with the Lord.'

Then I prayed to the cross, glad in spirit,
ardently, though I was alone,
with few friends. All my mind
was fixed on faring forth; I suffered many
hours of longing. Now my life's hope
is that I might seek that triumph-tree   *dreamer*
alone, more often than any man,
and honour it well. That is my wish,
which fills my spirit, and my protection is
focused on that cross. Nor do I have crowds of rich
friends in the world. They, forth from here,
have left the world's glitterings, have sought glory's King.
Now they in heaven with the High Father
dwell in glory; and each day
I hope for the time when the Lord's cross
which I saw once here on earth
will fetch me from this fleeting life,
and bring me to where there is great bliss,
happiness in heaven, where the Lord's host
feast   are sat to banquet, where there is lasting bliss,
and set me down where I might dwell
in glory, glad amid the saints,
sharing pleasures. May the Lord be my friend,
he who here on earth suffered once
on the cross for the sins of men.
He released us, and gave us life,
and a heavenly home. Hope was renewed,
with bounty, with bliss, for those who suffered burning.
On that venture the Son was victorious,
mighty and successful, when he came with many
crowds of souls to the kingdom of God,
the One Ruler almighty, to angel's bliss,
and to all the holy ones who in heaven already
lived in glory, when their Lord
almighty God came to where his country was.

THE MIRACLES OF ST NYNIA THE BISHOP (c. 780?)
Latin

This poem was written in the late eighth century by a Whithorn cleric, and seems to have found its way via York to Alcuin, who had been born and trained in that city, becoming master of the school there in 766. He subsequently travelled to the court of Charlemagne in Gaul and contributed greatly to the advance of scholarship and liturgical reform there from around 781 until his death in 804. Alcuin was so inspired by this poem that he wrote to the Whithorn monks of his devotion to Nynia, sending a silk cloth to them as an offering to ask for their prayers at Nynia's shrine. This was a period when Whithorn was under the control of English masters, both political and ecclesiastical. After Nynia himself, we do not know the name of any bishop of Whithorn until Pehthelm (c. 731–35) whom Bede calls the first bishop in the new Northumbrian see.

I.

God the eternal king, the worshipful power of the Father,
Christ, in the fullness of time, came from the summit of heaven,
clothed himself in flesh from the body of his own chaste mother,
that he might save us, every one, from anger.
The power eternal, who orders all God's works,
granted that the venerable mother's body should shine forever
with virginity's honour before all people, and established
the bright comfort of the life of salvation.
Many lights have shone on countless lands,
the Lord's grace flowing wide across the nations,
just as the psalmist in his lyric incantation sang,
filled with God's breath: 'The Lord is ruler of the earth;
let the nations exult and let every island be glad.'
So the lofty prophet spoke and his judgment was fulfilled,
for God almighty, who has strewn his shining lights across
the world,
has granted to his own folk, far and near, lights in profusion.
And from among these, for all the world, one has shone,
a brilliant teacher, Nynia by name in his own native tongue.
How he excelled, magnificent in merit,
strong with strength he drew from the fountain of heaven,
trusting in the gift of God.
Many and astounding are the signs he performed among us,
and many, through his speech, opened believing hearts to Christ,
a vast and zealous crowd seizing on Christ's mystical commands.
So he called and so he led a host of men
from grievous death to the red-gold stars of heaven.

For any heart dedicated to Christ's name
would rather turn from this world and find union with God
than yield to the pursuing serpent's raging throng.

*2. How the man of God came to Rome, where he was raised with
God's help to the rank of bishop*
The holy man went down to the shore of the wave-strewn sea,
found a broad boat, boarded it and berthed within.
And how they flew! – sails stretched by stiff winds,
the rough timbers carrying them across the sea,
till she emerged and fixed her prow in tawny sands.
Towards the Alps he turned his steps; he climbed
where milk-white fleeces slide through silent skies,
and snow lies heaped on the mountains' heights.
Pressing on, on holy feet he went to seek his confirmation,
his sacred ordination by the pontiff most high,
the holy man whose task it was those days
to man the defence of his predecessors of old,
the peak of apostolic victories.
At his coming, Rome's clemency rejoiced, and there he stayed
within the dazzling walls of the mistress of all nations.
He visited the holy shrines, day after day,
besought the bright ones in night-long vigilance,
and honoured in good order all the other saints
whom God has adorned with everlasting victories
and raised to the golden halls of flowering life.
But while radiant Rome embraced the holy man
he worked, by his glorious merits, extraordinary deeds,
and Christ the king adorned him with great honour,
for he received the lofty office of high priest,
that as the lamp of the holy shrine he might blaze out
and drive away the dreary darkness of the night,
appearing at the head of the lampstand, shining bright.

*3. How, returning home, he converted to the grace of Christ the
Pictish nations – those who are called Niduari*
Then turning his steps to his own lovely land,
the great master filled the ranks of the faithful on earth
and swiftly taught his own folk with wise speech—
a brilliant leader, constant in fervour—
so overcoming every danger in the present struggle
they might receive a kingly crown on the day of Christ's coming.
What shall I sing worthy of you, or who could compose in verse

songs equal to this bishop most honoured in all the world?
You gave the peoples – pious teacher – Christ's commands,
long awaited, drawing to yourself the Pictish hordes.
Revering idols in death's shadow, they were defiled,
but turned to Christ, his love their guide.
All then raced to be plunged in an everlasting spring,
the holy font where they washed away the shame of sin.
For as he sowed the seeds of life from his own holy mouth,
he gave growth to all their talents among the far-flung nations.
Many monasteries he made, together with new churches
which flourish now with choicest choirs of monks,
worshipping Christ truly and serving the monastic rule.
He taught by his teaching the furthest kingdoms of the world,
and when of itself that world shall pass away, Christ on earth
will come again, all men shall rise, and he shall have his reward.

4. *How he came home and built Candida Casa*
And so he left behind the Pictish people and their lands
and came in the Lord's own company to his British sons,
a pure shepherd, protecting his fold with mind and hand,
ardent defender of his cherished flock against the foe.
Then in our own lands he shone out, a brilliant bishop,
known by name to all those dwelling here.
He laid the first fair foundation of this shining house,
and erected the splendid summit of the towering temple.
Here our father shone in the splendour of his mind,
in perfect perpetual star-like brilliance.
Walls founded on hard-baked brick, and with its towering roof,
with the merits of Martin this honoured building gleams,
for our father, Christ's eminent and worthy priest,
dedicated it to the Lord in Martin's name.
This is the Lord's own house, and many have longed to see
the glories of this wondrous temple shining out on high.
For crushed by chronic illness many come hurrying here,
eagerly accepting what is given to obtain a saving cure,
and in all their members, by the same saint's power,
they are made new.

5. *How God punished that people's king, Thuvahel by name, with
blindness for his crime, and healed him again through the blessing
of the man of God*
The judge eternal, creator of all things,
has made the holy one shine out
128

far and wide among all races, brightly adorned.
A radiant splendour in our lands, truly in his holy heart
he was the image of the virtues to us all,
and has deserved – most honoured man – to shine on earth.
Called from earliest youth, the chosen one came forth
and now his holy deeds shine in the place of his birth.
This servant and shepherd of the heavenly fold,
powerful pillar of watchful protection over his flocks,
and guiding them according to the eternal law,
was subject to a king named Tudvael, as lustful as he was cruel.
The saint, from many races, gathered in his holy flock,
among whom many flourished in the good and heavenly life,
radiant in their virtues like the firmament's bright lights.
But the foresaid king drove out the blameless one,
thrust him out unjustly, an exile from his lands.
Now the rash man felt the wrath he had deserved,
and fell into sudden sickness and wasting of his eyes
till all his sight was shrouded in black shadows,
and blind he remained, though not for long.
For now the king, mindful of his wicked deeds,
addressed his servant: 'Look you, visit that noble man
and seek from him due penance for my sins,
for of the crimes I once committed – see I confess – I now repent.'
So he spoke; the messenger ran off in haste
and rushed into the kindly bishop's presence.
There he threw himself upon the earth, kissed his feet,
and poured out in prayer his tears upon the ground.
He spoke and begged the servant of Christ with groans:
'Ah, my dearest master lies, bereft of all bright light,
I confess, smitten by dark shadows and, if I judge alright,
will pay for his sins with his life.
Hurry, I pray, and scatter his pitchy night,
you, our splendour and rightly chief part of our fame,
for the weighty guilt of crime may yet find forgiveness.'
Having spoken thus, and in full flood of tears,
the fearful messenger filled the air with wailing,
while the prophet answered him in righteous words:
'Rise, now, quickly and wipe those dripping tears away.
Mind now, go to your master, bearing these new gifts:
set off and run ahead on hastened feet, for I am coming,
and forgiveness will completely cover the king's sin.'
He spoke, and the messenger ran rejoicing to his master's
inner chamber,

and there spoke truly, setting out all things in order,
all that had been said and done so piously by him.
Meanwhile the prophet and high-priest came
to where the king lay sunk in bitter illness.
Now the sick man's head he signed with his right hand,
and health, restored, crept up pushing back the dark,
as the merciful one restored lost light to his eyes
and at God's will the gloom was beaten back.
The king, now seeing, repaid with thanks and praise,
proclaiming how the Lord works marvels through his saint.

6. *How he freed a priest of his from the accusation of unchastity
through the speech of a new-born child*
There was, meanwhile, a priest and baptiser of souls
who stood accused of sins of lust – by some demented fool,
barking, shouting out his guilt of sins of sacrilege.
But the holy man, by his care, averted all disgrace.
While far and wide among the nations
his noble teaching flowed in splendid speech,
and as the words poured from his mouth
sowed seeds of fourfold flowing streams,
purifying floods which watered the hearts of the nations.
But as he refreshed believers with his bright teaching,
see, a tiny infant was brought forth among the people,
born that night past from his mother's womb,
and our saint's priest was accused of an ancient crime.
But asking for silence the older priest spoke out and said:
'This man is innocent, I believe. But you, my child,
must also speak. Tell us by the most-high Thunderer's rule
who is your begetter, and who is the author of this deed?'
And straight away the tender infant thundered forth,
astounding all, with learned words from his simple heart
– he who had only lived the space of a single night –
and breaking the impeding bonds of speech
he set forth holy mysteries from his faithful mouth:
'O holy and blessed man, Nynia by name,
with speech and pointing finger I will show to you my father,
just as you command in the name of the high-throned king.
Good folk, you see I'm forced to judge my father's case.
See, this is my father – turn you all and look at him –
for in marriage he begot me from my mother's body.
The priest remains as chaste in body as he is pure in thought,
and has succumbed to none of the devil's darkness.'
130

Having said these things, having broken the laws of nature,
he grew still, closing his throat in a silent knot.
And all the people, seeing it, re-echoed holy words to Christ,
repaying the Lord with praises and thanksgiving.

7. *How he commanded that vegetables, planted in the earth and
grown to maturity on the same day, be given to the brethren*
Throughout the world, the Lord of miracles made his
                                             honour shine,
and blessed him with the countless merits of his works.
Earth's almighty ruler, the worshipful power,
crowned him forever in honour with a beautiful diadem,
raising the great saint to be among the holy ones,
to perform through his help miraculous signs.
It happened once, when the Lord's servant and his brothers
sat indoors at table, there were found to be no greens.
And so he spoke to a certain man: 'Run now to the garden,
as fast as your feet will carry you, to our well watered rigs,
and bring to us whatever you find growing from the ground.'
But the brother replied who had care of the garden,
and uttered true words to the holy man:
'I have sown, only today, vegetables planted in furrows,
and from the green sod they have not yet grown
those dewy shoots which flower from within.'
But the priest spoke to the servant out of his chaste heart:
'Run, therefore, and look, believing in the Lord,
for God almighty can perform all things,'
Then, swifter than speech, going to the garden's depths,
all unbelieving, he saw the flowering of the seed of the earth,
of herbs springing up to grow as much in one day
as if they had grown green the whole summer season.
Seizing them in both his hands, he went back all amazed
to the brothers and the bishop, to share Christ's holy gifts
                                             with them,
and praised the Lord who works wonders by his saints.

8. *How he drove thieves mad through his prayer, and how he
restored to life their chief when he had been killed by a bull.*
About that time, Christ's servant and priest
foiled some thieves through his heavenly power.
Once, when the saint had blessed his own dear herd,
in the flesh he remained close by, in a herdsman's hut,
but in an ecstasy his mind passed beyond the clouds of heaven.

131

And when all things grew still in the sleep-inducing night,
suddenly and secretly thieves came at the run
to carry off the cattle, hidden by night's gloom.
But God almighty would sooner ruin the guilty, and swiftly,
than bring grief to his chosen one by robbers' thievery –
the stupidity of those who wished to harm a man of deeds so pure!
Immediately, then, he snared the thieves in dizziness,
hemmed them in, all alike, in dreadful madness,
until with bellowing roar a bull advanced,
whose curly head bristled with dreadful shagginess;
menacingly he charged at them and with his horns he gored
their flesh,
tossed and shook them all with furious blows,
until their leader breathed out his soul in death.
And where the unspeakable chief of robbers lay,
marvellous to tell, the wild bull impressed
his footprint in the granite rock as if in softest wax,
and under his tender hooves the hardest rock gave way,
for all things are possible to the Father of Christ,
and in his bright-shining saints he brings about all things.
But when dark night's colourless shadow had lifted,
the saint went out, the Holy Spirit guiding him,
and found them all in terror licking the dust,
and the leader dead and still, his limbs all frozen,
who had tried to lead the thieves to the byre at first.
But standing by the stricken thieves, the priest spoke thus:
'Why, pray, did you wish to harm one who had not deserved it,
who never sought to deceive you in even the smallest theft?'
This he asked, and then released them from all sickness and
from blame,
and from the fullness of his own pure heart, he spoke:
'I beg you, high-throned Lord, give life to this unmoving corpse,
to its frozen joints, and warmth to the whole body,
and let the spirit enter to restore the gift of life.'
He spoke and lifeless limbs revived – the dead man lived!
All stared in terror then when they saw his life return,
and all alike repeated, piously, praises to the Lord.

9. *How the man of God, after the many miracles which he
performed, was attacked by illness and passed over to eternal joys
and how he was buried in his own church.*
Such things for many years the wonderful man had done:
the darkness of blind folk he changed into brightest light;
132

he cleansed from scaly bodies their leprous swellings,
he cured for many the lameness of their feet,
and deaf ears he penetrated with his piercing voice.
Many folk, fallen under foul disease,
he restored again to health, by Christ's own healing power.
Then came the time when the happy man, full of years,
                                                    was smitten.
Little by little he was consumed by illness' decay,
and all the bishop's body bore his pain.
But even in sickness his heart could rise to heavenly things,
and the exalted champion of justice called this to mind:
'The potter's furnace shakes the pots with the fiery force of
                                                    its flames,
but for the just their souls are scorched by dreadful burdens.
So now I wish to be dissolved, to see Christ face to face.'
And when the beloved bishop had said these things in order,
his time accomplished, his blessed spirit left his icy members,
and drawn from his pure body it pierced the clear and
                                                    starry heights of heaven.
Therefore, when breath of life had left his dying limbs,
encircled by a shining host in snow white garments,
shining now like phosphorous in the heavens,
he was borne on the arms of angels above the starry sky,
and passed among the crowds of saints and all the eternal hosts,
to enter into the high-throned king's most intimate presence.
Joyful in the heavenly hall, joined with heavenly company, .
lifted up on high, he now beholds clearly Trinity's glory,
with God's kingdom's foremost citizens, singing songs of joy.

10. How he restored to health a paralytic carried to his tomb
Even then God's grace, present in his holy members,
could not die or lie buried in the bowels of the earth.
Far and wide it began to run among the faithful folk,
bringing light to all the world through countless ages.
So now I will begin to sing what must be told in brief,
what holy Christ has done through him since his burial in earth,
and in true verses I will speak of the miracles our saint
                                                    has worked.
A certain man of the people begot a son in marriage,
deformed in all his flesh, and racked in his exhausted body
by a great host of diseases. From the very womb
he had never known what it was to run on firm feet,
for by his injuries his feet were twisted backwards.

Every day all his body knew a living death;
the wretched boy, consumed by wasting illness,
always wounded, lay dully in death's shadow.
His parents, with nothing but their faith, brought him to
the temple
and were at pains to visit there the saint's body and his dust.
The great hall's heavenly heights they sought on foot,
and entered carrying the boy between them as they wept,
flooding their faces with sorrow's hot tears.
They begged on bended knees for the gift of life,
and at the shrine's sacred tomb, in a shower of prayers,
entreated and lamented, wept, and in a murmur spoke:
'O God's beloved, who now gaze on heaven's lights,
whom Christ gave as a respite to the weak of the earth,
the ruler of Olympus has made you healing for our hurt.
Make this lame child run on loosened feet, confessor,
and restore him to health by your own heavenly power.'
When, falling down in prayer, they had poured out all
these words,
as the sun's light died they left their dying son and his
diseased limbs;
they went outside and with its groaning bolt they shut the
temple gate.
These things at last performed, the frozen night with
darkening gloom
swept down and hid the gleaming stars of heaven.
Then at midnight's very turn, where the young boy
wrapped in darkness, crushed by bitter illness
lay inside by the tomb, light shone forth.
Suddenly he saw the bishop, now vested as in snow,
enter and place his right hand on the child's head.
From his hand into those wasted limbs healing power flowed,
and strange to say, he turned those feet, by his very speech,
into their right position, and all his frozen feebleness left him,
quicker than it takes to say, as he moved forward on his feet.
Made whole, he rose and leaped across the temple's marble floor,
and henceforth he has lived, a monk within our walls
for many years, called by name Pehtgils.

*11. How a man with leprous elephantiasis was cleansed of his
illness at the body of the man of God.*
Meanwhile, a man corrupted in all his frame
flew to the tomb where the blessed bishop's body lay

134

in furrowed marble, according to fatal destiny.
At those sacred feet, holding out discoloured limbs,
he fell and worshipped in supplication, and so he prayed:
'See, all my flesh is deformed with besieging corruption.
My skin is discoloured, the leprous mass erupted.
I pray you, free me from my sickness and distress
through the merits of your own abounding grace;
let disease's danger pressing on me be subdued,
and command without delay that health flow into your suppliant.'
So he prayed, and swiftly the heavenly power of God's kindly one,
through his mounting merits, cleansed his lurid limbs,
and by this new gift his former aspect returned to him.
And when he saw what the living power had done,
he heaped up praises, marvelling at the gifts of salvation.

*12. How God returned a woman to health who had been blind for
a long time when she was led to his body.*
There came a woman in blind and horrid darkness,
seeing nothing from the blackness of her staring sockets,
her eyes obscured by night, long ago bereft of light,
while chaos bathed her mind in misery
but did not dry up the fountains of her tears.
At last her parents led the tormented woman
to where the lofty walls of the sacred temple shine.
When she arrived, oppressed by her long sleep,
where the bowels of the hollowed rocks hold fast
the holy body in their stony inner parts,
throwing herself to the ground and worshipping she spoke:
'O beloved man of God, daylight is all gone
and pitchy darkness covers the two windows of my face,
and long night, illumined by no light, is all that remains to me.
But I pray, I beg by the most high Thunderer's reign,
shatter the black shadows, put darkness to flight,
shed on me the day's own brightness and give me health.
Cast out the heavy darkness and make me see the light,
for your loving hand never delays its gifts
as long as men's hearts are constant in faith.
Sure it is that the Lord himself thundered forth such words
when he taught his beloved band of disciples:
"To him who asks it will be given, whoever seeks will find."
So I, least among men and trusting in that promise,
crying out in tears, I beg Christ's gift
that he now deign to grant light to this wretch.'

With such words and with these entreaties she prayed –
this woman blind, yet faithful – throwing her whole body down.
With her brow she pressed the ground, she lay in the
                                        hollowed cavity,
and then leaped up as radiance filled her eyes and darkness
                                        fled away.
So the rejoicing woman, made well by the grace of God,
began to run across the famous sanctuary
and sing praises to the Lord throughout the earth.

*13. How a certain priest celebrating Mass at the body of the man of
God, in answer to his prayers, saw Christ the son of God sitting on
the dish in the form of a very beautiful child.*
There was a noble priest – Plecgils his venerable name –
devout and lovely was the just and modest life he lived.
This worthy man of righteous deeds
would often storm the Thunderer with prayer,
and with holy words the honoured body
where the saint rests in the tomb's embrace.
He had heeded, since his youth, the commandments of the law,
and now in serving Christ grew strong in heaven's might.
He had left his native land, the farms and fields,
that he might learn the mysteries of the Lord. An eager exile.
Then, returning home, he visited those famous walls
and day by day served in the altar's godly ministry,
brought gifts to offer to the Lord, his peaceful heart
full of fervent loving adoration.
With gifts he worshipped at the altar, days on end,
and out of his pure heart he made pure offerings.
Diligently, day after day, he begged the Lord
to manifest the nature of his own loving body
and his holy blood. He offered precious gifts
and often prayed in floods of bitter tears,
since Christ, the universal God, whom the whole world
                                        cannot contain,
lay hidden in the likeness of bright bread.
So he prayed, not because he doubted the body,
but in his pious prayers he longed to see the Christ in bodily form,
whom no one weighed down by the flesh now sees,
shining as he is above the stars of heaven.
So came the day, in the heights of the tall temple,
when the suppliant at the altar stood in prayer
where rests the buried body of bishop Nynia,

yet all the while his joyful spirit shines on Olympian heights
ministering before the high-throned king.
Offering in piety the holy Mass's mysteries
in his accustomed way, flooded by a fount of tears,
he bent his knees in genuflection,
and prostrate on the marble spoke these words:
'I pray, all-powerful Father, manifest Christ's mysteries:
reveal him in the nature of his own loving body
and grant me to see him present face to face.
The shepherds longed to see him in his mother's embrace,
the boy who filled the stable air with his tiny voice,
the very voice which turns heaven's stars.
Then they understood what angels had sung before.'
While the priest spoke from his humble heart,
from heights of heaven an angel appeared, came down
and spoke to him, standing at his right hand:
'Rise, therefore, in haste if you wish to see the Christ
present now in bodily form, dressed in garments of flesh.
Here, see Christ the Lord, earth's author and creator.
This is that boy who for his holy ones prepares
heavenly stores above the stars. With a constant heart,
look upon the Thunderer, revealing now his sharing in your flesh,
the one the holy mother bore in her womb's lodging.'
The priest fell prostrate on his face in fear, and then
rising from the ground he saw, amazed,
on the high and holy table the Father's Son, most venerable.
He saw him sitting on the dish, the blessed boy
whom old Simeon, filled with joy, had carried in his holy hands
under the roof of the ancient temple, worshipping the
                                                    infant child.
Then he heard the radiant angel speak:
'Away with fear, if you wish to see the Christ,
he who was always hid under cover of bright bread
which you were wont to consecrate as you sang the
                                                    mystical words.
Handle him now with your hands, and see him with your eyes.'
Trusting heaven's gift, the priest – wonderful to say –
took the child into his trembling arms
and pressed his holy breast against his own,
gave kisses to the holy face as in his embrace he lay,
touching with his own the beautiful lips of Christ.
These things done, he restored at last the lovely limbs
of the life-giving body to the top of the noble table.

Then once again he prayed to heaven's Lord,
once more he pressed his fearful breast against the ground,
that Christ's body to the form of bread might be restored.
Rising then, on the high sides of the dish he found
the bright oblation, returned to its earlier form.
So devoutly he deserved to feed on the holy offering,
and, having eaten, from his throat he belched out sacred praises.

*14. Of miracles left out of this account, and that it would be
impossible to tell of all his works.*
Since his death, there shine such signs of power
from the body of the saint, from his tomb to the world,
no one could ever encompass them in worthy verse;
Some such wonders I have told, unskilled as I am,
rather than fail to speak of them at all.
Christ, the all-present God, has shown forth many miracles
and, since his death, garlanded his body with shining honours.
Diseases are put to flight, miracles flow from his body,
now he praises Christ in sacred songs.
The loving witness, his deathless honour shining still,
brings healing after death, just as he did in life,
to show the radiance of his marvels gleaming under heaven.
Here Christ is always present. He, at this holy body, brings about
all things the faithful pray for, unassailed by doubt.
He was an excellent priest in all his deeds—
reader, who could encompass them all?
Again, in writing I must omit countless things,
but out of reverence for the saint I will begin
to tell a few, setting out the harvest of my poor garden.
He was a humble man and wise, just and good and kind;
ever pure, pious before all, he offered life's healing
to the people, brought them the gifts of heaven.
Generous to all guests, he opened up his stores,
pressed food on them devoutly with lovable words,
to the naked he gave the most beautiful garments,
he cared for men oppressed by pain in prison,
for the pangs of the hungry he brought relief in bread,
and quenched thirst's misery with the sweet draughts he brought.
He was a father to orphans, to widows a kindly judge,
in him the poor received their share in this present life,
but to all the wicked he was an authority to be feared,
no less than he was loved by good men with great love.
He was a happy man who never did harm to anyone,

joyful beyond measure, the glory of our affairs,
learned in devotion, who would despise no man.
He was worthy of his Lord, thrice and four times blest,
radiant before all and bright in the power of Christ,
in words and deeds worthy of the world's praise,
by his merits a confessor, illumining all lands.
He shone like heaven's brightest star, his people's glory;
in a cave of dreadful darkness, there this man
would meditate within his heart on heavenly wisdom.
He walked in the way of a teacher, gave gifts of salvation;
worthy was he to understand books in learned tongues,
from which he preached, powerful in words made good by
                                                   his deeds,
for whatever he taught to other men he first fulfilled himself.
The hearts of his chosen ones grew strong by his eloquence,
and marvelled as he thundered out sweet sounding melody,
speaking to his servants of eternal life's true joys.
Flying to the stars, he opened their ears to heaven's favours.
To all alike, races and peoples, the holy man gave teaching
worthy of those who are called to enter a heavenly kingdom.
And having performed such deeds among countless peoples
                                                   and races,
a man so good, with a teacher's tongue, the joyful one
was carried to the courts of the Lord, his voyage over,
where now in sacred harmonies he sings Christ's praise.

HYMN FOR SAINT NYNIA THE BISHOP (c. 780) Latin

The hymn celebrates Nynia, the saint of the *Miracles* above, and is quite possibly written by the same person. There are similarities, not only in the devotional imagery of sanctity (light, height, stars etc), but also in the description of God as 'the Thunderer', which is used four times in the *Miracles*. Certainly the poems seem to have emerged from the same literary environment in Whithorn.

Like the *Altus Prosator* and the *Adiutor Laborantium*, the hymn is abecedarian. Twenty-three stanzas begin with the letters of the alphabet in order, except for J, U and W. The final four stanzas begin with A, M, E and N.

A more unusual feature is the repetition of the first line of each stanza in the fourth, suggesting that our poet has been influenced by the hymn in honour of Æthelthryth which is found in Bede's *Ecclesiastical History* (IV, 18), and which also uses this technique.

A   The judge enthroned on high,
      One, God and maker of all things,
     powerful in majesty,
       the judge enthroned on high.

B   Sweet in heaven's citadel,
     he has begotten, light from light,
     the beginning and the end,
      sweet in heaven's citadel.

C   Everywhere grows manifest
     the glory of the eternal king;
     the holy king our Lord
      everywhere grows manifest.

D   Sinners in due punishment
     he held for the ancient crime.
     In the Lord he had left
      sinners in due punishment.

E   Error fell and fled the world
     when the heavenly healer came;
     in the suffering of Christ
      error fell and fled the world.

F   The flowering one begot him
     without a father, fertile mother

– joyful her virginity –
  the flowering one begot him.

G Everlasting joys are hers
    whose virginity is honoured.
    She who gave birth to the Lord,
      everlasting joys are hers.

H The Father's supreme offering
    delivered the earth from death.
    Now he claims the rule of heaven,
      the Father's supreme offering.

I Red-gold, rightly shining bright
    is the glory of the saints in heaven,
    a light to be honoured above,
      red-gold, rightly shining bright.

K Loved one, shining in heaven's halls,
    one with the folk who dwell therein.
    Holy bishop Nynia,
      loved one, shining in heaven's halls.

L He whose heart is full of light
    will blaze out brightly on all lands;
    now above the stars he shines,
      he whose heart is full of light.

M Gentle father on the earth,
    many the miracles he wrought;
    steadfast covenants he bears,
      gentle father on the earth.

N He, our splendour in this world:
    scaly bodies' leprosy most foul,
    from his tomb he cleansed them all,
      he, our splendour in this world.

O Granted power to do all things
    by the Thunderer's abundant blessing,
    he in purity of faith was
      granted power to do all things.

P   The holy one's body rests,
        the bishop buried in the flesh;
        housed beneath the church's heights
            the holy one's body rests.

Q   The God of heaven took him,
        rightly adorned by his victories,
        bore him to heaven's starry heights.
            The God of heaven took him.

R   He dwells in a blessed kingdom,
        who here by the pureness of his ways
        had dwelt always in the Lord.
            He dwells in a blessed kingdom.

S   His spirit reaches for the heavens,
        raised up from his own pure body;
        borne aloft by angelic hands,
            his spirit reaches for the heavens.

T   Through your healing power, O God,
        he cures so many of men's wounds;
        all disease is put to flight
            through your healing power, O God.

V   From deep within he brings it forth,
        carefully poured out, most powerful,
        an overflowing cup of miracles—
            from deep within he brings it forth.

X   Christ in the hall of heaven
        has crowned with garlands of bright honour
        the holy bishop Nynia—
            Christ in the hall of heaven.

Y   In the world the serpent groans,
        now Christ rules over all the earth.
        Now the light of God is here,
            in the world the serpent groans.

Z   The great cauldron stands ready,
        heaped up full of pitchy darkness
        to which the wretched will return.
            The great cauldron stands ready.

A Good folk in sweet stillness
    are at rest for endless ages,
    praising the Lord for ever—
      good folk in sweet stillness.

M They sing in mystical words,
    faithful to their royal vows.
    Holy the throngs in heaven,
      they sing in mystical words.

E And unto you forever
    stately songs are sung O king;
    ceaselessly, by night and day,
      and unto you forever.

N The noble one of heaven,
    with the holy ones singing there,
    keeps watch in obedience—
      the noble one of heaven.

GAELIC VERSES ON KINGS OF THE PICTS

More fragments, this time a poem, probably for the Pictish king Óengus, son of Fergus, who conquered Dál Riata and other parts of northern Britain, preserved in a tract of versecraft, and attributed to a legendary Pictish poet Gruibne; and an elegy for Cinaed son of Ailpín, the Gael who took over the kingdom of the Picts, and whose dynasty continued to rule a united kingdom of Picts and Gaels throughout the Middle Ages.

On Óengus, son of Fergus (†761?)

Good the day when Óengus took Alba,
   hilly Alba, with its strong chiefs;
He brought battle to towns, with boards,
   with feet and hands, and with broad shields.

On the death of Cinaed son of Ailpín (†858)

That Cinaed with his hosts is no more
   brings weeping to every home:
no king of his worth under heaven
    is there, to the bounds of Rome.

GAELIC SATIRICAL POEMS

On Gille-Phádraig

This poem, from 10th-century metrical tract, is written in a 'Pictish' metre called *etalsheisidach Cruithentuath*. Aside from that, it has no Scottish claims. It is an extremely obscure piece, an invective, perhaps, against a bad poet: only a tentative translation is offered here.

Gille-Phádraig, plague of versecraft,
has not found the musicians' sound measure:
a handful of a wether's belly-wool for bedding;
a treasure-chest bandits can't get at;
the horn of a cow, snarling fiercely;
a horn player, inside, on a yew-wood vessel.

On Eithne, daughter of Domnall

Also from a metrical tract, this piece is connected with Scotland only by virtue of its attribution to a legendary Scottish poet, Eochu Echbél (Eochu horse-mouth). Nonetheless, we have included it as a plausible example of an early Gaelic pub-crawl poem.

A blessing from me on excellent Eithne,
    daughter of Domnall
    who deals out spears,
with whom I've drunk (after touring towns,
    on top of snake-poison)
a load for an octet and quartet of peasants
    (long-headed, and hauling pack-saddles)
        of streams of mead.

EARL TURF-EINAR OF ORKNEY (10th century) Norse

Second earl of Orkney, but founder of the dynasty of the Norse earls, he was an illegitimate son of Earl Rognvald of Moer in Norway and, according to legend, the brother of Gongu-Hrolf, first duke of Normandy. The name Rognvald subsequently became dynastic amongst his descendants and, of those mentioned in this poetry, two further earls of Orkney bear this name.

An anonymous couplet celebrates Turf-Einar's clearance of Viking pirates from the Isles. After his father was killed by sons of King Harald Fairhair of Norway, he took vengeance by killing one of Harald's sons, and celebrates this in vv. 1–5. These are preserved in *Orkneyinga Saga* and are metrically archaic; it is therefore possible that they are genuine.

Anonymous
Turf-Einar is praised for killing some pirates

He gave Treebear to the trolls,
Turf-Einar slew Scurfy.

Turf-Einar
Avenging his father

In the following five verses, he boasts of avenging his father by killing Halfdan Long-leg, son of King Harald Fairhair of Norway.

I see not from Hrolf's hand
nor from Hrollaugr's
a spear flying into a host of foes;
we must avenge our father;
yet at evening, whilst we press on,
over the cask-current, battle,
silent sits now
Earl Thorir in Moer.

I reckon I've avenged Rognvald's death
– the fates rightly ordered it –
now is the army-prop fallen –
in my quarter.
Cast, bold lads,
for we rule victory,
– I chose hard tribute for him –
stone at Long-leg!

Ever shall I be glad, since spears
– it is good for a man to work valour –
of strife-eager soldiers
bit the king's young son.
I am not ignorant that it will displease
– there flew early to the wounds
the carrion-vulture – around the Isles
the gut-hawk's gladdener.

There are for my life many
men, for real conflicts,
from different quarters
unlowborn eager,
but that they know not at all,
before they have felled me,
who under the foot-thorns
of the eagle has to stand.

Many a man is outlawed for a sheep,
a fellow with a fair beard,
but I at the fall in the Isles
of the all-ruler's young son;
perilous men tell me
it is against the grief-stricken lord;
I have hewn a cleft (and fear not for it)
in Harald's shield.

cask-current 'ale'.
Long-leg: Halfdan Long-leg, son of King Harald of Norway, who had killed
    Turf-Einar's father, Earl Rognvald of Moer.
carrion-vulture, gut-hawk 'carrion-bird, raven'; its *gladdener* 'warlike man',
    i.e. King Harald.
foot-thorns 'claws'.

ORM BARREYJARSKALD 'Poet of Barra'
(10th century) Norse

Only the name and these incomplete fragments of poetry are known of this figure, who, to judge by his nickname, was of the Christian Hiberno-Norse population of the Hebrides.

1 . . . In what way, goddess of Draupnir's cord,
   – I hear the lord to be mighty;
   that ruler governs the realm
   of the cart-way – he will welcome me.

Draupnir mythological ring; its *cord* 'gold ring'; its *goddess* 'lady, woman'.
cart-way possibly 'Milky Way'; its *realm* 'the sky, heaven'; its *ruler* 'God'.

2 Outside there crashes on the shingle
   Ymir's blood, of good journeys . . .

Ymir 'the primaeval giant'; his *blood* 'the sea'.

HAFGERDINGADRAPA (10th century) Norse

Fragments of a work by an anonymous poet, supposed to be composed on a sea-journey from the Hebrides. The account is given in *Landnamabok*: 'Herjolf was the name of a man, the son of Bard Herjolfsson; he went to Greenland with Eirik [the Red]. In his ship with him was a Hebridean, a Christian, he said the words of *Hafgerdingadrapa*.' Herjolf's son Bjarni first saw Vinland, though he did not land.

1 Let all listen to our cup
   of Dvalin's hall of the dark fells.

Dvalin dwarf-name; his *cup* 'poetry'; dwarfs conventionally live within rocks and mountains.

2 I beg the monks' tester
   unmarring to direct my voyage;
   may the lord of the land's high hall
   hold his hawk's stall over me.

monks' tester 'God'; *the land's high hall* 'sky, heaven'; *hawk's stall* 'resting-place of the hawk', i.e. hand.

THE DEATH-SONG FOR EIRIK BLOODAXE
(Eiriksmal) (c. 954) Norse

Skaldic

A memorial lay for Eirik Bloodaxe, who was briefly king of Norway before being expelled by his brother, Hakon the Good, and then became king of the Norse kingdom of York; he fell in a skirmish at Stainmore in 954. His widow, Gunnhild, 'Mother of Kings', fled to the Norse earldom of Orkney after Eirik's death, and it is usually assumed that this lay was composed there. It is probably incomplete in its present form.

1 'What joyous sounds are they? *said Odin*;
I thought I rose before day,
to clear Valhall
for a slain host:
I woke the Einherjar
told them to get up,
to strew the benches,
to clean the beer-casks,
valkyries to bear wine,
as if a lord were coming.

preparing for a king

2 'For me from the world
I hope for men,
some nobles,
so my heart is glad.

3 'What thunders there, Bragi,
as if a thousand quiver,
or a multitude too great?'
'All the bench-boards creak
as if Baldr would come
back into Odin's halls.'

4 'Wise Bragi must not, *said Odin*,
speak foolishness,
for well you know:
before Eirik it resounds,
who shall come in here,
a lord into Odin's halls.

5 'Sigmund and Sinfjotli,
rise swiftly

and go to greet the king;
invite within,
if he be Eirik,
hope of him is certain for me.'

6 'Why do you hope for Eirik, *said Sigmund*,
rather than for others?'
'For in many a land, *said Odin*,
he has reddened a blade
and borne a blood-stained sword.'

7 'Why did you take victory from him, then,
when he seemed bold to you?'
. 'It's uncertain to know, *said Odin*,
the grey wolf gazes
[grim] at the dwellings of the gods.'

8 'Hail now, Eirik, *said Sigmund*,
you must be welcome here,
and enter the hall, wise one!
That I wish to ask of you,
which come with you,
kings from the edge-thunder?'

9 'There are five kings, *said Eirik*,
I shall tell you the names of all,
I am the sixth myself.'

THE FALL OF RHEGED (9th or 10th century) Welsh

This is a sequence of poems, mostly in the voices of various characters in the events it recounts, which describes the internecine strife between rulers of the British North which led to the death of Urien of Rheged. It thus complements the earlier tradition concerning Urien, which had one of his fellow Northern kings instigating his assassination. Unlike most of the other Welsh 'saga poems', the poetry of what is usually termed the *Urien Cycle* but which is here called *The Fall of Rheged* was not transposed in setting or characters to the Welsh countryside, and it seems to preserve various northern traditions. It is arguably, then, a product of the last phases of Welsh literature among the northern British, who in the years around 900 were expanding back into northern Cumbria, what had once been the kingdom of Rheged, the demise of which is described by these poems. The meditation on the deserted Hearth of Rheged could be taken, in such a context, as a contemplation of a vanished British heroic past.

It is questionable whether the Welsh 'saga poems' were originally given a context by prose narratives that have not survived or were never recorded. The nature of the poems themselves is fairly clear: they are, in essence, dramatic monologues, and sometimes dialogues, in which the speaker is a character involved in events that took place several centuries before the composition of the poems. So, in contrast to the poems of Taliesin and Aneirin, the speaker is someone other than the poet.

The best-known group of saga poems has as the speaker Llywarch Hen, presented as a cousin of Urien of Rheged, who in old age seeks refuge in Powys, which is then the setting for his monologues and dialogues. Llywarch has also been thought of as the speaker in the present group of poems, since these come in manuscript between two of the Llywarch poems, but it now seems probable that poems from one or more earlier sagas centring on Urien were later copied into the Llywarch saga.

The identity of the speaker or speakers of the Urien poems is, therefore, uncertain, as is the question of whether, in the poems dealing with Urien's head and corpse, the speaker fought on his side or in opposition. What is supported by historical tradition is that Urien fell in battle against other British rulers, among whom were Morgant and Gwallawg.

1 Unhwch would counsel, savage warrior,
Enraged in peace parleys:
Better slay than supplicate.

Unhwch would counsel, savage warrior,
He wreaks carnage in combat:
I will lead Llwyfenydd's war-bands.

Unhwch would counsel, savage warrior:
It was said at Drws Llech
Dunawd ap Pabo will not run.

Unhwch would counsel, savage warrior,
Bitter wrath, the sea's laughter,
Inciter, triumphant lord.

Urien of Rheged, ardent, eagle's grip,
Foe to Unhwch, bountiful, bold,
Fierce in war, victorious ruler.

Urien of Rheged, ardent, eagle's grip,
Foe to Unhwch, ample owner,
Sea's store, comely streams, men's table.

2 A head I bear at my side:
He led the charge between war-bands;
It was Cynfarch's proud son owned it.

A head I bear at my side:
Kind Urien's head, he ruled a host,
And on his white breast, a black crow.

A head I bear on my belt:
Kind Urien's head, he ruled a court,
And on his white breast, crows banquet.

A head I bear in my hand:
He was shepherd for Yrechwydd,
Noble-hearted, expender of spears.

A head I bear next my thigh:
He was the land's shield, he was battle's wheel,
He was war's pillar, foe's snare.

A head I bear on my left side:
Better his life than his grave.
He was the old folks' bulwark.

A head I bear from Penawg's slope:
Far-roving his war-bands;
Head of Urien, lavishly praised.

A head I bear on my shield:
It did not dishonour me.
Woe's my hand, for slashing my lord.

A head I bear on my arm:
He furnished for Brennych's land,
After battle, a burden of biers.

A head I bear from beside a stake:
Head of Urien, valiant lord,
And though Doomsday come, no matter.

A head I bear in my hand's hard grasp:
Bountiful lord, he once ruled a land;
Prydain's pillar-head, it was removed.

A head I nurse that nursed me:
I know it did me no good,
Woe's my hand, it wrought harshly.

A head I bear from beside a hill:
On his mouth the frothing
Blood: woe's Rheged from today.

It has twisted my arm; it has savaged my ribs;
My heart it has broken:
A head I nurse that nursed me.

3 His slender white body is buried today
Under earth and stone:
Woe's my hand, Owain's father slain.

His slender white body is buried today
Within earth and oak:
Woe's my hand, my cousin slain.

His slender white body is buried today;
Under stone it was left:
Woe's my hand, the fate that befell me.

His slender white body is buried today
Within earth and turf:
Woe's my hand, Cynfarch's son slain.

His slender white body is buried today
Under earth and gravel:
Woe's my hand, the fate that beset me.

His slender white body is buried today
Under earth and nettles:
Woe's my hand, the fate designed for me.

His slender white body is buried today
Under earth and grey stone:
Woe's my hand, the fate that was mine.

4 Hard to find till Doomsday, our gathering
Around drinking-horns, around dipper,
Lord's retinue, Rheged's war-band.

Hard to find till Doomsday, our welcoming
Around drinking-horns, around dish,
Lord's retinue, Rheged's men.

5 Efrddyl's cheerless tonight
With many another:
At Aber Lleu, Urien slain.

Efrddyl's sad for his tribulation tonight
And the fate that beset me:
At Aber Lleu, her brother slain.

6 Friday I saw the great
Sorrow of Christendom's war-hosts,
Like a swarm that lacks a queen.

Rhun Rhyfeddfawr, he gave me
A hundred troops and a hundred shields,
And one troop was by far the best.

Rhun, suppliant's lord, he gave me
A hundred homesteads and a hundred oxen,
And one homestead was better than any.

In life, Rhun, ruler of war,
He curbed those with wicked ways,
Shackles on the steeds of the wicked.

7 How well I know my affliction:
Lively everyone, every summer;
None know anything of me.

8 Dunawd was bent, slaughter's horseman,
On making corpses in Yrechwydd,
Facing the onslaught of Owain.

Unhwch was bent, region's lord,
On wreaking carnage in Yrechwydd,
Facing the onslaught of Pasgen.

Gwallawg was bent, strife's horseman,
On making carcasses in Yrechwydd,
Facing the onslaught of Elphin.

Bran ab Ymellyrn was bent
On banishing me, on burning my hearths,
Wolf who'd yelp at a gap.

Morgant was bent, he and his men,
On banishing me, on burning my land,
Shrew who'd scrape at a crag.

9 I saw when Elno was slain
A blade scourged the rampart
Of Pyll and his people's camp.

Again I saw, after the war-cry,
A shield on Urien's shoulder:
Second best there was Elno Hen.

10 Need has come on Yrechwydd
From a horseman's death under spears:
Will there ever be another Urien?

Bald is my lord, bold is his nature:
Warriors love not his hatred.
He poured out a ruler's riches.

Urien's passion is grievous to me,
Raider in every region,
In the wake of Llofan Llaw Ddifro.

Tranquil the breeze next the slope.
A rare thing, one worthy of praise.
Save for Urien, no leader matters.

11 Many a lively hound and vigorous hawk
Were fed on its floor
Before this place was ruins.

This hearth, with its blanket of grey,
More common, once, on its floor
Mead, and drunken men pleading.

This hearth, nettles hide it:
While its defender was living
[It saw many a suppliant].

This hearth, borage hides it:
When Owain and Elphin lived
Its cauldron would stew plunder.

This hearth, grey lichen hides it:
More common, once, for its food,
A savage fearless sword-stroke.

This hearth, a layer of briers hides it:
Blazing wood was its due.
Rheged had the habit of giving.

This hearth, thorns hide it:
More common, once, for its warriors
The friendly favour of Owain.

This hearth, reeds hide it:
More common, once, were bright
Tapers, and true companions.

This hearth, dock leaves hide it:
More common, once, on its floor
Mead, and drunken men pleading.

This hearth, a hog roots in it:
More common, once, were men's
Revels, and mirth around mead-horns.

This hearth, a hen scratches it:
Hardship could not harm it
While Owain and Urien lived.

This pillar, and that one there,
More common, once, around them
War-band's revels, and path to reward.

MUGRÓN, ABBOT OF IONA (†980) Gaelic

Mugrón was successor of Columba as abbot of Iona and head of the Columban family, 965–81. At his death he was called 'successor of Colum Cille both in Ireland and Scotland'. He seems to have been abbot at a time when Iona was renewing some of its prestige, lost more recently to the Irish monastery of Kells. Under the patronage of Norse kings, Iona may have been undergoing something of a renaissance. The king of Dublin, Man and the Isles, Olaf Cúarán, died as a pilgrim on Iona in the same year as Mugrón. Mugrón's successor seems to have been resident also on the island, where he was killed, along with 15 of the elders of the monastery, by Danes from Dublin on Christmas Night, 986.

His name seems to mean 'seal-slave'; does this help to explain the odd imagery of the first poem, in which Colum Cille is called 'high heaven's noble seal'?

In Praise of Colum Cille

Colum Cille, Alba's head,
keen for fierce fame over rough seas,
matchless barque of bards' rewards,
eager author, high heaven's noble seal.

Our high apostle of Aran,
unhindered by the world's gold;
blameless sun, fine stride of Cualann,
shoulder bird of the flood's God.

From Conall, Christ brought desire,
sorrowless, for fervent free knowledge,
the son of Heaven's King – he broke great chains:
chief of Conn's household is Colum.

Christ's Cross

This is an example of the very common form of Gaelic devotional verse, the lorica, or breastplate, in which God or the saints are invoked in a systematic, incantatory fashion. The contrast between this poem and the previous one, if both are by Mugrón, is striking. However, the final work attributed to him here, the Litany of the Trinity, is a similarly functional Gaelic prayer, rather than an exercise in praise-poetry.

Christ's cross across this face,
across the ear like this,
Christ's cross across this eye,
Christ's cross across this nose.

Christ's cross across this mouth.
Christ's cross across this throat.
Christ's cross across this back.
Christ's cross across this side.

Christ's cross cross this stomach,
(like this it is just fine).
Christ's cross across this gut,
Christ's cross across this spine.

Christ's cross across my arms
from my shoulders to my hands.
Christ's cross across my thighs.
Christ's cross across my legs.

Christ's cross with me before.
Christ's cross with me behind.
Christ's cross against each trouble
both on hillock and in glen.

Christ's cross east towards my face,
Christ's cross west towards sunset.
South and north, ceaselessly,
Christ's cross without delay.

Christ's cross across my teeth
lest to me come harm or hurt.
Christ's cross cross my stomach.
Christ's cross across my heart.

Christ's cross up to heaven's span.
Christ's cross down to earth.
Let no evil or harm
come to my body or soul.

Christ's cross cross my sitting,
Christ's cross cross my lying.
Christ's cross, my whole power
till we reach heaven's King.

Christ's cross across my church,
across my community.
Christ's cross in the next world.
Christ's cross in the present-day.

From the tip of my head
to the nail of my foot,
Christ, against each peril
the shelter of your cross.

Till the day of my death,
before going in this clay,
joyfully I will make
Christ's cross across my face.

The Litany of the Trinity

Have mercy on us, God, Father almighty.
God of hosts.
Noble God.
World's ruler.
Ineffable God.
Creator of the elements.
Invisible God.
Incorporeal God.
Unjudgeable God.
Immeasurable God.
Impassible God.
Incorruptible God.
Immortal God.
Immovable God.
Eternal God.

Perfect God.
Merciful God.
Marvellous God.
Fearsome God.
God of the earth.
God of the fire.
God of the varied waters.
God of the rushing storm-tossed air.
God of the waves from the ocean's deep house.
God of the constellations and all the bright stars.
God who formed the mass, who began day and night.
God who ruled over hell and its rough crowd.
God who governs with archangels.
Golden good.
Heavenly Father who are in heaven.
Have mercy on us.

Have mercy on us, almighty God,
    Jesus Christ, Son of the living God.
Twice-born Son.
Only-begotten of God the Father.
First-born of the virgin Mary.
Son of David.
Son of Abraham.
Beginning of all things.
End of the world.
Word of God.
Path to the heavenly kingdom.
Life of all things.
Eternal Truth.
Image, Likeness, Form of God the Father.
Hand of God.
Arm of God.
Strength of God.
God's right hand.
True Knowledge.
True Light that lightens every darkness.
Guiding Light.
Sun of Truth.
Morning Star.
Brightness of the Godhead.
Shining of the eternal light.
Wellspring of eternal life.

Perception of the mystic world.
Mediator of all men.
The church's promised one.
The flock's faithful shepherd.
Hope of the faithful.
Angel of the great counsel.
True prophet.
True apostle.
True teacher.
High priest.
Master.
Nazarene.
Fair-haired one.
Eternal fulfillment.
Tree of life.
True heaven.
True vine.
Branch from Jesse's stem.
King of Israel.
Saviour.
Door of life.
Choice Flower of the field.
Lily of the glens.
Rock of power.
Cornerstone.
Heavenly Sion.
Bedrock of faith.
Innocent lamb.
Diadem.
Gentle sheep.
Redeemer of the human race.
True God.
True Man.
Lion.
Calf.
Eagle.
Christ crucified.
Judge of doom.
Have mercy on us.

Have mercy on us, God almighty, Holy Spirit.
Spirit who are highest of every spirit.
Finger of God.

Guard of Christians.
Comforter of the sorrowful.
Gentle one.
Merciful Intercessor.
Giver of true wisdom.
Author of the holy scripture.
Governor of speech.
Sevenfold Spirit.
Spirit of wisdom.
Spirit of understanding.
Spirit of counsel.
Spirit of strength.
Spirit of knowledge.
Spirit of fondness.
Spirit of awe.
Spirit of love.
Spirit of grace.
Spirit by whom every noble thing is ordered.
Spirit who burns up guilt.
Spirit who washes sins.
Holy Spirit who rules all creation, visible and invisible.
Have mercy upon me.

Almighty God, heavenly Father and only-begotten Son.
Have mercy upon me.
Have mercy on me, father, Son, Holy Spirit.
Have mercy on me, only God.
God of heaven, have mercy upon me.
Have mercy on me, God, from whom and through whom is
    the rule of all creation for you, God.
To you be honour and glory for ever and ever. Amen.

HERFID'S SONG ON THE BATTLE OF CLONTARF (1014)
Norse

The Battle of Clontarf, fought on Good Friday, 1014, between the forces of the kings of Munster in Ireland, and the kings of Leinster and the Ostmen of Dublin, supported by a large gathering of forces from the Hebrides, Man and the Northern Isles, is famous for the Pyrrhic victory of Brian Bórama of Munster. Nonetheless, it seems to have had cataclysmic resonances in the Norse world, especially since the powerful Earl of Orkney, Sigurd was slain, according to tradition, with a raven banner wrapped round him. Two verses concerning the battle are preserved in *Njal's Saga*. This first is spoken by a 'dream-man', Herfid, to a local ruler in the Hebrides, Earl Gilli (an apparently Gaelic name), who was based at least sometimes on the island of Coll. The poem is introduced in the saga as follows:

[Earl Gilli in the Hebrides dreamt that a man came to him and gave his name as Herfid, and said that he had come from Ireland. The earl seemed to himself to ask for news. He said this:]

I was where men fought;
a sword rang in Ireland;
many, where shields clashed,
weapons crashed in the helm-din;
I heard of their keen assault;
Sigurd fell in the spear-din,
sooner wounds bled;
Brian fell and held the field.

DARRADARLJOD (11th or 12th century) Norse

Also preserved in *Njal's Saga* in the account of the Battle of Clontarf is this semi-mythological lay in the same metre as the mythological and heroic lays of the Elder Edda. It is part of a continuous narrative; the prose preamble and conclusion are given here in square brackets. It is only found in *Njal's Saga*, composed in the late 13th century, but is likely to be older than the saga, which seems to misunderstand the name *Dorrud*. It may, however, not be older than the 12th century, since it is similar to pieces of 'pastiche' legendary and mythological poetry likely to have been composed then, while pagan subject matter seems to have been avoided for most of the 11th century, presumably while paganism was still a threat soon after Conversion.

[On the Friday morning it happened in Caithness, that a man called Dorrud went out. He saw that people were riding, twelve in all, to a mound, and all vanished there. He went to the mound and looked into a window which was in it, and saw that women were within and had set up a loom. Heads of men were used as the loom-weights, but guts for the woof and yarn, a sword was used for a beam but an arrow for a beating-rod. They then spoke some verses:]

1   Wide is cast
    for falling of the slain
    the loom-beam's swung cloud;
    blood rains;
    now before the spears
    is come up the grey
    weaving of mankind,
    when those friendly women
    fulfil with red thread
    Randver's fate.

2   That weaving is cast
    with guts of men
    and hard-weighted
    with heads of men;
    blood-spattered javelins
    are used as the beams,
    iron-clad is the frame,
    but beaten with arrows;
    we must strike with swords
    this weaving of victory.

3   Hild goes to weave
    and Hjorthrimul,

Sanngrid, Svipul,
with drawn swords;
the shaft will crack,
shield will shatter,
the helm-hound
will strike the buckler.

Hildr etc. are names for valkyries ('choosers of the slain') and troll-women;
helm-hound 'that which hunts a helmet like a dog, i.e. weapon'.

4 Twist, twist
Darrad's weaving,
that which the young king
once possessed!
Forwards let's go
and wade into battle,
where our friends
deal in weapons.

Darrad ('spear-warrior') is probably here a name for Odin. The *young king* is
probably Sigtrygg Silk-beard of the Viking kingdom of Dublin.

5 Twist, twist
Darrad's weaving,
and then let's
go with the king!
There see men's
blood-stained shields
Gunn and Gondul,
who protected the lord.

Gunn and *Gondul*: valkyrie names.

6 Twist, twist
Darrad's weaving,
where sanctuaries wade
of warlike men!
Let us not allow
his life to perish;
Valkyries have
choice of the slain.

7 Those peoples
will rule lands
who before
dwelt on far capes;

I declare for the mighty lord
death determined;
now before spear-points
the earl has bowed.

8 And the Irish
will endure a grief
which will never
grow old for men.
Now the weaving is woven,
the battle-field reddened,
through the lands will go
the ill-tidings of men.

9 Now it is fearsome
to look around,
when blood-stained clouds
are drawn across heaven;
the sky will be stained
with men's blood,
when the battle-women
know how to sing.

battle-women 'valkyries'.

10 Well we spoke
of the young king,
many voices of victory,
let's sing good fortunes!
But let that one learn
who hears the voice
of the victory-women,
and tell men.

11 Let's ride our horses,
bear out harshly
with drawn swords
away from here!

[Then they tore down the cloth they had woven and tore it apart, and each had
what she was holding on to. He then left the window and went home, but they
mounted their horses, and six rode southwards, but the other six north.]

OTTAR THE BLACK (early 11th century) Norse

An Icelandic poet who performed at the court of King Olaf Haraldsson (St Olaf) of Norway, and also at the court of Olaf of Sweden and Knut the Great, king of England and Denmark. Although there is no indication that he ever worked in Scotland, this verse has been included as a statement of the network which existed between Norway, Iceland and the Northern Isles.

On Olaf Haraldsson, King of Norway (†1030)

Noble, hold with moderation
the realm of good kings of nations;
Shetlanders are acknowledged
to be your subjects;
No prince, terror-swift,
came on earth, who
sooner than you seized
the westward Isles into his power.

ARNOR THORDARSON, JARLASKALD (Earl's Poet)
(mid-11th century) Norse

The Icelandic poet Arnor 'Earl's Poet' was son of Thord Kolbeinsson, who figures as a poet in *Bjarnar saga Hitdoelakappa*. He spent most of his career outside Iceland, serving as court poet to kings in Norway, and for the competing earls, Rognvald (Brusason) and Thorfinn, in Orkney. His verses about them, preserved mostly in *Orkneyinga Saga*, are the most important historical source for Thorfinn's long reign (sixty years, according to *Orkneyinga Saga*), for his campaigns in Scotland, and in particular for the battle in which Thorfinn defeated Rognvald. Arnor is unusual for the personal tone with which he expresses his grief at conflict between his patrons, and for the death of Thorfinn in the long memorial lay, *Thorfinnsdrapa*, presumably composed at the earl's death some time before 1066.

In Praise of Rognvald Brusason
(†1046) (Rognvaldsdrapa)

Earl Rognvald is praised for his warfare, and for arranging a marriage into the earl's family for the poet.

1 It was granted of his life
   that the war-swift Njord of battle
   in Russia convened ten
   storms of the carved shield's file.

2 The offspring of Heiti,
   hostneedful, made kinship with me;
   the mighty marriage-bond of the earl
   brought us renown.

3 True governor of the sun's canopy
   aid bold Rognvald.

Njord of battle 'warrior'; *the carved shield's file* 'sword', its *storm* 'battle'.

An Elegy for Earl Thorfinn the Mighty
(†1064–65) (Thorfinnsdrapa)

This elegy for one of the most pivotal of the Orkney Earls begins by meditating on the poet's lord and goes on to detail his military career, beginning at the age of 14. It mentions important campaigns, such as his defeat of a Scottish king, often identified with the person called here Karl Hundason, in a battle off Deerness, and various other exploits, lamenting also the conflict between the competing Earls Rognvald and Thorfinn. The poem is mostly preserved in scattered form, interspersed with prose, in the *Orkneyinga Saga*, and further, though not necessarily always accurate, details about some of the events mentioned here may be found in that text. The order of the poem as presented here is not necessarily the original order.

1 I vowed, when each winter we sat
    opposite the raven's foodgiver – always
    the lord drank ale
    for the good ships' crews.

raven's foodgiver 'warrior, warlike lord'.

2 Through all the serpent's feller,
    excellent – the fen of yeast –
    the prince acted magnificently—
    Rognvald's kinsman drank.

serpent's feller 'winter'; *fen of yeast* 'ale'.

3 They begin to bear visible—
    for me, about the end of that lord's
    slaughter-known benchmate—
    heavy harms, my young sons.

4 Now I plan to tell men of the merits
    of the perilous-minded earl
    – slowly do my griefs lighten –
    All-father's yeast's surf roars.

yeast's surf 'fermented drink'; *All-father* Odin; his drink is poetry.

5 The lord reddened sword-edges
    in the helmet's storm;
    Hugin's foot-reddener set out

sooner than fifteen winters old;
ready no man said he was to defend the land,
brave-minded, and to attack for it,
nobler than Einar's brother
under heaven's hall.

Hugin Odin's raven; his *foot-reddener* is a warrior who gives carrion to the raven.

6 Yet I think the earl taught Karl
   the corslet's strange judgment—
   the land of the lord's son was not loose—
   east of Deerness;
   with five ships advanced,
   slow to flee, with stoutness of heart,
   wrathful the magnificent man
   against the king's eleven vessels.

the corslet's strange judgment 'battle'.

7 Men set ships in clear counter—
   the host fell on decking;
   iron weapons, frenzy-hard,
   swam in the dark blood of Scots;
   shook not – strings twanged,
   steel bit, but blood streamed,
   dart flew, arrow-points quivered
   bright – the prince's heart.

8 The clash was not the shorter
   (that was soon) with spears;
   glorious, with a lesser troop
   my lord drove the fleeing;
   shrieked, before the king's men fell,
   the war-gull over a wounded host;
   he won victory south
   of Sandwick; we reddened blades.

war-gull 'gull of battle, raven'.

9 Keen edges reddened the wolf's chew,
   where alone it is called Torfness,
   the young lord brought it about;

that was a Monday;
there sang there slim
swords, south of Oykel,
where the prince, swift in battle,
fought against Scotland's lord.

the wolf's chew 'carrion'.

10 High bore the Shetland's lord
his helm at the spears' uproar,
the terror-increaser reddened for Irishmen
a point, at the head of the troop;
my lord employed his strength,
generous, beneath a British shield;
Hlodvir's kinsman seized soldiers,
but battle happened.

11 Dwellings perished, when they burned—
peril that day did not fail—
there sprang into smouldering thatch
red flame – the Scots' realm;
the death-acknowledger repaid men
for crimes; in one summer
they got against the lord
three times the lesser lot.

12 I know, where it's called Vatnsfjord,
– I was in great peril –
against mankind's tester—
marks of my lord's deeds;
the nation bore swiftly from ships
a shield-fortress Friday;
clearly I saw that gaped
the grey wolf over wounded corpses.

13 Let the host hear, how the bold
king of earls sought the sea;
the outweighing lord did not
give way against ocean.

14 Manifold the wave's Baldr
accomplished – an Irish host fell –
when he attacked – or British men –
(fire burned) the Scottish realm.

wave's Baldr 'sea-going warrior'.

15 One there was that the English remember,
an edge-storm, (nor will there be after)
the ring-scatterer (a greater)
came thither against a helmeted host;
swords bit old Rognvald's child,
slender, but there rushed
south of Man
under their shields mighty armies.

ring-scatterer 'generous lord'.

16 His standard the earl bore
on the English homeland—
banners the lord bade to drive forward—
at times the host reddened the eagle's tongue;
flame grew, halls withered,
the warlike band drove the fleeing there,
smoke thrust, but the branch-bane
struck out light, nearer heaven. *no longer Valhalla*

branch-bane 'that which is the death of branches, fire'.

17 Many a horn-blast was between fortresses,
the generous lord pressed into battle,
where was shaken
the mighty-hearted leader's standard;
nought fearful startled, when war-bright seemed,
the stern host of the outlaw's feller,
(weapons trembled but wolves)
morning (chewed carrion).

the outlaw's feller 'the just lord'.

18 The warlike ruler got in each,
of Shetland, thunder of blades
(a poet wants to raise the lord's praise)
gain, he who was highest of men.

thunder of blades 'battle'.

19 I am, since men rejected
as I think reconciliation,
reluctant to tell of the earls' condition;
equally was carrion given to the ravens;
the all-ruler tore, out beyond the Isles,
a blue canopy,
the storm-chilled billow had
frosted the mast firmly.

blue canopy perhaps 'dark-dyed sail' torn by impetuous sailing.

20 An ill fortune came about
yet, when loud malice
taught many to fall,
hard, where the earls fought;
near attacked each other
our beloved ones, when arrow-storm
(afterwards many a generous man
got grief) happened before Raudabjorg.

21 I saw each of my two hew their
retinue on the Pentland Firth
(greater the harm was got)
my wealth-givers;
the sea was mingled, but blood spattered
dark on the flexing ship-seams,
blood shot on shield-rims,
the boat was sprinkled with blood.

22 That lord, battle-swift, would have brought
all the ancient land
under himself (he received
much the lesser man-loss);
if Endil's kin-stave
could have had (the host
betrayed the Shetlanders' lord)
a troop of native helm-Odins.

Endil's kin-stave Endil (legendary sea-king); his *kin-stave*, a supporting descendant, Earl Rognvald.
helm-Odin 'warrior'.

23 He who made warfare on rings
a host had to obey from Thurso skerries

(I tell men truly how Thorfinn seemed)
as far as Dublin.

He who made warfare on rings 'generous man' who gave rings away.

24 Bright becomes the sun a black one,
    sinks the land into the dark sea,
    Austri's effort shatters,
    all the sea will crash on the mountains,
    before in the Isles a lovelier
    lord than Thorfinn (God keep
    that keeper of his court)
    shall be born.

Austri's effort Austri (a dwarf who holds up the sky); his *effort* 'heaven'.

25 Mighty Turf-Einar's glorious kin-mender,
    God, keep from harms;
    but I pray for true mercies
    for the noble prince.

Turf-Einar's kin-mender Earl Thorfinn.

BJARNI HALLBJARNARSON GULLBRARSKALD
(mid-11th century) Norse

The Icelandic poet's nickname probably indicates that he was thought to have
composed poetry for a 'gold-browed' lady, but his surviving poetry was
composed for a Norwegian patron, Kalf Arnason, a political exile in Orkney
and later the Hebrides, who was allied with Earl Thorfinn of Orkney against
his nephew Rognvald Brusason. The poem relates to his intervention, on
Thorfinn's side, in the naval battle in which the two earls came into open
conflict.

In Praise of Kalf Arnason (c. 1045)

We heard how Finn's kinsman
you accompanied, Kalf, through hostilities,
and let on the sea swift ships
boldly attack the earl;
You destroyed the resolve
of the frenzied son of Brusi –
your courage grew hot – but mĭndful
of vengeance aided Thorfinn.

ADVICE TO MAEL COLUIM FROM MACDUIB Latin

Walter Bower, the 15th-century historian, in his *Scotichronicon*, tells how Macduff (MacDuib), the earl of Fife, fled from MacBethad, king of the Scots, who suspected him of treachery. Arriving in England, where Mael Coluim, son of Donnchad, was also in exile at the court of Edward the Confessor, Macduff sought to persuade Mael Coluim to return to Scotland and take the throne from Macbethad. Mael Coluim, after carrying out a strange loyalty test on Macduff, agreed to return, whereupon Macduff gave him the poetic advice that follows. When this dramatic speech actually dates from is impossible to say, though it is unlikely to be either as early as Macduff or as late as Bower.

In 1054, Mael Coluim III was finally installed as king of the Scots, known by his nickname Cenn Mór, but his control was limited to the southern part of the country, while Macbethad continued to rule in his northern stronghold until Mael Coluim defeated and slew him at Lumphanan in 1057 and took effective control of the consolidated kingdom.

Would you bring safety to helpless faithful folk,
those who till today have lacked all help?
For fifteen years the enemy has oppressed them, so
come kindly, relieve the wretched for the love of God.
Waste no time in idle speculation, but with ready strength
cast down our foe, relieve your still devoted people.
Let your sword be girded on your thigh, take up your arms,
for the strength of every fibre of your frame is clear.

You are a Scot, born of the line of kings of old,
and so advance in triumph, take up your father's rule.
I promise you, the kingdom's crown will be rightly yours,
for every right belongs to you, and none to him are owed.
Bold in your rights, therefore, be always battle-ready,
but do not reckon warfare to be entered into lightly.
And, barring ill chance, let you not rush headlong into strife,
for every man may fall through that for which he's unprepared.
But when about to fight, do not let your foe precede you on
the field,
but be there first yourself in the place where arms will meet.

THE BIRTH OF ÁEDÁN MAC GABRÁIN (c. 1060) Gaelic

This verse narrative tells a strange tale of baby-switching, suggesting that the progenitor of the dynasty of Scottish kings was really the son of an Irish king in Leinster. Although written from a Leinster poet's perspective, it seems likely that the audience was a Scottish one, and that the relationship described is meant to be complimentary. Political allusions suggest that the poem belongs to the mid-11th century, and the epithets referring to Scotland as rich in gold and horses, and to its kings as being based on the Forth, are historically interesting. The poem also contains what is probably the earliest reference to the Stone of Scone: Áedán's 'real' mother swears 'by the very famous eastern stone'. We have omitted the first part of the poem, which details the ancestry of the kings of Leinster.

Eochu and Fáelán, feast-rich—
you've not balked at their deeds—
   these men had bright bloody weapons
   fighting to rule the Uí Chennselaigh.

I have heard how brave Eochu
was driven across the sea's broad plain.
   far the rowing from Riadán,
   till they reached Gabrán's chamber.

He got honour at feasts,
great Eochu mac Muiredaigh,
   he prospered with Gabrán, steed-rich,
   he got every human gift.

A good woman, kind Eochu's wife;
Eochu was not a senseless man:
   he took her to keen Gabrán's house,
   far away, for his great love.

One grief fair Gabrán had,
the king of Alba, gold its measures,
   they never hid that hurt:
   his great wife bore no sons.

Alba's king, splendid his steeds,
loved the king of troop-filled Liffey;
   a friendship – no slender one –
   grew between the two queens.

To the great women it chanced
that both, unstayed, fell pregnant
   the women, with scarce a whimper,
   were brought to bed the same hour.

He went once on a hosting,
Gabrán, heading his host of Gaels;
   that man never girned at raiding:
   he took guest-rich Eochu with him.

Behind the men, on the Forth—
what business could be better—
   the women, still without complaint,
   began labour the same night.

Two sons – greatest under heaven –
Eochu of Inber's wife bore;
   oh man, the wife of Alba's king
   bore, unhindered deed, two daughters.

Four there were, sure the number,
two sorrowful, two full of joy;
   two silent, with blameless breasts,
   the two women found to attend them.

Joyful was Eochu of Enach's wife,
at her sons, with no deceit,
   sad was steed-rich Gabrán's wife,
   while singing to her daughters.

[Steed-rich Gabrán's wife said]
to Eochu's wife, another time,
   'Take a girl with you and lie down,
   and give me one of your sons.

'We'd both be better for it,
wife of pride-filled Eochu:
   a boy and girl for each of us
   to drive our sorows from us.'

'If it were better for me and you,
Feidlimid's words have come true:

you will take aid purely,
and take your choice, oh queen.'

She put a mark – I'll not hide it –
in her son, fairer than limed shields;
    she put a grain of fierce foreigners' gold
    happily under his shoulder-blade's crest.

She brusquely let go her son,
to the wife of horse-rich Gabrán,
    the woman took a good daughter
    with smiling undarkened cheeks.

Horse-filled Alba's king returned,
after welding realms, and great raids,
    with lively cheeks, godly the image,
    to ask freely about the birth.

'Let my druid be called swiftly,'
said Gabrán of the rough fields.
    'Let him explain the noble boys,
    let him say if they'll be chief-rulers.'

'Let the priest proceed with no *geis*,'
said the druid, pure and unblemished.
    'Steadily let it be read by him,
    let him boldly do the baptism.

'Let the boys be baptised outside,
king of Monad of the market;
    they will get fine, sweet, bright rule
    over Ireland and Alba.'

'Those boys are twins, my man',
says the druid from Dún Inbir.
    'Women, do not be ashamed:
    the two girls, too, are twins.'

The druid was not foolish, by my skill,
(though the one he worships, I'll not worship)
    he revealed the kinship, painless,
    only to Gabrán, fine and fierce.

'A better king, bright Gabrán,
has never taken ford-filled Alba;
    fame for Da-Thí's offspring in the east;
    Brandub, his brother, will be king.'

Eochu began a journey to his house
following the chiefly king of Alba:
    unbent arms in his dear right hand,
    he brought Brandub to his dwelling.

He left Áedán of the gold
in Alba of the feasting-horns;
    in Alba, our good young friend,
    Áedán, was not honourless.

Rough, splendid Áedán knew not,
he who took organ-loud Alba
    (he headed every hail host)
    that he was not sprung from Gabrán.

Well did Gabrán's wife call him,
and told Áedán sincerely,
    while she was dying – I know it –
    she could only lament her sin.

'Gabrán, who took foreigner's hostages,
is your fosterfather's name, Áedán of Arran;
    companion of the western wave,
    I am your fostermother, my soul.

'Your mother's from fair Cruachan,
of the race of blameless Da-Thí;
    the father of fond Brandub,
    of Catháir's clans, is your father.'

That conversation, carefully,
Áedán of Islay remembered.
    He came over here on a swift steed
    to talk with his land's peoples.

He came to Leinster in secret
to speak to his mother's son,
    the form who spoiled every plain,
    to the house of Brandub his brother.

His own mother was present
to meet the son I have praised,
   good at guarding clerics and crosses,
   he spoke to her after the crossing.

To fair Feidlimid's house
he came across the flood's ridge;
   of the curled-haired one, sweet her words,
   he asks a shower of truth.

'Eochu's your father, fine his steeds,
and Brandub is your brother;
   by the most powerful eastern stone,
   it is I, son, am your mother.

'It was till nine great months' end,
king of the Forth, feast-laden,
   along with sorrowless Brandub,
   you lay harmless in my womb.'

Free-handed Fedelm found
the rich golden grain
   she had put on Áth Gabla's Áedán:
   the omen was good in all eyes.

'It will abide to blessed doomsday,
your fame, Áedán of the armlets;
   for me this is no boastful saying:
   it will be full of excellence for Leinster.

'Though good for women and men
the armies of the Gáiléoin you spring from,
   the paths of your splendid steeds to Slemain
   are five times better for Uí Chennsalaigh.'

Áedán and famous Brandub
are not spurned by the Leinstermen:
   over Alba of the fair gardens
   and over Ireland, they ruled.

Prayer in St Margaret's Gospel Book (c. 1090) Latin

This poem tells a story which is also told in the *Life of Margaret* by her confessor, Turgot, in which a Gospel book fell into a certain river and was miraculously protected from harm. The story is one told of other books and other saints (Adomnán's *Vita Columbae*, for example, tells similar stories), but what marks this instance out as particularly interesting is that the sole manuscript of the poem exists in the very book that was the subject of the miracle.

Expressions such as *tempore nostro*, 'in our days', and *nuper* in the second last line, 'recently, only now', make it likely that the poem was written more or less contemporaneously with the event in the 11th century. The last three lines suggest that Margaret was still alive at the time of writing, so that we can date the poem prior to her death in 1093.

Queen Margaret, in whose personal Gospel Book this poem appears, was regarded as a saint. Her *Life* was written by Turgot, bishop of St Andrews. After her marriage to King Mael Coluim III, her influence in opening Scottish society to English and Norman culture – especially church influences – was considerable.

All thanks we pay to you, O Christ, always;
who in our days have spread out your wonders before us.
For certain souls, seeking to swear upon this book,
took hold of it unwrapped, uncovered, unsecured;
a priest received and wrapped it round in his clothes,
but let it fall – poor porter – dropped it in the flood,
not marking that the book had sunk beneath the waves.
But soon there fell on the book a soldier's gaze,
who thought he'd raise from the river the sunken tome,
but faltered fast when he saw it lying exposed,
thinking surely that the book was ruined utterly,
yet he plunged his body headfirst into the waves
and plucked the open gospel from the watery deep.

O power clear to all! Great glory!
The book remained throughout its plight unharmed,
save for the two leaves you see at front and back
where a certain watery shrinkage may be discerned,
proof of Christ's work on behalf of this holy book;
and the loss of one linen leaf washed out from its heart
makes the story of his deed more wonderful to us yet.

May the king be saved forever, and his holy queen,
whose book from out of the river was rescued only now.
And great glory be to God, the saviour of this self-same book.

A Verse on David son of Mael Coluim (c. 1113)
Gaelic

This brief quatrain is of major importance. It testifies to the continued work of Gaelic poets in southern or central Scotland in the early years of the 12th century. Probably written as a complaining or satirical verse on the future David I's claiming of Lothian by threat of force in 1113, it seems to represent the sentiments of a poet and also those he represents, who were disadvantaged by David's actions in their relationship with the Scottish king, David's brother, Alexander I.

It's bad, what Mael Coluim's son has done,
    dividing us from Alexander;
he causes, like each king's son before,
    the plunder of stable Alba.

SIMEON (early 12th century)
Prayer to St Columba (1107–22) Latin

This prayer for Columba's patronage was written by an otherwise unknown author called Simeon, evidently some time between 1107 when Alexander I became king, and 1122 when his queen, Sibylla, died. It had been attached to a manuscript of a *Life of Columba*, transcribed at the behest of Alexander, and the poet makes use of Columba's traditional role as protector of Scotland and of its rulers, as found in the *Life* itself. The saint is addressed as *Iona sacer*, holy dove, playing on the Latin *Columba* and the Hebrew *Iona*, both of which mean 'dove'.

Where the Island of Bishops is, the *insula pontificum* of the poem, we cannot say. Anderson and Anderson (1961, p. 10) suggest the monastery of St Serf on Loch Leven as a place of composition, but perhaps the monastery island of Inchcolm is the most likely location for a poem to Columba. Inchcolm was under the control, from as early as we hear of it, of the bishops of Dunkeld.

Who is William, who, according to the second last line, had some hand in the writing of this manuscript? One suggestion has been Bishop William of Man, into whose jurisdiction Iona fell at the time. But Iona and Man were then in the Norwegian political sphere, which would make the poem's reference to Alexander a little odd if it were written on Iona. The question of William's identity remains unanswered.

The manuscript is damaged, and the original Latin text incomplete in two of its lines.

Holy Columba, our father, born of mother Ireland,
given by Christ's command to be the church's light,
may what we have written for you be pleasing to you, we pray.
For unworthily, yet lovingly, we have written down your deeds,
your life of virtue, heaven-adorned, we have set down.
We beseech you, through him . . . for ever
protect all those devoted to your service.
. . . and for everyone pour out your prayer.
Increase King Alexander's virtue, bring him help
and guard his salvation, for in your honour
he commanded that your triumphs – see! – be written down.
Be close to him, O father, when the dark spirit flits about,
that no temptation carry off the king to a worse estate,
but may a good spirit come, to whom he may entrust himself
and his own.
May the king shape his royal acts according to the rule of law,
for when the king is ruled by law, the realm is kept from harm.
Protect the queen and let her know no desolation,
and may the Island of Bishops know you to be its friend.

With the clergy, rule the people in Christ, the true Ruler;
and help them all, holy father and patron, Columba.
Be for the Scots a two-edged sword, be a mighty rampart,
and by your prayer bring goodness' help to Simeon your servant
who thought it fitting to write these words of prayer to you.
And William, who thought well to illuminate this book –
to him, O holy dove, impart your heavenly gifts.

ARRAN (mid- to late 12th century) Gaelic

This poem is contained in the long Middle Gaelic composite work *Agallamh na Senórach* (The Discussions of the Old Men), in which the legendary warriors Oisín and Caílte relate their many adventures all over Ireland, in story and verse, to St Patrick and his scribe. The text has attracted into it a number of poems which must have originally been independent compositions. This jewel-like poem on Arran is almost certainly one such.

Arran of the many deer,
   ocean touching its shoulders;
island where troops are ruined,
   ridge where blue spears are blooded.

High above the sea its summit,
   dear its green growth, rare its bogland;
blue island of glens, of horses,
   of peaked mountains, oaks and armies.

Frisky deer on its mountains,
   moist bogberries in its thickets,
cold waters in its rivers,
   acorns on its brown oak-trees.

Hunting dogs and keen greyhounds,
   brambles, sloes of dark blackthorn;
close against the woods its dwellings;
   stags sparring in its oak-groves.

Purple lichen from its rocks,
   faultless grass on its greenswards;
on its crags, a shielding cloak;
   fawns capering, trout leaping.

Smooth its plain, well-fed its swine,
   glad its fields – believe the story! –
nuts upon its hazels' tops,
   the sailing of longships past it.

Fine for them when good weather comes—
   trout beneath its river banks;
gulls reply round its white cliff—
   fine at all times is Arran.

Columba's Island Paradise (12th century) Gaelic

A great deal of poetry was written in the voice of St Columba during the later part of the early Middle Ages, especially in the 11th and 12th centuries. This poem, although it cannot be shown to be from a Scottish context, stands here for the multitude of these poems, as its theme links it inextricably with Iona.

Delight I'd find in an island's breast,
on a rock's peak,
that there I might often gaze
at the sea's calm.

That I might see its heavy waves
over the brilliant sea
as it sings music to the Father
on its constant way.

Might see its smooth bright-caped strand
(no dismal tryst);
might hear the strange birds' calls,
a joyful strain.

Might hear the shallow waves' crash
against the rocks;
might hear the cry beside the graves,
the ocean's roar.

Might see its splendid birdflocks
over the teeming sea;
might see its whales, greatest
of all marvels.

That I might see its ebb and flow
in their sequence,
that this might be my name, a secret I tell:
'Back towards Ireland'.

That help of heart might come to me
gazing on it;
that I might lament all my wrongs,
hard to mention.

That I might bless the Lord
who rules all,
heaven with its crowd of pure ranks,
land, strand and tide.

That I might ponder on some book,
good for my soul;
a while kneeling for dear heaven,
a while at psalms.

A while cropping dulse from the rock,
a while fishing;
a while giving food to the poor,
a while enclosed.

A while pondering the lord of heaven,
holy the purchase;
a while at work – not too taxing! –
it would be delightful.

EARL ROGNVALD KALI (St Ronald of Orkney)
(†1158) Norse

Earl Rognvald Kali was a Norwegian nobleman, nephew of St Magnus of Orkney, who thereby had a claim to the Earldom of Orkney. Under the guidance of his father, Kol, he conquered the Northern Isles c. 1136, having made a vow to build the cathedral in Kirkwall for his uncle. This building, the finest surviving Viking cathedral, is his greatest monument. He was a fine and prolific poet, and employed many court poets, mostly Icelanders. With one of these, Hall Thorarinsson, he is said to have composed the *Hattalykill*, 'Key of Metres', exemplifying every metre of Norse poetry. A text insecurely identified as this poem survives but in very corrupt form; it is not given here.

Orkneyinga Saga and fragments related to it are the source for all the surviving poetry from his court, apart from his verses 33–35; it preserves some incidental verses from his youth, and some dealing with a shipwreck at Gulberwick in Shetland (7–11), as well as part of a verse competition (with Oddi Glumsson) about figures depicted in fight on a tapestry (13, Oddi 1). The bulk of Rognvald's poetry (vv. 15–31) deals with his pilgrimage to the Holy Land, 1151–53, in which he stayed at Narbonne in the South of France and with his poets composed amorous verses towards its ruler, the widowed lady Ermingerd. This poetry shows the earliest datable troubadour influence in Norse literature. He also seems to have sacked a castle in Spain, indulged in some crusading piracy against Saracen shipping in the Mediterranean, and visited Byzantium, as well as swimming the Jordan and reaching Jerusalem via the Mount of Olives. There also survive two verses, 34–35, cited in late sources as examples of *ofljost*, a sort of extended word-play on implied homophones. Earl Rognvald's poetry is always technically brilliant; it is also often very sharply witty, for example, in his mockery of hermit-monks (4), and is sometimes touching, as in his verse on the descent from the Mount of Olives (29), or that on watching over his sick wife (34).

Rognvald Kali was murdered in Caithness in 1158/59, and his relics elevated in c. 1192 in the cathedral in Kirkwall, which he himself had built, where they remain to this day.

1. Earl Rognvald Kali lists the 'attributes of a gentleman'.
Chess I'm eager to play,
I know nine skills,
I scarcely forget runes,
book and handicrafts are frequent,
I know how to ski,
I shoot and row serviceably,
I know how to consider
both harp-playing and poetry.

2. He is glad to leave Grimsby at the end of a visit to England in his youth.

We have waded the mud-flats
five mighty-grim weeks,
there was no want of filth,
when we were in mid Grimsby;
Now across the gull's fens
mighty-gladly we let
the bowsprit's elk
thunder to Bergen.

gull's fens 'sea'; *bowsprit's elk* 'ship'.

3. He explores a cave on the Norwegian island of Dolls.

Here I have raised a high cairn
for the hard-hearted
Dolls-zombie in a dark cave;
so I seek riches.
I don't know, which thruster
of the wave-skis will go afterwards
so long and ugly
a way over the broad water.

wave-skis 'ships'; their *thruster* 'sailor'.

4. He mocks Irish monks on a windswept island.

I've seen sixteen women
at once with forelock on forehead,
stripped of the old age of the land
of the serpent-field, walk together.
We bear witness
that most girls here –
this isle lies against the storms
out west – are bald.

women with forelock on forehead monks with Celtic tonsure, wearing habits which seem feminine in Norse dress; *old age of the land of the serpent-field* 'gold, on which dragons lie'; its *lands* 'women'; their *old age* 'facial hair' (i.e. the monks are clean-shaven); *bald* 'tonsured'.

5. He rebukes Kugi for plotting.

I see lying on the limbs
of the evening-wandering old

fellow (a lock forbids your rushing,
Kugi) the twisted fetters;
never hold, Kugi – you
will be restrained from your tricks,
oaths must be kept—
night-meetings, but keep agreements.

6. *He mocks a woman for her supposedly fine attire.*
Always I've heard that clad
all high-ranking women their hood-stall—
the ring-slayer does not prove
soft-worded – with kerchiefs.
Now the hawk-land's valkyrie
manages to tie around her neck – the woman
puts on finery for the feeder
of the wound-gaggle – a mare's tail.

hood-stall 'head'; *ring-slayer* 'generous man'; *hawk-land* arm on which a falcon rests, its *valkyrie* 'woman'; *wound-gaggle* 'group of carrion-birds', its *feeder* 'warlike man'.

7. *After being shipwrecked at Gulberwick in Shetland, he plays with his hands.*
I hang the hammer-rounded
hanged man of the ptarmigan's tongs,
for Grimnir's drink, on the gallows
of the serpent of the hawk's bridge.
So has the tree of the gleaming voice of
the cave's Gautar gladdened me,
that I play with my hollows
of the bay's towering feller.

ptarmigan (perhaps) 'woman', her *tongs* 'hand' or 'arm', its *hanged man* 'ring' formed by hammering (but also 'encircled by a crag'); *Grimnir's drink* Odin's mead, 'poetry'; *hawk's bridge* 'arm on which the falcon rests', its *serpent* 'arm-ring', its *gallows* 'arm'; *the cave's Gautar* 'giants', their *gleaming voice* 'gold', its *tree* 'woman'; *the towering feller of the bay* 'oar, that falls from above on water', its *hollows* 'hands'.

8–9. *He describes the shipwreck.*
It smashed, when a billow struck,
the wave threatened men,
wet weather gave
women sorrow, Hjalp and Fifa;
I see that this voyage

of bold-hearted earls—
the crew certainly got wet work—
will seem memorable.

I shake out a wrinkled leather cloak here,
there's very little finery for me—
much is the prow-field which
stands around our cloaks—
whenever yet we go from the spray-swept
steed of the eel-plain—
surf drove the mast-head's stallion
against cliffs – finer-clad.

Hjalp and *Fifa* were the 'women', Earl Rognvald's ships wrecked off Gulber-
wick in Shetland.
prow-field 'sea, sea-water'; *eel-plain* 'sea', its *steed* 'ship'; *mast-head's stallion*
'ship'.

*10. He puts words into the mouth of a wet serving-maid who comes
in while he and his companions are drying themselves after the
shipwreck.*
You roast yourselves, but Asa—
atatata – lies in water—
hutututu – where must I sit?—
I'm rather cold! – by the fire.

11. He rebukes Einar for inhospitality after the shipwreck.
Einar says he wants to look after
none of Rognvald's men—
Gaut's flood comes to my
lips – except the earl himself;
I know he failed in his promises,
this unpleasant man;
I went in, where Yggr's fires burnt
late in the evening.

Gaut Odin, whose 'flood' is 'poetry'; *Ygg* Odin, whose *fires* are probably
'hostility'.

*12. A woman laughs at the earl, who has been out fishing incognito
with a Shetland crofter.*
The Sif of silk guffaws
in her wisdom at my get-up,
the girl laughs much more

than would be fitting;
few recognise an earl
clearly – but earlier, generous,
I dragged the roller's oak from the waves
before – in fishing-clothes.

Sif of silk 'woman'; *roller's oak* 'boat' (beached on rollers).

13. He challenges his court-poet to describe a scene on a tapestry.
The aged victory-Freyr, who stands
further out on the tapestry, lets
Svolnir's goddesses' scabbard-wand
swing down by his shoulder;
he, though the arrow-askers'
terrifier grows angry,
the battle-icicles' gleam-bush,
bandy, will not go forward.

victory-Freyr 'warrior'; *Svolnir* Odin, his *goddesses* 'valkyries', their *scabbard-wand* 'sword'; *arrow-askers' terrifier* 'a warrior who intimidates other warriors'; *battle-icicles* 'swords', their *gleam-bush* 'warrior'.

14. An idiot tries to grab hold of him.
There grabbed at the lord's gown
a strong-grasping wretch;
the man tried hard to pull
at the generous battle-lord;
the steels-Bjarki was strong,
they said the lord stumbled somewhat;
the ill-mouthed edge-skirmisher
has force instead of thought.

steels-Bjarki 'Bjarki of weapons, warrior, man'; *edge-skirmisher* 'man who fights in petty skirmishes'.

15. He praises Ermingerd of Narbonne for her hair.
Truly excel far for the better
women, well-tasselled
with Frodi's milling,
your tresses, wise lady.
The hawkland's prop lets hair fall on
her shoulders –
I reddened the greedy eagle's
claw – yellow as silk.

Frodi's milling 'gold' (milled for King Frodi), *well-tasselled* (with gold) 'golden-haired'; *hawkland* 'arm' on which the falcon rests, its *prop* 'lady'.

16. He claims that Ermingerd has sent him on his quest to the Holy Land.

Ermingerd's words long
the glorious warrior must remember;
the noble lady wishes us to ride
Ranworld to Jordan;
but when the wavesteed's trees
go back north across the sea,
home in autumn, we shall score
the whale's land to Narbonne.

Ran goddess of the sea, her *world* 'sea'; *wavesteed* 'ship', its *trees* 'sailors'; *the whale's land* 'sea'.

17. He contrasts Ermingerd's beauty with a battle in Spain.

The fair-haired, pure
broider-sister of the ell-drift bore wine,
Ermingerd's beauty was shown
to men, when we met;
now folk do attack
in fierce boldness with fire –
from scabbards swing
sharp swords – the castle-men.

ell-drift 'snow-drift of the forearm-length', i.e. 'silver', its *broider-sister* 'lady wearing embroidery and silver'.

18. He contrasts past holidays in Norway with a battle in Spain.

I'll remember Yules that we spent
east with the bold steward,
woundflame's Ull,
at Agdir's fells, Solmund;
Now I make during others,
as glad as I was there,
the sword's tumult
at a southern castle.

woundflame 'gleaming sword', its *Ull* (god) 'warrior', i.e. Solmund

19. He contrasts Ermingerd's company with a battle in Spain.

I was well content when

the wine-oak grew used to my talk –
I was welcome to the French woman
doubtless – in the autumn;
now again I make, for we love
the noble-born lady well –
stone must loosen
in its mortar – the eagle fed.

wine-oak 'woman'.

20. *He claims that his valour in war makes him worthy of Ermingerd.*
I look for – out in Spain
the fleeing were swiftly driven,
many a torc-tree fled
in weariness – meeting the lady.
So are we, for splendid voices [of war]
were spoken to nations –
carrion covered the field –
worthy of Ermingerd.

torc-tree 'man (wearing a neck-ring)'.

21. *He claims that his voyage is fulfilment of his promise to a woman.*
I shan't be sad in storm
of the chill field, Hlin, while rope and
cord, cable at the warship's prow,
does not break;
so I promised the white
flax-prop, when I went south –
wind bears the seam-steed swiftly
at the sound – the fine woman.

flax-prop 'lady clad in linen'; *seam-steed* 'clinker-built ship'.

22. *The storm-wind blows him from Ermingerd.*
A wind for a winter's hour
from the hands of the French lady –
we put out the beam to tack –
has shot ships from the east;
we have to fasten [the sail] to
the middle of Svidrir's sailyard

somewhat firmly off Spain, the wind
drives swiftly in the sea.

Svidrir's sailyard the World-tree, hence 'tree', 'mast'.

23. He sails away from an unwelcome companion.
The land bends – but the sea
sports on the fair timber –
the man will be slow to
delay poetry – continuously north;
I score with slim prow
– Earth's neck-ring roars –
out from Spain, this envy-turn
for a single fellow.

Earth a giantess, her *neck-ring* 'sea'.

24. Erling attacks a Saracen dromond.
Erling went, terror-strong,
where our standards were reddened,
renowned, with valour and victory,
a javelin-tree, against the dromond;
we piled up – but widely
were folk deprived of blood –
bold men reddened keen swords –
champions of the blackamoors.

javelin-tree 'spear-bearing warrior'.

25–26. He describes the seizure of the dromond.
We're prepared to take
– you could call it killing now –
early has a warrior reddened his sword
in blood – the dromond;
The lady shall hear of that
spear-storm from north and south
– the people suffered ugly
life-loss from men – to Narbonne.

There went on to the dark dromond –
the warrior was swift for booty –
up with sufficient valour
first Audun the Red;

there were we able to redden –
mankind's God brought it about,
a black body fell on the planking –
weapons in people's blood.

*27–28. He and a companion swim across Jordan and as a token tie
a knot in bushes on the other side.*
I have laid a lock on the heath –
in grief of the path's thong
the wise lady will remember this –
beyond Jordan;
But I think that nonetheless it will
seem a long way to go there –
warm blood falls on to the wide
field – for all stay-at-homes.

We tie this knot for the wretch –
I come weary to a good place –
in a thick bush
this Laurence-day.

the path's thong 'snake', its *grief* 'winter'.

29. In pilgrimage he descends the Mount of Olives to Jerusalem.
A cross hangs for this poet –
uproar should be lowered – before my breast;
men flock forward on to the hill-slopes –
but a palm-branch between my shoulders.

30. A companion falls into an open sewer in Byzantium.
My friend won't call out –
he had all to fall in dirt,
there was almost enough bad luck
in that – *midhæfi*;
hardly I think that then seemed
the king's kinsman, when he went astray –
grey filth falls from the fool –
glad in Imbolar.

'*midhæfi*' probably a Greek word meaning 'don't cross' (on a footbridge across
an open sewer); *Imbolar* probably a suburb of Byzantium.

31. He sails to Byzantium.
We ride Ræfil's steed –
we don't drive the plough from the field
but furrow with a spray-swept prow –
out to Byzantium;
we take the prince's pay,
rush forward into the crash of steels,
redden the wolf's gums,
win the honour of the mighty king.

Ræfil a legendary sea-king, his *steed* 'ship'.

32. He complains of treachery at home in Orkney.
Now the lords have gone back –
hateful to God is it for men;
men's ill plans are uncovered –
on enough oaths;
it will never settle for him
who practises treachery at home.
We walk lightly on a low leg,
while I [can] hold up my beard.

33. An isolated religious half-verse.
Of what shall I tell you or other
wolf-waterers –
I praise the glad lord of the cloudless
high hall – other than true God?

wolf-waterer one who gives drink to wolves, 'warrior'; *the cloudless* (literally,
'bright, glorious') *high hall* 'heaven'.

34. He laments watching in sorrow beside his sick wife.
Yet I must often sit in my acre beside
the sick goddess of the fishes of the
island-watermeadows (red-faced for me
is the table of the neck-ring),
to accompany my falcon's land –
so I, cunning, express hawk,
seeking a seat
for sorrow, on each day.

acre = *salr* 'hall'; *fishes of meadows* 'serpents' = *hringr* 'ring'; *goddess* of rings
'woman'; *table of the neck-ring* 'woman wearing a neck-ring'; *falcon's land*

'arm', perhaps for *harmr* 'grief'; *hawk* = *harmr* 'grief':

'I must often sit in my hall beside the sick lady; she is feverish; to go with my grief each day I seek a resting-place for sorrow – so with skill I set forth sadness.'

35. *He comments on a sick horse.*

I don't know, when the frenzied
fleeter can knot the sea;
the beast of fishing tackle,
which we own, is likely to die.

sea = *marr* 'horse'; *knot* 'to bridle'; the *frenzied fleeter* of a horse is its rider; *fishing-tackle* = *taumar* 'reins', their beast is a 'horse'.

HALL THORARINSSON (mid-12th century) Norse

An Icelandic poet who worked in the circle of Rognvald Kali.

The poet seeks residence with Earl Rognvald Kali
I sent your son, Ragna –
true tales come to men,
his was a noble task –
to request residence at court for me;
the hoard-diminisher, who controls
greatest glory – he refused the
sausage's neighbour – said that he
had enough warlike men.

hoard-diminisher 'generous lord', i.e. Rognvald; *sausage's neighbour* 'Icelander'
(since Icelanders were supposed to live off mutton-fat sausages).

EIRIK (mid-12th century) Norse
Svein Asleifarson Causes Mayhem

An Icelandic poet from the circle of Rognvald Kali, Eirik here praises the famous Orcadian land-holder Svein, who lived on Gairsay. Svein meddled in Orcadian politics, lived 'an old-fashioned Viking lifestyle as raider and mercenary', until his death, probably in Ireland in 1171.

Farms are burnt,
farmers robbed –
so has Svein contrived –
six this morning.
He did enough
for any one of them,
rents out charcoal
to the tenant-farmer.

ODDI LITLI GLUMSSON (mid-12h century) Norse

An Icelandic poet in the court circle of Rognvald Kali, and one of his companions on his journey to the Mediterranean. The first of his fragments responds to Rognvald's challenge in his verse 13. The other verses also complement Rognvald's: a praise poem for Ermingerd, and a lament for a companion lost in the attack on Acre.

1. The poet responds to Earl Rognvald's challenge to describe a scene on a tapestry.

There stands and thinks of hewing
bent-shouldered with a sword
the belt-elf of the Rind that begs for
Baldr by the doorway on the tapestry;
he will be perilous to men with his blade;
now it's time that loaders of the roller's
leaping ski should be reconciled,
before harm is done.

Rind that begs for Baldr Frigg, Baldr's mother, *Frigg* name of an island, its *belt* is *mar* 'sea' = *mar* 'sword', its *elf* 'swordsman'; *leaping ski of the roller* 'ship', launched on rollers, its *loaders* 'sailors, men'.

2. The poet complains of being unworthy of Lady Ermingerd of Narbonne.

Scarcely are we, as I reckon,
worthy of Ermingerd –
I know that the wise
broider-ground may be called king of women –
for it befits the Bil of the fire of the
rings' stand altogether –
may she live blessed beneath the sun's
seat – much better.

broider-ground 'lady wearing embroidery'; *the rings' stand* 'arm', its *Bil* (goddess) 'lady'; *sun's seat* 'sky'.

3. The poet contrasts the ease of those who had stayed at home with Rognvald's valour.

The trusty friend of men
who drinks mead indoors
with the seafire's flexer
had seven daytimes somewhat easier;

but great-hearted Rognvald galloped,
with a shield-bearing troop,
on the roller's stallion, gleaming with
paint, to the Straits of Gibraltar.

seafire 'gold', its *flexer* 'generous man'; *roller's stallion* 'ship'.

4–5. The poet laments Thorbjorn's death at Acre in Palestine.
The ship of landowners bore
Thorbjorn the Black
before Freswick.
The roller-bear trod
beneath a chief poet
Ati's earth
to Acre.

There I saw him,
at a chief church,
the prince's friend,
sprinkled with sand.
Now stony earth,
sun-brightened,
lies still over him
in the south-lands.

roller-bear 'ship launched on rollers'; *Ati* a legendary sea-king, his *earth* 'sea'.

Armod (mid-12th century) Norse

Another Icelandic poet from the circle of Rognvald Kali, and another of his companions on the Mediterranean voyage.

1. The poet thanks Earl Rognvald Kali for the gift of a sword.
The glorious ruler,
enlarger of Ygg's storm,
does not compare with other men
in bringing gifts to the poet;
the land's keen guardian bore,
gold-gleaming, the best blood-taper,
most excellent lord,
to Armod's hands.

Ygg's storm 'battle', its *enlarger* 'warrior-lord'; *gold-gleaming blood-taper* 'shining and gold-decorated sword'.

2. The poet contrasts the sea-voyage with the ease of those who stay at home.
The surge before Humber's mouth
is steep, where we tack;
the mast bends, but lands lower
before Wallsend's sands;
no foam-capped wave
drives into the eyes –
the fellow rides dry from the meeting –
of him who now sits at home.

3. The poet laments his separation from Lady Ermingerd of Narbonne.
I shall never Ermingerd –
unless Fate turns out otherwise –
many a man nurtures grief
for a lady – see again;
I would be blessed if I slept
– clear grace it would be –
the lady has a very fair forehead –
one night beside her.

4. *The poet contrasts his voyage in the Mediterranean with the idle ease of those who stayed at home.*

We keep, where the sea spills in
over the stiff gunwale –
this have we to do –
watch on the prow-steed,
while tonight beside the excellent,
soft-skinned kerchief-tree
the feeble wretch sleeps;
I look over my shoulder to Crete.

prow-steed 'ship'; *kerchief-tree* 'woman wearing a kerchief'.

THORBJORN SVARTI (mid-12th century) Norse

An Orcadian (?) poet in the circle of Rognvald Kali, and a companion on his campaigns in the Holy Land.

The poet praises the valour of Earl Rognvald Kali.
I was at court with the hardener
of the sword-rush in Orkney;
the host-starlings' feeder earlier,
during winter, decided [to go] to battle;
Now we bear shield boldly
with an experienced earl
on to the spray-swept watch-tower (?)
of Acre on Friday morning.

sword-rush 'battle', its *hardener* 'warlike leader'; *host-starlings* 'carrion birds', their *feeder* 'warrior'.

SIGMUND ONGUL Norse

An Orcadian poet, associated with Svein Asleifarson, and one of the crusader companions of Rognvald.

1. The poet boasts of his valour in a battle in Spain.
Bear back, when Spring comes,
these words to the Skogul of embroidery,
the mountain-rib's polishing-tree,
across the skiff-plain to Orkney,
that no-one, where blows
resounded early, under the castle wall,
though he were older,
a glorious warrior, went further.

Skogul (valkyrie) *of embroidery* 'woman'; *mountain-rib* 'stone', its *polishing-tree* 'woman'.

2. The poet ties a knot in bushes across Jordan.
I will tie a knot for the fat-bellied
man who sits now at home –
truly we have rather risked
his child – today.

Botolf begla (fl. 1150) Norse

An Icelander, resident at Knarrarstadir in Orkney in the 1150s.

*Botolf tells Rognvald's enemies that he has gone grouse-shooting on
the moors, and thereby diverts pursuit and saves the earl's life.*
The lord goes fowling –
men use their arrows well,
the heath-hen can expect a neck-blow –
under the hill-slopes.
There the bow will be drawn often,
where the frenzied staves of the wound-serpent –
the prince defends the land with his sword –
encounter grouse.

heath-hen 'grouse'; *wound-serpent* 'sword', its *frenzied staves* 'swordsmen'.

CONFLICT IN ORKNEY (c. 1151) Norse

The poet discusses political conflict between the supporters of Earls Rognvald
Kali and Paul, after Rognvald had returned from pilgrimage.

I hear contrasting report –
our foes have dissimulated –
mighty lord, from the meeting
this decision of the land-owners,
that many lords wish
that you, wolf-sater,
should occupy the bows-steed
at sea, but Paul on land.

wolf-sater 'warrior'; *bows-steed* 'ship'.

THE MAESHOWE VERSE (mid-12th century) Norse

The prehistoric chambered cairn at Maeshowe, on the Mainland of Orkney, contains some 33 distinct graffiti-like inscriptions in Norse runes, carved on its inner flagstone walls by a number of people in the middle of the 12th century. This is the only one in metrical form and, although the metre is rough and irregular, the word order suggests it was intended as verse rather than prose. It has been suggested that the inscription was carved by the Icelander Thorhall Asgrimsson, who is mentioned in *Orkneyinga Saga* (ch. 90).

The man who is
most skilled in runes
west of the ocean
cut these runes
with the axe
once owned by Gauk
son of Trandil
in the south country.

WILLIAM, CLERK OF GLASGOW (fl. 1164) Latin
Song on the Death of Somerled

This is a contemporary, if fantastical, account of the death of Somerled (Somairlid mac Gille-Brighde) in the battle of Renfrew in 1164. Somerled is referred to as *Rí* and *regulus* in various sources, i.e. as king of Argyll and the Isles, but we can make no sense of the word *sitebi*, or *sicebi*, in the title. He had been loyal in the past to King David, and fought for him and probably paid tribute (*cáin*) to him. But he rebelled against Mael Coluim IV in 1154, and only made peace in 1160. Again, in 1164, he invaded western lowland Scotland, bringing an armed fleet up the Clyde as far as Renfrew. The invaders included, according to the annals, men of Argyll and Kintyre, men of the Hebrides and Dublin Norse, but they were repulsed, and Somerled himself was killed.

William, the author of this poem, who seems to be a Glaswegian clergyman, attributes the death of Somerled to the prayers of St Kentigern. These prayers were obtained by Herbert, the bishop of Kentigern's church in Glasgow, by rebuking the patron saint. This calls to mind the ritual 'humiliation of the saints' found in Europe in the Middle Ages, and the incident in Adomnán's *Life of Columba* (Bk. 2, ch. 45), when Columba is shamed into performing a weather miracle by something close to abuse.

How Somerled sitebi/sicebi, *the King, with his Immense Army, was Slain by Very Few.*

A king ruled by death, David lay entombed,
when the treachery of scheming Scots emerged.
Norsemen and Argyllsmen, who leaned on Scotsmen's might,
raging, slaughtered righteous men with cruel hands.
Though good men rushed to calm the fury of the wicked
who raved and ruined their churches and their towns,
war returned, peace was lost, the strong thrust out the weak,
the wretched slain and hurt by foes with fire and sword.

Gardens, fields and plough-lands were laid waste and destroyed;
the gentle, menaced by barbarous hands, were overwhelmed.
Wounded, Glasgow's people fled the blows of two-edged swords,
while Mark, of all the scattered clergy, murmuring remained
within the church's hard high walls, bearing his harsh fate,
weeping and lamenting the prosperous days of old.

Though far off, the bishop Herbert, gentle and noble,
suffered with him, and shared his lamentation.

He prayed to Kentigern to plead with the King most high
to grant his captive people's hopes, and curse their foes.
And as he prayed and sighed for an answer to his prayers,
which rose without ceasing yet won nothing in return,
he began to mock the Scottish saints and by his words
to rebuke, right reverently, the blessed Kentigern.

When these taunts had been laid to rest, almost forgotten,
Kentigern did not forget the bishop's clamour.
At length he called on Herbert for his vindication,
to wipe out every trace of the Scottish saints' dishonour.
At once the noble bishop, the praiseworthy old man,
rose from his bed, and made haste right away;
and with his household, his youth renewed,
diligently and willingly, he marched by night and day.

But even as he went, he did not know what drove him on,
for like Elijah he seemed inspired by heaven's breath –
which was proved by one who begged him to hurry home
and save himself from the hands of hate-filled Somerled.
For he was foul with treachery, the cruellest of foes;
he schemed and strove against the ministers of the Lord;
he, suddenly, with his huge army of accomplices,
threatened to lay waste the kingdom as he came ashore.

Herbert heard this as he went, groaning in his heart,
asking then, 'Who now urges me to go on or return?'
He called on Solomon, a young and warlike squire,
and then Elias who often helped him on the road:
'Come! make haste to help our poor abandoned countrymen;
let us pray that we may stand and stem their misery,
for a teacher and a ruler should defend his land.
Come! make haste, and let us fight. We shall have victory.

'For God, who is ever-mine, with neither sword nor spear
cares for his flock and guards his folk in battle's strife.'
When those defending heard the bishop had come near,
they were like dragons, and as bold as lions for the fight.
While Somerled stood with a thousand of our enemies,
ready to make war against a mere one hundred innocents,
our few men advanced and made assault upon the ranks
of treacherous Argyllsmen, soldiers most unfortunate.

Hear and be amazed! To the terrible the fight was terrible.
Broom thickets and thorn hedges tossed their heads;
wild thyme burning, orchards, brambles, ferns
filled them with fear, as they appeared as armed men to our foes.
In this life, there have not been heard such miracles.
Smoky shadows of thyme reared up to be our ramparts.
The deadly leader, Somerled, died. In the first great clash of arms
he fell, wounded by a spear and cut down by the sword.

His son, too, the raging sea consumed
and with him many thousands of wounded men in flight.
Their savage leader now laid low, the wicked turned and ran,
but many of them were butchered in the sea as on dry land.
They sought to clamber from the blood-red waves into their ships
but were drowned, each and all, in the surging tide.
Such was the slaughter, such destruction of the treacherous
thousands,
but not one of those who fought them was wounded here or died.

So the enemy host being driven off, deluded,
all the kingdom rang with Kentigern's loud praise.
A cleric hacked off the head of the wretched leader Somerled,
and placed it into bishop Herbert's outstretched hands.
He said, 'The Scottish saints are surely to be praised!'
yet wept as his custom was, to see the head of his enemy.
And to blessed Kentigern he attributed the victory,
so keep you his memory always, and that fittingly.

All that he saw and heard, William has written down,
an offering to the honour and glory of blessed Kentigern.

KRAKUMAL (c. 1200?) Norse

This anonymous poem purports to be the final words of the ninth-century viking hero, Ragnar Lodbrok, as he dies in a snake-pit, where he has been put by King Ella of Northumbria. Although there is a saga about Ragnar (McTurk 1991), this poem appears to be based on somewhat differing traditions. The title of the poem is given in the earliest surviving manuscript, from around or just after 1400, but cannot be said to fit the poem very well: it means 'Speech of Kraka', the nickname given to Ragnar's second wife Aslaug (who is only mentioned in stanza 26). As he looks back on his career, Ragnar remembers some of the battles in which he and his comrades took part. The sites of these battles are a mixture of real and mythological (or unidentifiable) places throughout the Viking world, and few of Ragnar's opponents are known from any other source. The poem is largely composed in the first person plural, but we get little sense of Ragnar's comrades (apart from his son Agnar in stanza 17). Some of these first-person plural forms clearly have singular reference to Ragnar himself (as in stanza 1, and probably the refrain), but they have all been translated literally, so the reader can decide which refer to Ragnar alone and which to the warrior collective.

The poem is based on the traditional *dróttkvætt* stanza (see Introduction: The Norse Tradition), but with the novelty that each stanza has ten lines (except 23 and 29, which have the usual eight). It also has a lax interpretation of the metrical rules of *dróttkvætt*: the poet uses rhyme only at random, and the alliteration is not always regular either. The poem is also unique in its use of the same first line in every stanza: this has the character of a refrain, but cannot be detached from the stanzas as it participates in their metrical scheme. Neither the date nor the place of composition of *Krakumal* can be established with certainty, though there is some scholarly consensus that it probably belongs to the second half of the 12th century. Norway, Iceland, Orkney and the Hebrides have all been suggested as possible places of composition. Of these, Orkney is probably the most convincing (de Vries 1967), as many links of various kinds can be made with its 12th-century culture, and its poetry in particular (see also *The Maeshowe Verse*, above).

Krakumal has an important place in European culture, as it was one of the first Norse poems to be widely known and extensively translated, after its first publication by Ole Worm in 1636. Two stanzas (25 and 29), translated into lively English verse, appeared in Sammes (1676) and a complete translation into English prose was published by Bishop Percy in 1763. These early translators are notorious for their misunderstandings of stanzas 13–14 and 25. Thus, they miss the negatives in stanzas 13–14 (Percy 1763, 34–36: 'The pleasure of that day was like having a fair virgin placed beside one in bed . . . The pleasure of that day was like kissing a young widow at the highest seat of the table') and do not understand that stanza 25 contains a kenning in which a drinking-horn (usually made from the horn of an animal) is called a 'curving skull-branch' (Sammes 1676, 436: 'And now I laugh to think/In Wodens Hall there benches be/Where we may sit and drink./There shall we Tope our bellies full/of Nappy-Ale in full-brim'd Skull'; Percy 1763, 40: 'Soon, in the splendid hall of Odin, we shall drink BEER out of the sculls of our enemies').

1 Slashed with our sword, we did.
   It's been a long time since
   the day we went to Gautland
   to do in that dragon,
   and then we married Thora;
   then the people called me
   Lodbrok from that killing:
   I laid low the ling-fish,
   I stabbed the loop of the earth
   with brightly-engraved steel.

ling-fish 'snake, serpent, [here] dragon'; *loop of the earth* 'the world-serpent, [here] dragon'.

2 Slashed with our sword, we did.
   I was so young, out east
   in Eyrasund, we made
   the fasting wolf a meal,
   and the yellow-footed bird
   we gave a great banquet,
   where hard iron sang on
   the high-studded helmets;
   the sea was rough, the raven
   rinsed in dead men's blood.

yellow-footed bird 'eagle'.

3 Slashed with our sword, we did.
   We carried spears on high,
   when I was twenty years,
   we turned all lances red;
   we overcame eight earls
   east of the Dina's mouth,
   we fed the wolves a lot
   of fine fare at that battle;
   blood flowed into the swell
   of seas, troops lost their lives.

4 Slashed with our sword, we did.
   The strife of Hedin's wife
   happened when we made Helsings
   go home to Odin's hall;

we sailed up the Iva,
spear-points got to bite then,
that river was ruddy
with red-hot wave of wounds;
sword-blades roared on breast-plates,
blood-herrings sundered shields.

Hedin's wife Hild, a personification of battle; *Odin's hall* Valhall, home of
warriors in the afterlife; *wave of wounds* 'blood'; *blood-herrings* 'spears or
arrows' (because of their metallic appearance).

5 Slashed with our sword, we did.
  I heard no one censure
  Herrod till he was struck
  down on Heflir's horses;
  no more famous earl will
  furrow with his sea-skis
  the puffins' plain again
  to anchor his long ships;
  that prince took his bold heart
  into battle everywhere.

Heflir's horses 'ships'; *sea-skis* 'ships'; *puffins' plain* 'sea'.

6 Slashed with our sword, we did.
  The army slung their shields
  when rushing carrion-dogs
  ran at the breasts of men;
  skirmish-scalpels bit in
  the Skarpasker battle;
  the gunwale-moon was reddened
  by the time King Rafn fell;
  hot blood streamed from squires'
  skulls onto their armour.

carrion-dog 'sword'; *skirmish-scalpels* 'swords'; *gunwale-moon* 'shield'.

7 Slashed with our sword, we did.
  The sabres sounded loud
  when out at Ullarakr
  King Eystein was struck down;
  our hawk-bases adorned
  with blazing gold we went

to that helmet-council
(corpse-candles probed red shields);
the neck's brew coursed from wounds
down the cliffs of the brain.

hawk-bases 'forearms'; *helmet-council* 'battle'; *corpse-candle* 'sword'; *neck's brew*
'blood'; *cliffs of the brain* 'head and shoulders'.

8 Slashed with our sword, we did.
Sufficient meat was then
for ravens to rend there,
round Inndyris island;
this time we fed breakfast,
a full one at sunrise,
to the troll-woman's mounts
(it was tough to feed just one);
I saw bowstring-sticks rise,
iron rammed helmet's rim.

troll-woman's mounts 'wolves'; *bowstring-sticks* 'arrows'.

9 Slashed with our sword, we did.
We soaked the shields in blood
when at Bornholm we gave
wound-starlings a banquet;
sword-storm clouds were sundered
elm-bows sent forth iron;
Volnir fell in battle,
there was no better king;
wolves enjoyed the booty
when bodies drove ashore.

wound-starlings 'carrion-birds (ravens or eagles)'; *sword-storm* 'battle', its *cloud*
'shield'.

10 Slashed with our sword, we did.
Battle was certainly
waxing when King Frey fell
in the Flemings' country;
hard and blue and dripping
with blood, the wound-etcher
bit Hogni's gold-covered
cowl that time in battle;

many girls grieved that dawn,
but the wolves got booty.

wound-etcher 'sword'; *Hogni's cowl* 'mail-coat' (Hogni was a legendary warrior).

11 Slashed with our sword, we did.
   Hundreds were slain, I'm told,
   where skis of Eynæfi
   gathered at Englanes;
   we sailed six days and nights
   to that slaughter of troops;
   we held a sunrise mass
   for the points of our spears;
   Valthjof was forced to sink
   before our swords in strife.

skis of Eynæfi 'ships'.

12 Slashed with our sword, we did.
   Sabres gave the pale hawks
   a surge of the brown dew
   of bodies in Bardafjord;
   the elm-bow whined aloud,
   as Odin's hammer-beaten
   shirts got arrow-bitten
   in the sheath-flames' flyting;
   blood-speckled snake, poison-sharp,
   slithered into wounds.

dew of bodies 'blood'; *Odin's shirts* 'mail-coats'; *sheath-flame* 'sword', its *flyting* 'battle'; *snake* here, a sword.

13 Slashed with our sword, we did.
   In battle-sport we held
   our Lokk's tarpaulins high
   outwith the Hjadnings' bay;
   the soldiers then could see,
   as we sundered the shields
   in the corpse-herrings' din,
   cloven helmets of men;
   not a bit like bedding
   a bonny bride it was.

Lokk's tarpaulin 'a shield'; *Hjadnings' bay* this may simply be a place-name, Hjadningavag; *corpse-herring* 'spear', its *din* 'battle'.

14 Slashed with our sword, we did.
   A hard storm hit the shields,
   bodies knuckled under
   on Northumbria's ground;
   there was no need that dawn
   to deplore men's deeds in
   battle-game, when sharp swords
   bit into helmet-stumps;
   not a whit like kissing
   a young widow it was.

helmet-stumps 'heads'.

15 Slashed with our sword, we did.
   Success was granted to
   Herthjof against our men
   in the Hebrides themselves;
   Rognvald was forced to sink
   in the rain of shield-rims,
   that greatest grief befell
   men in the gust of swords;
   helmet-shaker propelled
   palm of the bowstring-notch.

rain of shield-rims 'battle'; *gust of swords* 'battle'; *helmet-shaker* 'warrior'; *palm of the bowstring-notch* 'arrow'.

16 Slashed with our sword, we did.
   Stretched across each other,
   corpses gladdened the spear-
   storm cuckoo in swords' play;
   King Marstan, lord of Ireland,
   did not let eagle starve,
   nor she-wolf, in the meeting
   of iron sword and shield;
   the dead in Waterford were
   war-booty for the raven.

spear-storm 'battle', its *cuckoo* 'raven'.

17 Slashed with our sword, we did.
   Soldiers in their hundreds
   fell that dawn, I saw, before
   the sword in spears' flyting;
   my own son was soon hit
   by sheath-thorn in the heart;
   Egil robbed Agnar's life,
   a hero unafraid;
   spear clanged on the grey shirt
   of Hamdir, banners gleamed.

spears' flyting 'battle'; *sheath-thorn* 'sword'; *grey shirt of Hamdir* 'mail-coat'.

18 Slashed with our sword, we did.
   With their sabres, I saw,
   Endil's trusty offspring
   chopped ample meat for wolves;
   in Vikaskeid it wasn't
   like women serving wine;
   plenty of sea-mules were
   cleared in that din of spears;
   Skogul's mantle was scored
   in that skirmish of kings.

sea-mules 'ships'; *Skogul's mantle* 'mail-coat'.

19 Slashed with our sword, we did.
   A morning game of swords
   we held off Lindiseyr
   against three other lords;
   but few would have the joy
   (jaw of wolf got many,
   with hawk it tore their limbs)
   of leaving in one piece;
   a lot of Irish blood
   blended in the sea that dawn.

20 Slashed with our sword, we did.
   I saw the silken-haired
   lover-boy and widow's
   friend laid low that morning;
   it wasn't, in Alasund

221

before king Orn was killed,
like a wine-bowl goddess
bringing warm hand-basins;
I saw battle-moons burst,
breaking the lives of men.

wine-bowl goddess 'woman'; *battle-moon* 'shield'.

21 Slashed with our sword, we did.
Long sabres bit on shields,
while the gold-shrouded spear
jangled on Hild's shingle;
you'll always be able
to see in Anglesey
how commanders advanced
into their cutlass-game;
bloody was the winged
dragon of wounds offshore.

Hild's shingle 'mail-coat'; *dragon of wounds* 'spear'.

22 Slashed with our sword, we did.
Why must the soldier die
who stands in the first rank
in the ice-storm of spears?
He who never fattens
eagles in steel-blade-fight
has cause to rue his life
(cowards can't be spurred, they say);
what service is his heart
to a lily-livered sneak?

ice-storm of spears 'battle'.

23 Slashed with our sword, we did.
It seems to me it's fair
that one man face the other
when first they raise their blades;
noble can't fell noble,
that's always been the nub;
lover-boy must ever
be bold in din of swords.

24 Slashed with our sword, we did.
It seems to me it's true
that we must follow fate,
few can escape the norns;
I didn't think that Ella
would be there at my end,
when I served the blood-hawk
and launched ships on the sea;
far and wide in Scotland's firths
we got the wolf its food.

norns 'the fates'; *blood-hawk* 'eagle or raven'.

25 Slashed with our sword, we did.
It always makes me smile
to know that Baldr's father
has benches out for feasts;
we'll start by drinking beer
from curving skull-branches;
we won't regret life's end
in noble Odin's hall;
I will not come fearful
into Fjolnir's palace.

skull-branches animal horns, used as drinking horns.

26 Slashed with our sword, we did.
All the sons of Aslaug
would now with biting swords
bring about a battle,
if they knew exactly
how I was being treated,
that many poisonous
snakes were molesting me;
my boys got such a mother
so their hearts would be bold.

27 Slashed with our sword, we did.
My life will soon have ended,
there's fierce harm in that snake,
the asp lives in my heart;
I expect that Odin's
wand will go through Ella;

it will anger my sons
that their dad's been ensnared;
those courageous lads won't
sit around quietly.

Odin's wand 'spear'.

28 Slashed with our sword, we did.
Spear-meeting's inciter
took to the field in one
and fifty big battles;
I never imagined
that any other king
could ever surpass me,
who reddened spears so young;
the gods will welcome us,
there is no grief in death.

spear-meeting 'battle'.

29 But now I'm keen to stop,
spirits are calling me,
sent from Odin's hall to
summon me to Herjan;
I'll be glad to drink ale
when seated with the gods;
all hope of life is past,
and laughing I will die.

BJARNI KOLBEINSSON, Bishop of Orkney
(fl. 1188–1223) *The Song of the Jomsvikings*
(Jomsvikingadrapa) Norse

Bjarni Kolbeinsson was born into a Norwegian family that became powerful in
the Northern Isles, was bishop of Orkney 1188–1223, and is known from
Orkneyinga Saga and contemporary documents. He travelled to Norway and
had contact with learned men in Iceland. This poem (which is not preserved
in its entirety, though probably no more than four or five stanzas are lost at the
end) is attributed to him in one of the two manuscripts that preserve some of
its stanzas. It relates the well-known story of the Jomsvikings, a legendary
group of Danish warriors based on an island in the Baltic. Their story is more
fully told in the Icelandic *Jomsvikinga Saga*, preserved in a number of versions
and probably written at roughly the same time. The light-hearted, tragicomic
narrative concentrates on the attack by the Jomsvikings on Earl Hakon of
Norway and their defeat in the battle of Hjorungavag (c. 985–990), but shows
the defeated hero Vagn Akason nevertheless succeeding in his vow to marry
Ingibjorg. The poem is interspersed with the narrator's comments on his own
unhappiness in his love for a nobleman's wife. In this juxtaposition of love and
war, the poem resembles the stanzas composed by Rognvald Kali and his
poets (see above). Here, the theme of love-longing in part takes the form of a
refrain occupying lines 1, 4, 5 and 8 of stanzas 15, 19, 23, 27, 31 and 35. This
kind of refrain is known as *stælt* 'inlaid' and its 'baroque syntactical disruption'
(Finlay 119) is not possible to reproduce in an English translation. The metre
of the poem is *munnvǫrp*, a form of *dróttkvætt* (see Introduction: The Norse
Tradition), with a much less demanding rhyme scheme than usual. The
beginning of the poem plays ironically with skaldic conventions, in which the
poet requests a hearing for his poem and declares that he has his art from
Odin, and the style of the whole poem verges on the parodic.

1 I ask no sword-smashers'
    silence for my sequence,
    yet I've made an ode for
    the honoured paragon.
    I will serve Odin's ale
    to every man around,
    though none of the noble
    knights will listen to me.

sword-smashers 'warriors'; *the honoured paragon* the Jomsviking Vagn Akason,
hero of the poem; *Odin's ale* 'poetry, a poem'.

2 Cascades were not my school,
    I never cast a spell,

I learned not Odin's art
under a gallows-man.

Odin's art . . . gallows-man Odin was the god of the hanged, as well as of
poetry.

3 Sorrow's unhappiness
happens to me like others,
a lady with beautiful
arms has bound me in grief.
Yet I'm still very keen
to create this poem,
I've been so unlucky
in my dealings with ladies.

4 This lad loved a lady
long ago, and I've kept
my feelings for the fishing-
line-field's fire-carrier.
Though I've hardly composed
on the mead-pine's splendours;
yet it suits me to sing
of that server of ale.

fishing-line-field's fire-carrier field of the fishing-line = sea, fire of the sea = gold,
carrier of gold = woman; *mead-pine* 'woman'; *server of ale* 'woman'.

5 Something else must be said:
the poet sang of battle.
I offer an epic
ode to those not listening.

6 I've heard that south in Jom
five leaders once did sit.
(Lovely necklet-valkyrie
robs me of my delight.)
It's fitting to recount
the feats of those brave men,
those trees of weapon-moot
made material for odes.

necklet-valkyrie 'woman'; *trees of weapon-moot* weapon-moot = battle, tree of
battle = warrior.

7 I've heard of great campaigns
by Harald everywhere,
battle-eager kinsmen,
they bloodied biting swords.
The heathen ones could see
the heirs of Veseti
and thought that they would need
to nourish iron's din.

Harald, i.e. 'Bluetooth', King of Denmark and overlord of the Jomsvikings;
heathen ones 'Norwegians'; *iron's din* 'battle'.

8 I'll tell who had command
of those courageous men,
most valiant of all,
and praised for victories:
each martial warrior
was much the lesser man
than Aki's hawkish son
in all the hardest tasks.

9 Of the sprightly soldiers,
Sigvaldi was the chief,
and Thorkell ruled the force
of fighters valiant,
hard Bui and Sigurd
were at every battle,
but I've heard that Vagn had
the most valour of all.

10 The sturdy reddeners
of bloody spears then steered
their vessels to Denmark,
they were dashing and mighty,
when the war-gallant ones,
wealth-distributors, drank
their fathers' wakes (I've heard
many made ready that feast).

11 The officers resolved
to seek their own renown
(it's just such things that are
the stuff of poetry),

and they began to swear
solemn and daring vows.
There was much hilarity,
I hear, from all the beer.

12 Bold Sigvaldi, I heard,
he made a solemn vow,
carefree Bui was quick
to increase such manly acts:
they vowed that they would hunt
Earl Hakon from the land
(those keen men's loathing was
pretty grim) or kill him.

the land Norway.

13 Bui was raring to go,
bravely into battle,
with war-bold Sigvaldi,
into the rumble of swords.
The breaker of waves wished
to take Havard to war,
he was not averse, he said,
to Aslak in the squad.

rumble of swords 'battle'; *breaker of waves* 'seafarer', here Sigvaldi.

14 Tree of Hamdir's headgear,
the hardy Vagn, then spoke:
said he'd boldly follow
battle-practised Bui.
The ring-tree's vow was that
the radiant daughter
of Thorketil he'd wed.
(I suffer woeful grief.)

tree of Hamdir's headgear Hamdir's headgear = helmet, tree of helmet = warrior; *ring-tree* 'man'.

15 (That gentleman's wife, she
robs me of all my joy.)
Eager and bold the prince
ordered the launch of ships.

(The noble lady causes
me cruel suffering.)
The troops who could create
the clash of spears embarked.

16 It's said that from the south
the splendid men did sail
their fleet, the cold sea splashed
the trees of murder-flame.
The frosty bows battered
icy billows, the sea
roared cool on the planked hull,
the storm tested the crew.

trees of murder-flame murder-flame = sword, tree of sword = warrior.

17 It's said that on Yule night
Jomsvikings brought their fleet,
testers of crimson shields,
to the coast of Jadar.
The men were hankering
for some hard harrying,
the shield-snake reddeners
showed Geirmund their power.

shield-snake 'sword'.

18 Then the earls of Norway
called out every man
to meet in storm of spears
those coming from the south.
In a short time they gathered
a great national levy,
many murder-makers
were at that match of blades.

storm of spears 'battle'; *match of blades* 'battle'.

19 (That gentleman's wife, she
robs me of all my joy.)
Fire crackled in the islands,
dangerous to alders.
(The noble lady causes

me cruel suffering.)
Flames spurted from their houses,
spoiling their tranquility.

trees of the storm of helmet-destroyers helmet-destroyers = swords, storm of
swords = battle, trees of battle = warriors.

20 Three courageous chieftains
were with each company
(or so it's been repeated,
the people don't forget),
when the trees of the storm
of helmet-destroyers
met in Hjorungavag
in that historic event.

21 Hakon did what was needed
to defend his land, I hear;
and Eirik was not slow
to redden blades of swords;
and the third chieftain there,
he was cheerful to his men,
was said to be Armod,
always the warrior.

22 The strong men clashed their shields,
incited to battle,
there was a countless force
fighting to defend the land:
each and every viking
was up against five men
(that's not a tall story,
it's been shown to be true).

23 (That gentleman's wife, she
robs me of all my joy.
The noble lady causes
me cruel suffering.)

24 Sigvaldi urged his troops
(he would not have a truce)
on to a bold attack,
battle-strong, on Hakon.

The war-bold heir of Harald
sundered helmets and shields,
he kept on charging hard,
crouching behind his shield.

25 Keen Bui led the charge,
ahead of his recruits,
relentlessly (just as
men reckoned that he would),
the stalwart trees of spears
went stirred up into battle,
they made weapon-breakings,
dangerous with their blows.

trees of spears 'warriors'.

26 Inflamed, Gold-Bui split
helmets with Odin's fire,
he drove his chain-mail wrecker
right down to the shoulders.
Havard began to hand
out heavy blows to men.
Standing up to Aslak
was anything but easy.

Odin's fire 'sword'; *chain-mail wrecker* 'sword'.

27 (That gentleman's wife, she
robs me of all my joy.)
Storm of steel resounded,
bowstring sent off arrows.
(The noble lady causes
me cruel suffering.)
War-gallant soldiers grasped
the loops of their spears.

storm of steel 'battle'.

28 Squires fought back with weapons
as Vagn struck down their troop,
he cut open many
hundred broad brow-castles.
The song of slashing swords

was grim, lads saved themselves.
Aki's heir caused battle-
tumult, blood fell onto spears.

brow-castle 'head'.

29 In that hard conflict Vagn
   won all the victories,
   the lads advanced boldly
   with the brave and famous one
   when Aki's mighty son
   soon slaughtered (so I've heard)
   gallant-minded Armod
   in Odin's icy storm.

Odin's storm 'battle'.

30 The host made spear-din grow,
   and heroes everywhere
   yielded to the battle-
   bold trees of sword-blizzard,
   but the grim ruler Hakon
   offered the gods his son
   in that arrow-shower,
   showing his hatefulness.

trees of sword-blizzard sword-blizzard = battle, tree of battle = warrior; *arrow-shower* 'battle'.

31 (That gentleman's wife, she
   robs me of all my joy.)
   She-wolf trod on swollen corpse,
   wolf stood in the fodder.
   (The noble lady causes
   me cruel suffering.)
   Wolf drooled over marrow-hall,
   baby wolf was fattened.

marrow-hall 'bone'.

32 Then, I hear, Holgi's Bride
   called up a great hailstorm,
   fierce hailstones from the north
   fell booming on the shields,
   so the cloud-pebbles driven

232

by squalls pounded into
the snake-sharp eyes of men,
making their wounds gurgle.

Holgi's Bride Thorgerd, Hakon's tutelary goddess; *cloud-pebbles* 'hailstones'.

33 This was too hard a test
for the dog-tired earl
(I believe he was soon
under sail with his fleet).
In cold winds Sigvaldi
had the sail hauled up the mast,
waves rumbled on the bows,
winds filled the bulging canvas.

34 There, glory-eager Vigfus
sent Aslak to the shades
(but of that episode
there is no more to say).
The hard-striking Thorleif
got to break the thick legs
of the stalwart Havard
(he fought hard with his club).

35 (That gentleman's wife, she
robs me of all my joy.)
The current in the sound
took corpses past the islands.
(The noble lady causes
me cruel suffering.)
The maker of the din of spears
broke the fast of troll-wife's mount.

36 Bui made all his men,
battle-promoter, jump
overboard (Vagn's troop fought
back with their swords, I hear),
before, with heavy chests,
the brave sword-storm-maker
leapt right into the waves
(he held onto his wealth).

sword-storm-maker 'warrior'.

37 The fierce breaker of Ygg's
    flame then climbed overboard,
    brave Gold-Bui carried
    his caskets from the ship.
    And often afterwards,
    men who were unafraid
    could see a long serpent
    lying on that treasure.

breaker of Ygg's flame Ygg's flame = sword, breaker of sword = warrior.

38 Vagn and his men carried on
    defending their craft, I hear,
    (all their other narrow
    ships were empty by then),
    so the sovereign's men
    could not get on that sloop,
    the fierce friends of Eirik
    got forced back down again.

39 Only thirty were left,
    of those gallant young lads,
    still standing, the splendid
    squad supported Vagn well.
    I've never heard of so few
    fighting men defending
    themselves in buzz of spears
    right to the bitter end.

40 The brave fellow went ashore
    with the Danish foemen,
    the army lay dead on board,
    spears were reddened with blood.
    They could not rush away,
    Vagn said, from their rivals,
    so together they spent
    one night in a state of truce.

41 Then Eirik caused eighteen
    warriors all at once
    to lose their lives, I hear
    Vagn's host became smaller.
    The gallant heroes uttered

strong words to the others
(they are remembered still)
– that was very stalwart.

42 Then Thorketil Leira
lifted the helmet's bane
when the gem-giver sang
the ring-goddess a love-song.
He prepared to cut down
Aki's courageous son,
but Vagn, bold in fighting,
got to strike at him first.

helmet's bane 'axe'; *gem-giver* a (generous) man (here, Vagn); *ring-goddess* a woman (here, Ingibjorg).

43 The quick-witted donor
of rings said, 'Do you wish,
sweller of Odin's gale,
to get the gift of life?'
The young god of the sword-storm
said to the earl, 'I won't
accept my life until
I have fulfilled my vow.'

donor of rings a (generous) man (here, Thorketil); *Odin's gale* 'battle'; *god of the sword-storm* sword-storm = battle, god of battle = warrior (here, Vagn).

44 Generous Eirik gave
a truce and gifts to twelve
mighty warriors and Vagn
(that action's much admired).

45 Then the audacious god
of the din of shields wed
the dazzling Ingibjorg,
to the delight of many.

god of the din of shields din of shields = battle, god of battle = warrior (here, Vagn).

IN PRAISE OF RAGHNALL, KING OF MAN AND THE ISLES (1187–1229) Gaelic

Raghnall was the great-grandson of Gofraidh Crobh-bhán ('white-hand') or Méarach ('long-fingered'?), as he is known to this Gaelic poet and others. Gofraidh founded an independent dynasty, based in the Isle of Man, but with sporadic control also of Dublin and the Hebrides. Raghnall, who took power in 1187, was connected by birth and marriage to many of the leading players in the Irish Sea area, but had to contend with his brother, Olaf, who fought for the kingship for decades, eventually taking power after Raghnall's death in battle in 1229. Raghnall (the name derives from Norse 'Rognvald') was described by the *Orkneyinga Saga* as 'the greatest warrior then in the western lands', and his Norse heritage is also emphasised in this poem, in which many of the ship-faring and military terms are Norse loan-words.

The poem begins by praising Man as an otherworldly island, Emhain Abhlach, and plays with the image of the *sídh*, a mound, perhaps at an inaugural site on Man, with a link to the otherworld. The poet also dwells on the supposed eligibility of Raghnall to rule Ireland.

A fruitful place, the *sídh* of Emhain,
  shapely the land where it's found;
fair fort above all dwellings,
  where bright apple-trees abound.

Emhain Abhlach the freshest,
  the summer hue it takes is sharpest,
scarce a fort or hill is fairer
  in its clear fresh green garment.

Emhain, cool and pleasant fort,
  gladdest fort in its hollow;
on the road to the ancient hold,
  a new-horned calf being driven.

Many in fair, fresh-grassed Emhain
  the men a noble eye surveys:
a brown steed's rider, swiftly
  through a high new-branched *sídh*'s face.

Many in Emhain of the inlets
  which their brown feast has not left:
those fields tilled since the autumn
  for the Lord's body's pure grain.

Fine the region of the mound's man
    who has drunk the honey's fruit:
to go to the barrow's fair *sidh*
    is to go to mead's smooth fort.

Emhain Abhlach of the yews,
    glossy its trees' crests' colour—
fresh place of the dark blackthorn,
    where Lugh was raised, poet's offspring.

Emhain of the fragrant apples
    is without lie Man's Tara;
the noble brood of Sadhbh, they
    are Emhain's green-branched apples.

You, the son of noble Sadhbh,
    are the fairest apple sceptre.
What god from beside the Boyne
    conceived you with her in secret?

Raghnall, king of the stronghold,
    Da-Thí's great ridge seeks your head:
you will get, Sadhbh's noble son,
    speech from the slab on Tara's side.

Were yours the hosts of Ireland's men,
    from Boyne as far as Tiber,
better to you for honey and mirth
    were Lír mac Midhir's son's Emhain.

Son of fair, shapely Gofraidh
    who failed not to give return—
not right, for your father's sake,
    a churl's son, while you reign, in your mansion.

Not nobler than you, the Roman's king—
    your beauty is the free-handed beauty—
not nobler the grace of Syria's king
    than the curled-haired bloom of Leinster's griffins.

Today, Emhain will not get
    a lover like you – you are the helpmeet.

A hillock like it in aspect,
  find it on the earth's surface!

Many the doorways to your land,
  brighter than blue stretched skins,
of them, branch of Emhain's haven,
  are Fern's cave and Cnoghdha's fair cave.

I would arrive, with no great ship,
  in this Man which I extol,
so I'd be north beside your land,
  should I follow Corann's fair cave.

You will deal death from smooth-plained Man,
  slaughter by a great ship's host;
amidst your smooth fresh fields, hills
  have lured you from the fair Boyne.

You'll hold a man back, and plunder,
  you'll burn a house and smash.
Was metal laid on your anvil?
  You dry in its bed Colptha's strait.

You'll plunder disputed Dublin,
  your shield guarding your fine foot;
a house-site on coming to Dublin
  I ask beforehand, Raghnall.

Raghnall, king of the world,
  king to whom I give great love,
in your wake about Cnoc Ó Colmáin,
  will be organ-pipe, trumpet, horn.

Good your skill, stubborn your heart,
  bright-haired lord of Mull's harbour;
another warrior's stout sword
  you bear in a gold-cased scabbard.

Your crimson spear in your hand—
  each man pales at its sleek point—
you drive it, Raghnall, into him
  till its point is through his bright back.

From ship's prow you grasp a quiver,
    you grasp a brown, stripped-down shaft,
you sound your sleek, curved bowstring
    from the long prow of a ship.

You are the man of brindled barques,
    the shore you will reach is cursed:
you know how to foot a thwart
    to wound a knight's fair breast.

Gofraidh Méarach's fair offspring,
    you, man who shatters armour,
your vow, king, against a queen
    she has avenged on her eyes.

Lavish, manly son of Gofraidh,
    pleasant, noble son of Sadhbh,
with a mere splinter you shattered
    the straight bright gate of a court.

Offspring of fleet-rich Lochlann,
    offspring of bright Conn of the chains,
you'll seek harbour behind Aran
    while probing Ireland's cold shores.

Many a cup on your ship's floor
    unharmed by spray or downpour—
a dragon of yellow gold,
    with a man drinking from it.

Draughts of your ale fetter me—
    what mirth does not your mirth vanquish?
I have no trouble drinking them,
    the Norsemen's cold ales' madness!

Approaching your house for feasting,
    fian-men, king, are your captives;
a fine flask holds your pure cold ale
    like a blaze of burning blue embers.

Raghnall, king of Coll, all things
    you obtain in your trim ship:
from throngs, the Swan's thin cold wine
    has taken away the sea's care.

Easy the folk, doling great wealth—
    better than sharing it basely—
toughened the men for the fight,
    the hounds of the fine pack of Gofraidh.

You bring a finely cloaked band
    with you to the vast meadows;
for your sake the wind moves trees
    like fair lovely soft peat-moss.

Your head's well known to women
    from afar across the soft-grassed lawn.
The locks of your fresh-tressed hair move
    a soft blue eye against its will.

A face fairer than summer nuts
    in your crowd's view, fine noble,
the like of Gofraidh's heirs' eyes
    gave you: new cups' gems before them.

Your eye, like a curve of choice land
    besting the pick of straight-tipped grass;
the bloom of your long hair, like a strand
    of new smelted gold from the anvil.

Not rare, fresh lithe branch, is love
    for your grand hair, like a rich crop.
No woman dealt your foot envy,
    you bright brown-gloved great-limbed bough.

Norseman of the Brugh's best ones,
    as you travel the sea's foam:
splendid eyes, from the Swan's prow,
    shining feet and perfect cheeks.

Twined thatch on your brown head's crest,
    noble, sleek brown Amhlaíbh's offspring;
your smooth warrior-hand, Raghnall,
    is like a soft white strip of vellum.

I liken your hue to sea-spray's hue,
    Raghnall, king over Emhain;
a gentle blue star beneath your brow,
    like the sprig's fruit on the arum.

Good the array of locks and curls
   on which a green eye gazes,
lovely smouldering embers,
   your cheek's perfect side's beauty.

You've washed your fresh cheek's side; a green branch
   in your eye like summer rain;
on your hair's heath, Ferghus' offspring,
   the wind of Paradise has chanced.

Man of the splendid stallions,
   man of the Black Swan, roughly
you thrust and smoothly you whet
   a blade with smooth gold handle.

You brought a crushing defeat on Maelbheirn,
   your lively blows like war-gods,
many the man in a glen, loss-weakened,
   from a bright slim blue-eyed noble war-god.

Conn's offspring, Cormac's offspring,
   with the ship which is red brindled,
a herd of plunder for a worthy steed
   a man of unsure steed has traded.

Woe that his soft dry sleek hair
   holds not tonight the Glas Ghaibhnenn;
woe that the Dubh Saighlenn dwells not
   with fresh sleek blue herds of fair Norsemen.

Good to me my journey over,
   you pleasant head, brown and rippling:
your shoulder I had as my prop,
   noble king of Seghais.

Going from your good house
   my gifts were not worthless gifts:
worse the king's house where one would go
   than staying with Gofraidh's fair seed.

Gofraidh's son, of Mull's ploughed field,
   your fields will seize our notice:
to your hall's shores you take spoils
   from bright-barqued Tráigh Bhaile.

COLUMBA'S LEGACY (C. 1210) Gaelic

Another poem in the voice of Columba, this may have been composed at Derry, but was directed towards the disputed ownership of Iona, where in 1203 a Benedictine monastery was constructed by the son of Somerled, Raghnall. In 1204 it was torn down by the clergy of the north of Ireland, but their intervention was ultimately unsuccessful. This poem expresses the views of the conservative faction in the dispute, and probably dates from after a raid on the island by Norse adventurers in 1210.

Dead is my body tonight,
Oh noble sister's son.
I fear I'll not be allowed
to reach my destined land.

White-toothed Son who claims tribute,
warm my feet well!
Though great the hardship I've had,
henceforth I'll get more.

I'll get violent waves: they'll bring
me to unknown countries;
I will get a cold sea's storm,
I'll get ravens and monsters.

I will get rough cruel boulders
breaking my casket's lid;
the sea will be my cold dwelling
till the Lord's heart relents.

I am the son of Feidlimid,
son of Fergus, son of Conall.
A grievance for Gaels, the fate
which will fall on my body.

Myself, held captive by foreigners,
and they themselves on raids;
wretched I'll deem the foreign monks
who'll be after me in my place.

I will slay Clann Somhairlidh,
both beasts and men,

because they'll go from my counsel,
I'll lay them low and sap them.

Clann Cholmáin, Clann Somhairlidh,
Clann Chonaill and Clann Áedha,
fine-weaponed Clann Chairpri,
Clann Loingsigh from Tír Áedha.

Clann Luighdhech, Clann Aenghusa,
Clann Fherghusa whence I am,
those kindreds I recount:
their care for me will be bad.

Myself, though I am long-suffering,
a gush of rage will come to me:
a right-sharp, wounding disease
which will swiftly fill the graveyards.

The graveyards which I chose
both in Ireland and Scotland,
will be bright noble standards,
assisting my soul.

Reilig Odhráin of the pilgrims,
Reilig Martain in Derry;
the fine graveyard of Oireacht,
in it I would wish to lie.

Beloved, victorious Dunkeld,
Enach and Downpatrick,
Cuillech of the horns and feasting,
fierce-waved, deep grey Tory.

Leafy, bright-thicketed Derry,
Kells, the head of the clan,
renowned, windowed Durrow,
Swords, and Í Coluim Cille.

If my counsel had been done,
sinful folk of the graves' clans,
they'd not be in great diseases,
and they would not be in want.

[. . .]

My graveyards, my chapels,
my strongholds, my forts,
my congregation, while it lasts,
with me under the Creator's guard.

My Lord, my true Brother,
and my mother's only Son,
he is my Grandfather,
and my mother's Brother.

My churches, my monasteries,
my Creator guarding them,
my brothers, my sisters:
may they not be destroyed.

My tenants, both near and far,
those under my power,
let them not touch forbidden women;
may they not be in torment.

My pilgrims, my pupils,
may they live forever,
though they might cause grievances
which one dare not mention.

My Lord, my protection,
from each hour to the next,
Christ, head of every counsel,
till judgment and after it.

The bold son of Norway's king
goes under Iona's care;
he himself with his wealth
will fall by me for God's sake.

Mighty Gregory gave to me
the abbots of Ireland and Scotland,
my being over them, no scant thing,
though pride of place is Patrick's.

I got from him for my successor
to be without bishop over me after me,

except famous Gregory the pope,
from whom I'll get the Lord's honour.

Everything I got from Gregory
I wrote with my long hand,
at the end of the books of the battle
lest the dissolution be keen.

Oh, gentle, warm wee Báithín,
shelter of my heart's piety,
though you gain power from it,
forsake not heaven's King for a share.

Lively, babbling people,
most of your churches in Ireland,
quarrelsome, talkative peasants:
bad the life of scholars.

My beloved, my close kinsman,
avoid a bigger crowd;
let their fierce foes not attack
Iona's lovely community.

Iona's community, Derry's community,
a community which will reach heaven;
dear to me pale-brown Derry
and my heart's Reilig Odhráin

Marvellous Reilig Odhráin
on which I spread Roman soil,
generous true-judging Mary
comes to bless it every noon.

Every morning on rising early,
I used to go sunwise round the graveyard,
your sorrow and your awful burden
are forgiven you when you go in it.

Dear fresh-countenanced Durrow,
solitary, prayerful, lovely,
gentle, tranquil, well-beloved
as is wished for by scholars.

The wilderness owned by the true devil,
secluded, dark, black Dubhghlenn,
two years less two quarters it is
that we have been seeking it.

Two bishops, two great scholars
I brought west with me,
the friendly bishop of Cairpre,
the bishop of Áedh ón tSliabh.

Their choice and their tenants' dues,
will be brought east from them,
the foreigner's destruction will leave
them under the legs of dogs.

My poor and my weak ones,
wretched as they'll be there,
a foreign folk will spread
over them, since I'll be dead.

GILLE-BRIGHDE ALBANACH (fl. 1200–30) and
MUIREADHACH ALBANACH Ó DALAIGH (fl. 1200–24)

These poets are two of the earliest-named practitioners of the strict-metre verse termed 'Classical Bardic Poetry'. Gille-Brighde was, by his own testimony, from Scotland, but beyond this we know little. All his extant poetry, with one exception, was composed for Irish patrons, notably for the king of Thomond, Donnchadh Cairbrech Ó Briain (†1242), and the king of Connacht, Cathal Crobhdherg ('Redhand') Ó Conchobhair (†1224). The reigns of these patrons date Gille-Brighde to the first quarter of the 13th century.

Muireadhach Ó Dálaigh is rather the opposite: he began life as a prominent member of the foremost poetic family in Ireland, and was himself poet to the king of Tír Conaill, Domhnall Mór Ó Domhnaill (1207–41). In 1214, according to an account in late annals, Ó Domhnaill's steward came to Muireadhach's door, and feeling insulted, the poet split the steward's head with an axe. Fleeing through Ireland from patron to patron, Muireadhach ended up in Scotland, where, during 15 or more years of exile, he acquired land, family and the epithet Albanach. He is, by reputation, the progenitor of the famous and prolific Scottish Gaelic learned family of MacMhuirich.

Both poets clearly shared patrons and adventures. They appear to have been on crusade to the Holy Land, c. 1218–24. For this reason, their poems are presented here mingled together, to show two different but similar poets at work for common patrons and with a common poetic language.

Gille-Brighde Albanach
On Cathal Crobhdherg, King of Connacht
(1198–1224)

The Redhand has come to Cruachan.
 I see his badge in his hand:
through the patron saints' deeds are gained
 those promised to Ireland's bright-grassed land.

He has come, as Berchán promised;
 sure our knowledge, Cruachan's Red-Hand.
At Carn Fraích he's donned his kingship.
 First, he has hushed the land's wind.

Cruachan's Redhand has made fertile
 the green woods of the warm land;
struck with a mallet, each white hazel
 will pour down the fill of a vat.

His reign has put grain in the ground,
  brought blossoms through branches' tips.
The laws of that bright Greek candle
  have brought acorns to the oaks.

Banbha has recognised her king,
  in one month, it's borne a quarter's growth.
The wood which trembled with decay
  has in his reign once more borne fruit.

When autumn comes, the fruit will reach
  Galway's lord of the swift mounts:
cluster on cluster, ear on ear
  will stretch from Ceis Corrain to Cruach.

I shall tell you, men of Ireland,
  Cathal's appearance: hear me!
he, with his left hand now reddened,
  the fair, pale-curled, bright-haired one.

A shield-ridge which scatters onslaught
  is the tip of his red hand;
the pin's great boll on a ring-brooch
  is the tip of his white hand.

Whiter than a shirt on washing day,
  .his sure hand, like the sun's beam;
his left hand is scarce paler than
  the stones' hue in his own ring.

Hand of Toirrdhelbhach of Tara's son,
  which Marbhán (now dead) foretold:
you got a badge from Mary's Son
  all great Ireland's sceptre thereon.

Palm of the Redhand, Tuam's candle,
  you are the fairest I've seen;
the twin of your hand, fresh, deadly
  is alongside Níall's dark knee.

Upon his white-soled foot below
  he put a dark thread-worked shoe;
about his hand, broad, fine, half-dark,
  he puts a smooth mottled glove.

He dons, after rising early,
    a scarlet mantle, refined his body,
the soft-eyed king of Moy's mantle:
    braiding and green fringes on it.

If there's a battlecry in his court,
    it's not heard, from the crowd's depth;
you can hear every whisper there
    when a man recites his poem.

Ireland's five fifths would not restrain
    sleekhaired Cathal's assembly;
a flawed poem from bard or rhymster
    curbs the great curled fair man's bright throng.

Great Toirrdhelbhach, Ireland's high-king,
    the father of Flann's fort's king,
if it's asked which father's better,
    Cathal's pledge will reach his sons.

Toirrdhelbhach's son, of branched tresses,
    white his calf, crimson his hand;
no spouse like Cathal has taken
    Ireland since his father died.

A night in the south by the Shannon:
    the grand kin of Cruachan in sweet talk;
a night in the north by his long cheeks,
    by the fair Moy, full of trout and swans.

One night in Medhbh's great Cruachan
    Toirrdhelbhach's son spends the night.
Around him, mead-horns are drunk down,
    fair lads are braiding their hair.

What has excited the world's women
    among the Connachta of Cnoc an Scáil?
What in the lad's cheeks has harassed
    the fair-haired women of Fál?

Was it a big fire or good king's mead
    which reddened Ros Cré's king's face?
Or was it rage set his cheeks a-glow,
    or is the red always there?

The moon's paleness, when he's wounded,
  is in the Connachtmen's cheeks;
the host's faces are like the sun's burning
  when Ireland comes on his heels.

Boyle's king's never without a host
  going to fetch his herds,
Cruachan's king does not move a foot:
  though they be small, he's not grieved.

When he rises early on a summer morning,
  the curled-haired one, to hunt deer,
there's dew on the grass, a blackbird singing,
  the frost has spent its force.

Swift horses beside the Shannon
  in green meadows with white flowers,
a slender stud on the Moy's meadows,
  green-headed ducks in each ford.

Bowed to ground each apple-tree's elbows
  in Cathal of Cruachan Aí's land;
every fresh hazel has to
  incline its knee to the ground.

Every jutting nut dons its shell
  at branch's end, at farmland's edge;
the yellow grain puts on its husk
  on a fresh bent thicket's end.

On purple leaves, a red cluster,
  in green woods with luscious turf,
down from them, in heavy hailstorms
  come hazelnuts in brown shells.

It's in the Short Book that Conn's Half
  always belonged to Tara's king;
it would be madness for Mugh's Half
  to go against our books.

You did a wrong, I think, Redhand,
  when dividing soft-turfed Ireland.
The northern folk had three choices:
  you kept Ess-dara and Ess-ruaidh.

No one of the Redhand's offspring
    dares bend a branch for its nuts;
no fosterchild of his, so harsh his rule,
    breaks a hazel branch for fruit.

The Lion of Linn Féic creates
    justice between friend and foe;
quiet weather comes from his judgments,
    he kills no truth nor nurtures lies.

Royal tribute, for Ó Conchobhair:
    sacking a farmstead for nutshells;
his fine for his white hazel-stalks:
    a drove of white-horned heifers.

Ó Conchobhair of Cnoc Muaidh's law
    has brought sense to every thief;
if any get horse or cow on loan
    he calls it to witness itself.

His wealth to me: twenty milch-cows,
    Cruachan's Redhand, sweet his talk;
a cattle round-up, to be in his mansion:
    he keeps only two cows in ten.

Since the kings of Connacht enkinged
    Cathal Redhand, women's love,
there's no barren field in his land,
    milk and produce abound there.

From Scotland, for Cathal Crobhdherg

Long I've had my back to Ireland.
    Waves have rent me from its borders.
My eyes turn back toward Ireland
    under a fair fresh green surface.

The whole bright sunny island
    I recollect while weeping:
land of round, wooded hillocks,
    wet land of eggs and birdflocks.

Fairest land on flood's surface,
　　fresh to the core, its expanse;
land of smooth yews and berries,
　　pure nutbrown land of Ireland.

Bright land, filled with eggs, forests,
　　great flowering plains of horses,
tree-lined roads flanked with wild garlic,
　　full of swans, calves and blackbirds.

Fair land of grave-ringed churches,
　　of strewn blankets and flockbeds,
gentle, rich, well-loved island,
　　land of herds, boars and birdflocks.

Country of calves and milch-cows—
　　smooth its side, smooth its sea-coast—
fields filled with herds and rivers,
　　place of blackthorns, sloes and apples.

Ireland's king, this land's ruler—
　　splendid is his fleet's extent—
Crédh's offspring, tree of the island,
　　pathway of bright sleek tresses.

Toirrdhelbhach's son, since it's happened,
　　his succeeding his kindred:
guard, God, Duí Galach's offspring;
　　to poets he bears no hatred.

Cathal of Ceis, tall slim branch,
　　the swan's charm in his white cheek;
dear the one who makes us think,
　　king of Imdhán with red-haired troops.

Birches are cut for bothies
　　when his armies go raiding;
crushed hazel leaves for pillows
　　under the broad round eye of Cathal.

He made me head of the province
　　from his furrowed hair in branches;
curved head of winding tresses,
　　he raised me, fresh tree of Édar.

He gave me his blue horse-herds—
    stand by, Mary, Medhbh's offspring—
I'll praise, in the east, Sadhbh's offspring:
    may he get in God's house what he's given.

Fresh thick hair, lush and furrowed,
    with good eyes and brown eyebrows,
refined mouth full of dimples:
    that fresh bright manly chess-piece.

Fresh rippling hair, bright yellow,
    head of fine abundant thickets,
shock of rich fresh curled tresses,
    freckled cheek, soft eye, thick eyebrows.

The black-branched brow of fair tresses
    is Banbha's very Lugh for foot's fleetness,
the lord of red spears, white-tipped,
    is Imdhán's bright blue-eyed archway.

Bright hand, long-backed and loving,
    with hard spears, stout their spearshafts,
amorous branch with rayed lashes,
    winding, mounded hair in tresses.

Hand which no one's dared challenge,
    may it exalt the earth's surface;
lad who bloods a slim branching body,
    brave curled-haired tree of Fódla.

Lad of brown shields, good for battle,
    lad of bossed shields decked in plumage,
lad of pronged, fork-shaped ramparts,
    of fresh, winged, brindled banners.

The best lad of the men of Ireland,
    before pass's fray he'll not whiten,
he boasts not of his killing,
    Magh Málann's slim-flanked raven.

Soft eye who has few rulers,
    head like gold or like flax-skeins,
hand which holds a hundred for guarding,
    royal branch, charming, blue-eyed.

Long life to my dear tutor—
   I wish no parting in anger,
but to meet back in Ireland
   the fair, curled-haired, slim-fingered archway.

Cathal Crobhdherg, eversoft hair,
   I'll choose to seek his brown hillside;
Shannon's lord, spears strong in plunder,
   I'll praise the lad, his face mad and daring.

A Vision of Donnchadh Cairbrech, King of Thomond (1210–42)

Donnchadh Cairbrech Ó Briain was king of northern Munster (Thomond), and leader of the dynasty descended from Brian Bóramha. Their main military and economic centre was the originally Norse town of Limerick. This vision poem may date from early in his career.

Long ago, I saw a vision
   on ship's deck, in a straight bed:
I was borne to Limerick's tall castle
   by a fine pleasant skilled youth.

From the rock of high-hilled Limerick,
   rising towards me, I could see
a pleasant man, fierce and brilliant
   sitting in the champion's seat.

Fingers never played, on willow board,
   strings as sweet-voiced as his speech,
nor did a lad's bright hand play on
   instrument sweeter than his mouth.

The shape of him I saw in my sleep,
   as I recall, I shall sing:
two slender brows, both as new,
   lovely blue eyes in his head.

A slender calf and deep-blue eyes,
    gentle hands and a brown brow,
soft strong fingers like hazel withes,
    branching eyelash, curved and long.

Broad his countenance, trim his neck,
    smooth his face, handsome his frame;
the sprig's eye, like the harebell's blue;
    like bronze wire's shimmer, his hair.

Flower-like foot, throat like bog-cotton,
    swan-like skin, a breast like foam,
a head like round twisted ringlets,
    lively black eyebrows like coal.

A cloak of red dark-brown and gloves,
    a shirt which wreathes his soft skin,
new light brown silk tunic around
    the great-peaked brown-rayed blue eye.

I will tell, as much as I know,
    the gear of Magh Fód's horseman:
on a fierce flaming short-maned horse,
    a comely steady young man.

Reckon for me whom I saw,
    his curling hair like furs' gold;
it's right to reckon it with care:
    who's the slim bright red-cloaked one?

Is Cashel his, is Limerick his,
    or is Frémhonn his? Tell me.
Is Tara his, the house of chains,
    or is he one of Ireland's men?

If you do not recognise him,
    I know the dragon of the shields,
the folk of God's house at his right hand:
    he is the sleek-skinned tree of Cliú.

He is fair-haired Donnchadh Cairbrech
    whom we saw, pleasant the branch;
at last, I shall praise Domhnall's son,
    a branch as good as twelve men.

Donnchadh Ó Briain, Shannon's salmon,
  here's health to his fame, the dear lord!
his actions set Ireland aflame,
  but burned not Cliú's fair-haired branch.

Soft his heart, rewarding all poets,
  silky-haired Donnchadh Cairbrech,
hard his heart when bloodying blades,
  the bright-haired tree of Clann Chais.

Donnchadh Cairbrech's Harp

Bring me the harp of my king
that on it I may shed my grief;
  anyone's sorrow would break
  at the voice of the sweet tree.

He whose the music-tree was
is a fine lad for sad singing;
  many a smart verse he sang neatly
  on the pure smooth sweet-voiced tree.

Many lovely gems he scattered
behind the knotworked tree;
  often he spent Uí Cuinn's wealth,
  its bright peak to his shoulder.

Dear the hand which used to strike
the trim broad-sided clarsach;
  a slim graceful lad, playing
  it deft-handed, artfully.

Whenever his hand would touch
the instrument, so deftly,
  its great swelling gentle voice
  would strike from us our sadness.

When they would come within,
Cas's kin of the waving hair,
  Cashel's noble branches had
  a harp with sad strings inside.

They would recognise that girl
throughout wet boggy Banbha:
    everyone knew Donnchadh's harp,
    so slender and so fragrant.

Ó Briain's harp, sweet its sound,
before fair Gabhran's feast,
    Gabhran's bright arch used to strike
    a plaintive sound from the strings.

No pale Gael's son will obtain
waving-haired Ó Briain's harp;
    no foreigner's son obtains
    the magical knot-carved one.

Alas for thinking to ask for you,
harp of fair Limerick's ruler;
    or for thinking of buying you
    from me for wealth, Irish woman.

I find your smooth fresh voice sweet,
woman who was the high-king's;
    to me your voice is soft, mad,
    woman from Ireland's island.

Were there left me in the east
the lifetime of the yew tree,
    the shepherd of fair Cnoc Brenainn—
    I would tend to his hand-harp.

Dear to me (my heritage),
Scotland's lovely yellow woods;
    though still more dear to me yet
    is this tree of Irish wood.

Muireadhach Albanach Ó Dálaigh

Two of the poems attributed to Muireadhach were composed for Scottish patrons, both members of the family of the *mormhaers* (earls) of Lennox, whose base was at Balloch in Dumbartonshire. The first of these appears to be for the first officially named *mormhaer*, Alún mac Muiredhaigh, who must have died c. 1200. If so, Muireadhach's poem to him must date from an earlier journey to Scotland, before his exile. It has generally been taken in the past as being addressed to the second earl, Alún's son Alún, who died c. 1217, but the genealogical references in the poem suggest otherwise. The second poem is probably for the second Alún's son, Amhlaíbh, progenitor of the Dumbartonshire MacAulays, and lord of a territory around the Gareloch. From this poem we learn the name of Muireadhach's landholding in Scotland, the unidentified Ard nan Each.

For Alún, Mormhaer of Lennox (c. 1200)

Muireadhach recounts (and might even be the source of) an origin legend which has the founder of the ruling dynasty of Munster, Conall Corc of Cashel, journeying to Scotland, and marrying the daughter of the king of Alba. As in many place-name tales, the woman drowns in the river, giving it her name. The implication is that Alún is descended from royal Irish stock, and also, in a sense, from the river which flows through his lands.

Noble your lover, Leven:
young Alún mac Muiredhaigh,
   his waved hair, without blackness,
    Lughaidh's offspring, from Liathmhuine.

Good your fortune in fair lads
since you loved your first husband,
   the son of Balloch's king: his fate,
    that Leven should be his lover.

'Gearr-abhand', your name once,
in the time of great rulers,
   till Corc of Munster crossed the sea,
    the waving hair above his eyes.

Then Fearadhach Finn arrived,
son of gold-skinned Scotland's king;
   he made a compact with Corc
    when he came into his lordship:

Fearadhach gave – I think it good –
his daughter to fair-haired Corc.
   Meath's Tara is full of her fame:
   the daughter's name was Leven.

Leven bore a regal child,
Maine, son of long-haired Corc.
   She nursed the chick at her breast
   for Corc of hound-rich Cashel.

One day when Leven, mother
of slender-fingered Maine
   was with fifty white-soled girls
   swimming in the river's mouth,

she is drowned within the harbour,
Leven, Fearadhach's daughter:
   thence you are christened Leven,
   a memory not bad to tell.

Rare was the stride of Norse troops
on your green borders, river:
   more common for you, Leven,
   young deer above your river-mouths.

Young Alún, Muireadhach's son
of smooth roads has grown near you;
   lovely the hue of his fresh fair hands,
   offshoot of the first Alún's pack.

No lonely drinker of ale,
young Alún, Ailill's offspring:
   the branch of Alún's family has
   a hundred to drink the same gallon.

Though there be but one tun of wine
for the fair king Corc's family,
   not content, Corc's fair-haired seed
   to keep the wine all shrouded.

Smooth-cheeked Mormhaer of Leven,
good son of Ailín's daughter:
   white his hand, his side, his foot:
   noble your lover, Leven.

To Amhlaíbh of the Lennox (c. 1217?)

Woe to him who neglects us, Amhlaíbh
of the green apple-filled field;
   though great your charm and your threat,
   you've not been helping me enough.

Twenty milch-cows are due me,
swift, fresh Scottish chargers,
   the choice of fair hazel-fresh lands,
   from your soft young eye, Amhlaíbh.

Amhlaíbh, you dark eyebrowed man,
we don't prosper on your land:
   being yours at Ard nan Each—
   woe that you plot my bondage!

Neither marshland nor damp bog
do we deserve to get from you:
   a bit of church land is our due,
   fair bright one, for our foreign wares.

If you don't wish, for my lay,
to give herds and land, Amhlaíbh,
   keep your land, pay the cattle's price:
   you don't owe me your holdings.

Put twenty milch-cows in stock,
that I may leave your country;
   I'll seek a post, curled haired one,
   for I've always been for travelling.

I thought to journey wholly
from you, white skin, yellow hair,
   to make for swan-filled Ireland,
   to slim-fingered Clann Muiredaigh.

None of you, trailing-haired one,
engaged me but the mormhaer;
   scarce one of the crowd stopped me
   but that slim, soft-eyed archway.

Twenty lovely calving cows
for me from your white-gloved face,

a noble stead in Strath Leven,
a fort beside the chieftain.

Cattle, meal, a share of malt,
I got from Arbhlatha's son;
    good the one from whom I got
    meal and malt and livestock.

Good the lineage that's here now
at plundering my livestock.
    O God, strengthen this weakling:
    give a plough-team for his plough-team.

Since you heard, hair all shadows,
how I got the mormhaer of Lennox,
    envy and spite grows in you,
    with your tender soft-topped hair.

Recall the curled-haired Clann Conghail,
good your way with your professors;
    Clann Gofraidh recall in your duty,
    beautiful noble Munsterman.

Remember, above your ale,
great Lughaidh son of Ailill;
    recall Ailill his father
    above the rain-cloaked Burren.

Recall great Corc, Leven's son,
the warrior of Tara's slope;
    recall Corc of Cashel's honour,
    he of the lovely, smooth-curved hair.

Your brilliant face they surround,
Maine's children and Munstermen;
    Munstermen and Maine's children:
    heed them and call them to mind.

If they are all brought, young man,
to your attention, Amhlaíbh,
    they are worthy men, soft hair,
    over there, round you in crowds.

Known to me, your father's folk,
and your mother's noble folk,
 that I may count them in my lay,
 you white candle, Amhlaíbh.

I brought a choice sweet-voiced poem
to you, Amhlaíbh, from Ireland;
 your lay, lord, I fashion now—
 there's no rain without a shower,

no lovely cow without young,
no stripling without a calf;
 no praise-worthy poem lacks its lay,
 you bright splendid one, Amhlaíbh.

Amhlaíbh, regal-headed one,
my friend and my companion,
 your scholar of a bard – his lay's sweet:
 woe to him who neglects us, Amhlaíbh.

Gille-Brighde Albanach or Muireadhach Albanach
Donnchadh Cairbrech's Knife (c. 1217?)

This poem is anonymous in the manuscripts, though Muireadhach has been
suggested as the author by the poem's editor. On the other hand, the tone is
quite reminiscent of Gille-Brighde's poem on Donnchadh's harp, and the
Tonsuring Poem below, probably by Gille-Brighde, refers to a knife given to
him as a present by Donnchadh.

My friend's knife at my left side:
 my love for the girl's not lax;
my daily love for her won't go
 till he whose she is comes safe back.

She's not bad, her form's not base;
 though fair her beauty, it's not coarse.
He who poured the blue knife forth
 is free with arms, horses, horns.

She has her fill of gold,
    a smooth circlet near her lips;
the brown-browed branch gave to me
    the sharp new blue-sheathed gem.

Sharp and long is her point,
    smooth and slender is her side,
the curling haired one bestowed
    the hard grey iron on my belt.

A braided sheath guarding her,
    splendid and new; round her side
a border, heavy and gold;
    a bare saffron branch on her back.

Woman of the southern land,
    with ivory, wondrously carved,
fair Munsterwoman on my belt,
    with lovely blue bright-ridged side.

Donnchadh Cairbrech of fair hounds,
    no plunderer of poets' herds;
fair graceful tresses like gold:
    his knife under my cloak seems fine.

Mael Rúanaidh, the king's carver,
    his braided hair yellow, curled,
chaste face like blood or like wine:
    till all are filled, he rests not, knife.

Poems from the Fifth Crusade

In 1215, at the Fourth Lateran Council, the Fifth Crusade was declared. It had been preached throughout Europe, including Scotland, since 1213 and finally took place in 1217. By this stage, crusading had become much more than a warrior's activity, and the two motivations for journeying to the Holy Land, pilgrimage and the attempt to win back the Holy Land for Christendom, had become fused. Our two poets appear to have joined the crusade, essentially as pilgrims, in the company of an Irish prince and one other companion. The Fifth Crusade was one of mixed success and failure. Forces assembled at the crusader stronghold of Acre, before going on to besiege the Egyptian fort of Damietta in August 1218. Damietta, after a costly campaign, was gained, and then eventually evacuated in 1221.

Crusading had become an activity engaged in as an act of penitence. Our two poets describe in their poems on tonsuring the conversion of lifestyle and appearance they are undergoing. There were rewards, spiritual and material, for these pilgrims, but also dangers – disease, death in battle and loss of property while away were among these.

The group of four appears to have reached Acre too late for the main army in 1218, and Gille-Brighde's poem describes them making their way through stormy weather for Damietta. This seems to accord with the appalling weather of the autumn and winter of 1218. Finally, Muireadhach describes in his poem from Monte Gargano how their party had dwindled. These poems are a rare and valuable insight into the lay-person's experience – seemingly rather detatched – of a crusade.

Gille-Brighde Albanach (?)
Tonsuring Poem (c. 1218?)

Though this poem is ascribed to Muireadhach and a companion, traditionally one of the kings mentioned in the final verses of the poem, it has been plausibly suggested that Muireadhach's known poet companion in the Mediterranean, Gille-Brighde, is a more likely author. Given the references to both poets having been given knives by Donnchadh Cairbrech, and the fact that Muireadhach seems to have a companion piece to this poem in his tonsuring poem, this seems a good suggestion. Although tonsuring as such does not seem to be part of an official crusader ritual, it may be that the companions, setting out on a long journey, shaved their heads as a symbol of their religious intentions, and as a practical measure as well.

Muireadhach, sharpen your knife,
let's shear ourselves for the High-King.
   Let us sweetly give our vow
   and our two crops to the Trinity.

I will shear myself for Mary
(this vow is a passing vow),
   to Mary shear off this hair,
   you slender, soft-eyed fellow.

You find it rare, bright-cheeked one,
a knife shaving you across your pate:

more common a soft queen, sweet-voiced,
combing her hair before you.

All the time the fresh wavy heads
were washed for us and Ó Briain;
   and another time we would wash
   before Bóraimhe's fair-haired arch.

I used to swim with Úa Cais,
in the cold waters of Forghas;
   coming to land from the lake with him,
   Úa Cais and I would play at leaping.

These two knives, side by side,
Donnchadh Cairbrech gave to us.
   There are no two knives better:
   Shear smoothly, Muireadhach!

Sharpen your sword, Cathal, you
who fight for rain-cloaked Banbha.
   I've not known you vexed without cause,
   excellent Cathal Crobhdherg.

Guard us from cold and great heat,
noble daughter of Joachim;
   protect us in the hot land,
   you gentle great branch, Mary.

Muireadhach Albanach
Upon Tonsuring (c. 1218?)

This hair is for you, Father God.
   A light gift, but a hard one.
Great till tonight my share of sins:
   this hair I give you in their place.

Good its combing and its keeping
   within Ireland's soft-grassed land;
I'm sad for the poor ugly thing.
   This fair hair, Maker, is yours.

I promised to you, Father God,
   My hair shorn from its curling head;

it's right, Father God, to accept it—
  it would have gone on its own.

My hair and my comrade's curled hair
  for your waving hair and soft glance:
this fair hair and the yellow hair—
  I think they'll be too dark for you.

The shearing – small the sacrifice –
  of these two heads for fear of doom;
these two tonight, Son of Mary,
  offer you their fine yellow locks.

Better is your body, wounded
  for our sake – cruel the deed –
better your hair's grace, and purer,
  bluer eye and whiter feet.

Brighter the foot and slender side,
  whiter your breast like trees' flower,
whiter the foot, heart's hazel nut,
  which was pierced, fairer the hand.

Whiter the teeth, browner the brow,
  finer body, gentler face;
lovelier the hue of your curled locks,
  smoother the cheek, softer hair.

Four years has this whole head of hair
  been on me until tonight;
I will shear from me its curved crop:
  my hair will requite my false poems.

Gille-Brighde Albanach
Heading for Damietta (autumn–winter 1218)

See introduction to the crusading poems, above, for the context of this poem.
The description of the weather seems to accord well with the stormy con-
ditions of late November, 1218.

Lad who takes the helm, often
you go to an unknown land;
    you've nearly earned displeasure:
    you've called at many harbours.

Gentle lad . . .
. . . cause of distress:
    the unknown ports you travel
    bring sorrow to my heart.

[. . .]

Let's make a hard decision.
These clouds are from the north-east:
    let's leave the rough Greek mountain's feet,
    let's make for Damietta.

These clouds from the east are dark,
coming towards us from Acre.
    Come, O Mary Magdalen,
    and completely clear the air.

My ship tacks this way and that,
long-fingered Mary of plain-secrets;
    may your praying set us straight,
    fine bright Mary of plain-secrets.

I have turned towards you in
the Christ's name, your good husband.
    Come, you of the smooth branched hair,
    to plead for us to the Creator.

One night's suffering, or two,
for me would be no trouble;
    long, great Mary, this string of days,
    a whole season in distress.

You have held us here, waved haired one,
on the bright-beached Mediterranean
    the whole length of the autumn,
    womanly yellow-haired one.

Brighid of the pure breast,
though we've been some time sailing,

enough for me, our sailings here,
maiden of Europe, dear soul.

As you travel, take good care
to steer the rudder aright.
    If the barque bears us away,
    what shore, lad, will we gain?

Muireadhach Albanach
From Monte Gargano (1220–24)

Probably following the fall of Damietta, the Gaelic pilgrims set off for Ireland
again. This poem suggests that only two of originally four companions
survived: probably Gille-Brighde and Muireadhach. The siege of Damietta
was a long catalogue of disasters, especially in the winter of 1218/19, when
disease, cold and floods led to perhaps one-fifth of the crusading army dying.
One of their dead companions, referred to here, was a potential heir to the
kingship of Connacht, Áedh mac Conchobhair Máenmhaighe Ó Conchob-
hair. Cathal Crobhdherg, to whom this poem is addressed, may already have
been dead when this poem reached Ireland.

Far off is help from Cruachan
across the wave-edged Mediterranean.
    There's a spring's journey from us
    to the verdant-branched valleys.

May God be thanked –
. . . up against Monte Gargano.
    From Monte Gargano, it's not close
    to Cruachan's fair-ditched wilderness.

Like Heaven's pay, tonight, to touch
Scotland of the high places,
    to see the harbour . . .
    to breathe the air of Ireland.

I'd sleep safely, were I touring
with easy gentle Síl Muireadhaigh,
    in Cruachan, with its graceful band,
    on the green rushes of Ireland.

268

Ireland . . .
island of cups and drinking horns,
   fine island of brown collars:
   noble the island we've left.

If all of it were mine, all
Ireland, Laeghaire's island,
   Cathal's share would be wealthy,
   . . .

If I chanced, one day, near Ireland,
upon Abhdhán, Ibhdhán's son,
   his belt, off him awhile, would be
   round curled-haired Cathal's body.

I would bear his grief from him,
from Ó Conchobhair . . .
   . . . of the brown shoes,
   about his young graceful heir.

The horns of the world's proud kings
are west in Ó Conchobhair's house;
   the radiant troop of the pale peaks,
   . . .

We were four; we met sorrow:
half our company were lost.
   Split – it's no short departure –
   is the little band we were.

The two little ones who followed,
we left them in deep sorrow;
   we shall go, half our number,
   to the house of our chief counsellor.

If we see Cathal's fine face
in Conn Céadchathaigh's scion's house,
   beside Medhbh's fertile country,
   our sad spirits will leave us.

His father's form and honour
have seized hold of fair Cathal;
   his father's wildness and wrath
   have rushed to Cathal Crobhdherg.

To us from Cruachan will come
a salmon . . .

  . . .

  . . . , to the foot of our companion.

We'll not linger with our women
till we see Cathal of Cruachan;
  to Tuathal Techtmhar's offspring
  in Cruachan, let's give the first week.

Furs, featherbeds and fringes
will take from us the sea's rust;
  a change of colour will come to me
  on the soft silk of Cathal's company.

* * *

A pilgrim, good at praising,
and his hand which gives gifts,

  . . .

  Far off is help from Cruachan.

ascribed to Muireadhach Albanach Ó Dálaigh
On Returning from the Mediterranean (traditional)

This short verse is meant to be what Muireadhach exclaimed when he
returned to Scotland. It is unlikely to be actually a composition of Muir-
eadhach's, and instead is more likely to derive from a story concerning him,
yet we have included it here for completeness's sake. It was preserved in the
MacMhuirich family tradition in Kintyre into the late 18th century.

As I sit on the hill of tears
without skin on toe or sole –
  O King! O Peter and Paul! –
  Far is Rome from Loch Long.

Muireadhach Albanach Ó Dálaigh
Returning from the Mediterranean,
to Murchadh na nEach Ó Briain (c. 1224?)

Here, Muireadhach, returning from the Mediterranean to a world of changed patrons, presents his calling card to one of the minor members of the Uí Briain dynasty of Munster, looking for employment. Though the poem is magnificent, the use of stock imagery, such as lists of comparisons with Gaelic heroes, is prominent.

Guess who I am, o Murchadh!
Good your claim to a fine cast:
   for discernment, your father
   surpassed the ranked battalions.

What discipline befits me?
Guess, if you are Murchadh.
   Go and ask Ó Dálaigh,
   ruddy, mild, well-loved one.

Guess for me what place I live,
man who's not meek with high-kings!
   Guess what I seek in a house,
   fair-haired, white-skinned shining one.

Guess what is the name I bear,
noble blue-eyed young mastiff.
   Gentle lad, bright and slender,
   guess from what country I come!

I come, waved, wispy-haired one,
across the bright-edged Mediterranean.
   I am going round the world,
   you nut of autumn's hazel.

Muireadhach Albanach my name,
modest lad, never savage.
   Clann Bhloid summon me to them,
   though I may have thieved, I reckon.

A pilgrim and a poet
addresses your soft bright face.
  Give me something for my poem:
  it's almsgiving at the same time!

Donnchadh Cairbrech and Clann Táil
protect me and see me prosper;
  you are the best father's son,
  stalk from the field of Ireland.

I've never seen you, round eyed one.
We've not made fast our union.
  Murchadh, diadem of eyes,
  we'll be friends when I return.

You will sit in Munster, Murchadh,
fair-hilled, grassy, blossoming.
  You will sit, Murchadh, in Munster,
  over its fountain-filled hills.

There's no limit to your bounty
on Munster's plain, Murchadh.
  I don't think the Munstermen
  have steeds for you, Murchadh.

I will call you other names,
Brian Bóramha's offspring.
  I've used your baptismal name
  some time, noose of Ireland's prowess.

You Cú Chulainn for feats;
you Oscar for debates;
  solid stealthy Ó Duibhne
  for beauty, courting, bounty.

Cermad for fairness of voice,
pleated dark-satin banner;
  Ábhartach, slender, noble,
  comely, strong and affable.

Bodhbh Derg for redness of cheeks;
Manannán for herds of steeds;

luxuriant plaited tresses,
you Mongán for handsomeness.

You Midhir, the Daghdha's son
for humour, conversation—
    in your plaited hair, there's nought
    but Midhir's manner, Murchadh.

Murchadh of the brown brows, now
I call you by your own name.
    Much more befits your praising:
    gold's not refined in one heating.

Blue is your eye, pale your neck,
king of the fair-streamed Shannon,
    white your hand, slender your foot:
    your mother had the pick of sons.

Whiter your side than the wave.
Your hair's yellower than apples,
    more curled than a whole-pared shaving.
    The tang of perfume's in your speech.

The spring's rage on your weapons,
your discourses and your words;
    griffin's rage on your warring flesh;
    towards your friend, a dove's meekness.

Receive from me your own name,
Murchadh, smooth-soled Brian's son.
    Enter swiftly another company:
    good is the pilgrim's ability.

I will give your true nature, white teeth—
a satire which yet is praise—
    comely branch of the heavy hair—
    I have never heard before.

Guaire's largesse, slender face,
towards your scholars and your poets;
    fair Conall Cernach's fervour
    in your noble well-shaped flesh.

The poise of warlike Conchobhar
and Cú Roí of the fringed eyes,
   and Cú Chulainn of the skills
   who never suffered insult.

Yours, Almha's great-grandson's name,
Oisín's smooth shape on his cushion,
   Oscar's manly dignity,
   chess-king, blue-eyed and shining.

The poise of Mac Lughach of the blades,
Cliú's king, in your comradeship,
   and of Lir's son who drives steeds:
   happy he who got the gifts.

You will bear still other gifts,
the best of fame and form;
   no farmer's son in your house,
   but the king of Munster, Murchadh.

Murchadh mac Briain Ó Briain,
tree of the vineyard of fair Cliú,
   the weapons which you reject
   no person on earth can guess.

Allow me to go to my land,
gentle skinned Donnchadh Cairbrech,
   in wooded grassy Scotland,
   full of feasts and heights and isles;
I will come to Ireland again,
it's not you I leave – so guess!

Elegy on Mael Mhedha, his Wife

This translation is based, like all previous ones, on those verses edited and
'restored' by Bergin from the unique and difficult manuscript, the *Book of the
Dean of Lismore*. There are a further fourteen unedited quatrains.

My soul parted from me last night.
   In the grave, a pure dear body.

A kind, refined soul was taken
   from me, a linen shroud about her.

A fair white flower has been plucked
   from the weak and tumbled stalk.
The love of my heart is bent,
   the heavy stem of yon house.

Tonight I am alone, God.
   Bad is this bent world you see.
Dear was the young body's weight
   who was here last night, my King.

Wretched I find yonder bed,
   my long blanket set a-swim:
I've seen a body, fine, long,
   with curled hair, bed, in your midst.

There was a soft-gazed woman
   lay on one side of my bed;
none like her but the hazel's flower,
   that dark shadow, womanly, sweet.

Mael Mhedha of the dark brows,
   my cask of mead at my side;
my heart, the shadow split from me,
   flowers' crown, planted, now bowed down.

My body's gone from my grip
   and has fallen to her share
my body's splintered in two,
   since she's gone, soft, fine and fair.

One of my feet she was, one side—
   like the whitethorn was her face –
our goods were never 'hers' and 'mine' –
   one of my hands, one of my eyes.

Half my body, that young candle—
   it's harsh, what I've been dealt, Lord.
I'm weary speaking of it:
   she was half my very soul.

My first love, her great soft eye;
  ivory-white and curved her breast;
neither her fair flesh nor her side
  lay near another man but me.

We were twenty years together.
  Our speech grew sweeter each year.
She bore me eleven children,
  the tall young long-fingered tree.

Though I am, I do not thrive
  since my proud hazel-nut fell.
Since my great love parted from me,
  the dark world's empty and bare.

Since the day a stout post was fixed
  for my house, it's not been said:
no house-guest has put a charm
  on her fresh brown shadowy head.

People, do not restrain me.
  The sound of weeping's no sin.
Fierce bare ruin's come to our house:
  the warm bright brown-haired one's gone.

In his anger, He's taken her,
  the King of hosts and of roads.
Small the sin of the branched hair:
  she died; her husband's fresh and young.

Dear the soft hand which was here,
  King of the churches and bells.
Och! that hand never swore false oath.
  Sore, that it's not under my head.

A Poem to the Virgin Mary

O great Mary, listen to me,
  praying to you would be my joy:
on your brother, turn not your back,
  mother of creation's strong King.

I recall your mother's tale,
  they have long been telling it,
a gentle brown eyebrowed girl,
  heavy terraced locks on her head.

She was Anna, God's grandmother,
  from whose fair brother a king was born;
no woman surpassed her in mirth;
  she was married to three men.

She bore a girl to each good man;
  the fresh fair one gets from them
three daughters, her gentle clan,
  sleek, white their sides, curled their hair.

Blue their eyes, lovely their faces,
  not delightless, to visit them;
the whole crowd is after them,
  three women, Mary each one's name.

They took three men, these three
  Marys from the saints' heaven,
till the three fine lush-haired ones
  became pregnant, slow of foot.

Then the women bore three sons.
  Great prosperity they had.
Was there a better gentle six?
  The youngest of them was God.

One girl was the mother of James,
  a good shield from all griefs she got;
one was Mary, mother of John,
  a tale none has known in a poem.

You are Mary, mother of God.
  None has exhausted your fame:
A royal tree, cleft in three:
  true heaven's King was in your womb.

Wholly at your will, I am
  in your house and in your fort.

O friend, o mighty Mary,
  fragrant apple, yellow gold.

O food, o clothes you have to give,
  branching hair like the fenced field,
mother, sister, o my love,
  steer this poor brother right.

My brother is your great Son,
  noble mother, pliant branch.
To guard a true kinsman is right:
  a fine grandmother you both had.

Till I let your Husband shepherd me,
  fair Mary, o deep-haired one,
many the black embers in my heart.
  It's time today to wash them.

Mother of God, let's make peace,
  rich brown the hue of your hair;
great Mary, restrain His rage,
  red gold in a pot of clay.

From heaven He came, white his side,
  as noble as the stream his thigh;
have I not enough blood-tie
  from your Husband, hair curled and bright?

Trinity, Mary most kind,
  flowing, all glories but yours.
Foursome, listen to my poem,
  it takes from you no gift of gold.

Virgin Mary, black-browed one,
  great thornbrake, brilliant garden,
give me, chief of women's love,
  for my humbleness, heaven.

Soft, great one, you're David's kin;
  sought for, there's no tree like you;
of Abram's stock, your crowning hair,
  your head's spray of fragrant fronds.

Carrying your Husband and Son—
   bright his grasp, bright his fore-arm—
your Husband-Father in by your side:
   thus a glimpse of your Husband's wisdom.

Strange nursling for your white breast,
   and for your fresh, radiant hair:
your Son and your Husband both,
   pale noble wand, on your knee.

You were a beautiful pair,
   sheltering from glen to glen,
brown-haired, black-browed, white-armed Son,
   fair woman, heavy and slow.

He twirls your hair; He's your burden,
   guarding Him upon an ass.
Your hand, fresh virgin Mary,
   twirled the King's yellow-streaked hair.

You were always calm with Him,
   with His hand at your white breast.
When you washed the supple Branch,
   you kissed the dear foot and hand.

A yellow heath on your head, like gold,
   tender-eyed Mary, my sister;
a heavy smooth-white breast on your side,
   a fine brown-haired baby there drinking.

Woe to him who slights your fair hair
   (hard, since you have done no wrong).
Lady, if your womb's not chaste,
   no white forest branch bears fruit.

Useless for thieves' kin to speak,
   branching soft head, curled and waved,
to doubt you would be bad sense,
   with your splendid terraced hair.

Your womb below was all full,
   like the belly of a trout;

the Lord, without lying to you,
　fashioned on you Mary's Son.

Great Mary, it would not be clear
　without you, for a base man;
it's peaceful for a man, curled hair,
　not to be with a bad woman.

Your one Son has your waved hair,
　noble branch of the bright eyes;
the slender lad has your hands,
　and your lovely bright brown nail.

Radiant and blue-eyed your face,
　brown-arched eyebrows guarding it,
long and splendid-branched your hand:
　a poem without lie is my due.

Fair, full and yellow your hair,
　a brake of curls round your head;
pure your sure, thin-fingered hands,
　strong, slender, nobly-made foot.

No woman like you has died;
　none will – it's true – come near you;
no woman like you's tasted life,
　white womb into which God went.

Give to me shelter and drink,
　head that the earth does not touch.
May the false, unending feast
　not be mine, strong white-toothed one.

May your black brow plead fiercely
　for love of my soul, o pure love,
Mary, your husband won't be jealous
　at your prayer, bright-toothed one, for me.

Your bent yellow terraced hair,
　Mary of the slender brows,
don't leave me to another's doom,
　save your heart's ale for me.

Let's make a feast, great lively one,
    to your shapely form, side by side.
Take my share of fine verse and poems
    from me, fair noble comely one.

Let no woman but you be in my house,
    that you may be the man of it.
The false women I see, and their wealth,
    let what's mine not be drawn to them.

Without care for hounds or wealth,
    nor for horse herds, splendid swan,
lacking others' horns and their hounds,
    their sleek horses and their women.

Lift those black brows for me,
    and the face like a calf's blood;
lift, that I myself may see
    the fine fair-branched plaited head.

Lift for me, strong shapely head,
    and the round young sharp blue eye,
foot and hand, that I might taste
    the feast, near your tender hair.

A Poem of Renunciation

The ascription of this poem, and the one that follows, to Muireadhach is not
entirely secure. Although some of the language is similar to that used in his
tonsuring poem, it may be nonetheless that this dates from towards the end of
his life – he was still alive in 1228, when he composed a poem (not included
here) asking to be allowed to return to Ireland.

Soothe the heart, o Son of God—
    a sinner like me: great tale—
that I may now make my vow,
    Christ Jesus' cross over my lips.

Christ Jesus, bless with your hand
    my two feet and my two hands,

and bless me, by your will,
    in blood and flesh and bone.

I did not stop doing wrong,
    confused by my wayward flesh,
o gaping grave, till your deceit
    was over my head and my flesh.

Soothe me, great mother,
    about every grief I've known,
before I go beneath the turf,
    that before me all roads be smooth.

Poem when Dying

It's time I travel to the house of Paradise.
    When You will it for me, it is easy,
striving for the stronghold, without blemishes,
    with no one holding anything against me.

Examine yourself before your confessor,
    strictly remember your many misdeeds;
do not make a patchy penance:
    an account and origin will be asked of you.

Make no little secrets of your sins,
    though your evil be ugly to tell;
leave off your secret habits,
    lest you be at the Devil's call.

Make your peace,
    like it or no, with your body;
leaving the world, part from your wrong,
    lest its evil and fear be on you.

Woe to one who spurns the High-King's house,
    for love of sin, when he might.
The evil which one does in secret
    many the witnesses there to the deed.

Here's a saying for Adam's seed,
    for I think it no deceit:

he avoids death's pains a brief while,
  he who's not left, till he leaves.

He who bought the seed of Adam
  by His body's blood and flesh,
by His will, I am steadfast,
  though that shields me not from my sin.

Verses on the Death of Alan of Galloway
(c. 1234) Latin

A verse recorded by Walter Bower in his *Scotichronicon* of the 15th century. Alan son of Roland, Lord of Galloway and Constable of Scotland, died and was buried at Dundrennan in 1234. He left three daughters and a bastard son, and on his death his lands were divided only among his daughters, giving rise to a rebellion by the men of Galloway seeking to have Thomas, the son, rule over them. Bower tells how the rebellion was crushed by Alexander II in 1235 and many of Thomas's Irish allies were slaughtered by Glaswegians as they tried to flee back to Ireland after their defeat.

The poem, combining wit and prayerfulness, is a later addition to the *Scotichronicon*, but may well incorporate an original verse of 1234.

One thousand years, a hundred twice, and add three tens
and three:
Alan made his journey on the path of death this year.
Scots men's glory, rose of clergy, flower of all the laity,
swift his generous hand to give, here lies the noble Alan.
Seldom was, or is, or will there be a man who gave so much
of good.
O you who can read, or you who see these words,
learn now to do good deeds. For dead am I, as you will die.
I am Alan, who used to feed and nourish one man's men,
but now I'm feeding worms. From *alo*, 'I feed', I have my name.
So when the priest says, '*Miserere*', it is for me he sings.
    You who on this, my rock, may read these lines,
    pray that Christ, my Rock, may bear me to the heavens.

SNAEKOLL GUNNASON (mid-13th century) Norse

An Orcadian, great-grandson of Earl Rognvald Kali, who was in Norway in 1239.

The poet complains of being captured while on business in Norway.
I shall never,
though I live for ever,
ask for business
in South Moer,
since enemies
took me from there
to Bergen
at the king's command.

On the Death of Alexander II,
King of the Scots (c. 1249) Latin

Another verse preserved in the *Scotichronicon* of the 15th-century historian
Walter Bower.

In 1249 Alexander II set out on a military expedition to Argyll in order to
wrest control of the Western Isles from the Norwegians, having failed to bribe
or otherwise induce King Hakon IV to hand them over. On the island of
Kerrera, however, he fell ill and died, 'receiving the sacraments of eternal
salvation', but having failed to achieve his military goal. His remains were
taken to Melrose and buried there on 8th July of that year.

Much of the praise of the king's virtues here is fairly conventional, but
Bower suggests that he had a considerable reputation for piety, and he had a
particular affection for the newly founded order of the Dominican friars.

Church's shield, the people's peace, leader of the wretched,
an upright king, stern and wise, honest, well-advised,
a pious king, a mighty king, the best of kings and wealthy.
He was the second to bear his name, the name of Alexander.

For three decades he was king, and five years more,
but now the isle we call Kerrera has taken him away.
His spirit seeks the high places, joined with heavenly beings,
but Melrose here on earth now guards his buried bones.

Epitaph on the Tomb of Geoffrey,
Bishop of Dunkeld (c. 1249–50) Latin

Geoffrey, or Galfridus, was made bishop of Dunkeld in 1236 and died in 1249, according to Walter Bower who records this poem, or 1250 in other sources. The close connection of Dunkeld with 'our father Columba' began in 849 when the relics of Columba were taken from Iona to the newly established church and political centre of Dunkeld. Dunkeld also had close links with Inchcolm, of which Bower was prior. As bishop, Geoffrey had greatly enhanced the honour of the old church.

Galfridus rests here
entombed, in our father Columba's care;
he who was the shield,
sword and glory of the clerks of Dunkeld.

POEM TO AENGHUS MÓR MAC DOMHNAILL, KING OF THE ISLES (c. 1250) Gaelic

Though clearly by an Irish poet, and one who purports never to have crossed the sea to Scotland, this poem illustrates the ties of patronage which the rulers of the western seaboard of Scotland fostered in the period between the death of Somerled and the official beginning of the Lordship of the Isles. Aenghus Mór was Somerled's great-grandson, and seems to have led, from a base in Islay, the fragmenting Clann Somhairlidh. The poet had clearly worked for Aenghus's father, Domhnall, also, and the poem is essentially a well-dressed demand for Aenghus to pay his father's arrears.

Purchase your father's poem, Aenghus,
    the house of the king is yours,
you are the tree's root and blossom:
    all say it's right you buy it.

To you he left his position,
    yours each breastplate, each treasure,
his hats, his staves, his slender swords,
    yours, his brown ivory chessmen.

Yours your father's hounds' slender chains,
    each treasure chest's in your share;
all his houses and his tax,
    yours, Domhnall's horses and herds.

In his legacy he has left you
    each house from Mull to the Mull.
Yours, Aenghus, are the ships he left,
    arch of green-branched Druim Cáin.

Yours his assembly and swift steeds,
    yours his farmers, loyal to you,
you are the son who leads our battles,
    yours, what your father owes me.

Admit you should buy my poetry,
    sheer summit, Bann's fierce one.
If you don't, tell another story:
    I'll load your claim upon you.

I'm jealous of the wealth poets
  get from you, Loch Cé's lion.
Who knows if the envy's proper:
  I'm smothered by sea-terror!

Coire Dá Ruadh, Tuam's king,
  lies between us, it's my fear.
Coire Bhrecáin's part of my path,
  a groan of fear has grabbed me.

No less is Coire Bhrecáin's case,
  being between us, music-king;
its pride when it is in anger
  warps the sturdy masts of sails.

I say, for fear of the tempest,
  lord of Coll, woman's friend,
over sea to Aenghus of Islay
  sad there's not one dash of land.

One of my feet I put before me,
  king of Lewis, in the ship,
the other foot behind as prop,
  brown-haired patron, when going east.

I'd be bad on the savage sea
  at taking an oar, blue-eyed one:
on a peaceful river, I quiver
  taking the rudder of a boat.

The right way to arrange myself
  I don't know, crossing the waves;
I don't know if sitting's better,
  I'm afraid to lie in the ship.

It's my grip, grabbing it to me,
  which holds the ship, Ireland's king;
lest the thwack of the waves break it,
  I keep the ship's sides in my hand.

In my home-country people ask,
  Norsemen's king, how a ship's made.
There's little to see of the sea
  from the highest steep height there.

Though there were land to the sunrise,
  I'd find more dangerous, near you,
what there was, Aenghus, to Scotland,
  of white, green-washed, swelling sea.

Your father proposed – the lie's pleasing—
  to bear me prone in his galley,
me on a bed from Ireland to Scotland
  proposed fair-haired Conn's offspring.

My snatching without my knowing
  the blue-eyed king set about:
the great gentle one hatched a plot
  while I was sleeping off my wine.

I hate the leap of the sailing galleys,
  your ship's yard-arm was not turned;
Mac Domhnaill from Ceis Cairrgi,
  beneath you the sea's wave-ridge roared.

Attacking a strand, frequent raids,
  these your wish for yonder folk;
often from now a tide of blood
  lapping splendid Innse Gall.

You've circled Ireland, scarce the shore
  where you've not taken cattle;
nimble galleys are sailed by you
  you're otter-like, branch of Tara.

To Loch Foyle, on to Erris,
  you go straight from Innse Gall;
Erris harbour, truth's fountain,
  there you discovered Islay's host.

Islay's host, with you by Aran
  to prove their feats, far as Loch Con;
that fair host of Islay's taken
  cattle from placid Innse Modh.

Your fleet has reached Corco Mruadh,
  Corco Baisginn by its side;
from Galway-foot to Cúil Cnámha,
  you, a salmon who probes each strand.

Mac Domhnaill, heir of Manannán,
   his battle's been in Dún Baloir,
till he came, bright stalk of Gabhair,
   the lad who brought Ireland from bondage.

It's from you Colum Cille came
   across three times to our aid;
Ireland's men have paid for this poem,
   from you the scholarship has spread.

Your forebear, Síl Colla,
   Cairbre Lifechair, warrior of Mis,
when Conn's offspring died – Gabhair's veteran –
   the ridge of Ireland's fortune broke.

Torcuill, Ímhar and Amhlaíbh
   surround you, Loch Riach's man,
the earth's wave of ruin in fury,
   bright-hazelled Dublin's host.

Clann Somhairlidh, Síl Gofraidh,
   whence you're born, they hoarded no herds;
well-plotted orchard, apple branch,
   noble all blood from which you come.

Síl Cellaigh about you in Ireland,
   the Airghialla in Innse Líag,
the family tree's branches, you've heard:
   I have visited them all.

In Ireland or Scotland there is not
   an Aenghus like you, slim flank.
The Aenghuses of the Brugh's green-washed turf
   send to you, Aenghus, gifts.

HYMN FOR ST MAGNUS, EARL OF ORKNEY
(late 13th century?) Latin

The poet celebrates the martyred earl of Orkney, Magnus Erelendsson, killed by his own cousin Hakon, with whom he had shared the earldom of the islands. According to such legends as the *Orkneyinga Saga*, Magnus abandoned the raiding parties of his youth and eventually became a just and peaceful ruler as earl. He married, but his marriage is said not to have been consummated – this is confirmed by his story in the *Orkneyinga Saga* (ch. 45), though this may say more about the attitudes of the author than about the saint. At least this story would prevent anyone making a claim to be the rightful earl of half of Orkney as Magnus's descendant.

Magnus's cousin Hakon had him slain on the island of Egilsay in c. 1115, and his body was brought for burial to Birsay, which thereafter became a place of pilgrimage, even though Birsay's bishop William called the tales of Magnus's virtues heretical. The *Saga* tells how the bishop was finally forced by Magnus to dig his body up and transfer it to the altar of the church at Kirkwall, where he continued to attract popular devotion and perform miracles, driving several sinners insane and then curing them.

Noble,
humble
Magnus, steadfast martyr,
mighty and
kindly one,
our honourable earl,
praiseworthy protector,
save us, your servants,
framed in our fragile flesh,
weighed down and burdened.

Granted
by heaven,
by the Holy Spirit's gift,
so to live
fully free,
keeping to your noble task.
Lower passions you subdue,
deep your devotion,
so the spirit comes to rule
in flesh's prison.

A partner
right royal—
she had never known a man—
led to you,
given to you,
man and woman chastely joined.
Neither one is brought to ruin:
ten years pass, and still
the burning bush was not consumed
nor burned up in fire.

Envious
and raging
Hakon – cunning enemy –
would lay waste
and grind down,
seize your substance for himself.
You yourself he sought to slay –
razor-edged malice –
forging a false covenant
by a kiss of peace.

Injuries,
weariness
you bore in the cause of right.
You were seized
and deceived,
but in that last deadly blow
you are lifted up from earth,
rising to heaven.
So you are joined with Christ,
sharing his passion.

Wonderful,
glorious,
countless signs you worked for us.
What is done
now is sung
as the name of Christ is blessed,
and to you is given praise,
in church all honour.
How joyful Orkney now appears,
henceforth, forever.

By the power
of your prayers
win for all who sing your praise
graciousness,
forgiveness,
glory in eternity.
Help us who love your memory,
O loving father,
and this, your own family,
save from all danger.

Amen.

Song for the Wedding of Margaret of Scotland and Eirik, King of Norway (1281)
Latin

In 1281 a Scottish princess, Margaret, daughter of Alexander III, was married to the 14-year-old Eirik II, king of Norway, as part of the peace-making between Scotland and Norway which had begun with the Treaty of Perth in 1266. Eirik's father had died in May 1280 and the wedding was proposed to the King of Scots only days afterwards. After some negotiations over the contract, the marriage took place at Bergen in the following year, and Margaret was crowned queen on the same day at the hands of the Archbishop, Jon. The queen died only two years later, but not before she had borne a daughter, Margaret, later known as 'the Maid of Norway', who died in 1290 on Orkney while sailing from Norway to Scotland, causing a new crisis of succession in her mother's country.

From you arises, sweet Scotland, a light
whose brightness is seen shining in Norway;
how you will sigh when she is borne across the sea,
when the daughter of your king is taken away.

When the flame of peace is kindled, its grace
proclaimed to the nations, gladness makes reply.
Every nation's length and breadth now celebrates,
but above all England shares your joy.

To Eirik the king the royal maid is sent,
and with highest honour there received;
everyone breaks out in wild applause,
the people dancing while they sing her praise.

A crowd of clergy solemnly comes forth,
and wholesomely the holy priesthood prays.
Swiftly now come every class of folk,
men and likewise women, joy resounding.

The king leads forth the maid – a cause of joy
throughout the world is their sweet union.
May the God of all pour blessings on this bond
and of their marriage grant them children.

One flesh with the king, the queen now sits
upon the kingdom's throne and wears the crown,
worthy to preside and guide the nation's life.
Praise be to him who makes it so, God's Son.

How to praise this partner of the king,
so gentle, kindly, full of prudence?
Humble, she gives to all, strong in her speech,
made lovelier yet by noble continence.

May she be loving to her man as was Rachel;
may she be pleasing to the king, as Esther was.
As Leah begot, may she be fertile in offspring,
and like Susannah may she live in steadfastness.

Living conjoined in the service of God,
may they in happiness grow old
that when the race is run of this, their passing life,
they may be worthy of a lasting reward.

From you, sweet Scotland, there comes forth
a cause to sing your praise across the earth.

Scotland after Alexander (c. 1300) Scots

This has traditionally been regarded as 'the earliest specimen extant of Scottish poetry' and, while that is clearly not the case, it may be one of the earliest pieces of Older Scots preserved. It is included in Andrew of Wyntoun's *Original Chronicle*, as a song sung generally after the disastrous accidental death of Alexander III. The variants in different manuscripts are considerable. We present here one of the versions, untranslated. Notes are provided for the vocabulary.

Qwhen Alexander our kynge was dede,
　That Scotlande lede in lauche and le,
Away was sons of alle and brede,
　Off wyne and wax, of gamyn and gle.
Our golde was changit in to lede.
　Christ, borne in virgynyte,
Succoure Scotlande, and ramede,
　That stade is in perplexite.

lauche: law; *le*: protection
sons: abundance, plenty;
gamyn: sport; *gle*: enjoyment
ramede: remedy, cure
stade: stood

ON THE BATTLE OF STIRLING BRIDGE (? c. 1297)
Latin

William Wallace met the English army on the field of battle on 11 September,
1297 at Stirling Bridge on the River Forth. The English were put to flight and,
according to Bower, Hugh de Cressingham was slain – though Hugh was not,
as Bower suggests he was, commanding the English forces.

Wallace's armed struggle continued the next year, and involved a further
defeat of the English at Stainmore on St Cuthbert's Day, 20 March, and in the
spring of that year he was made sole *custos Scotiae*, 'Guardian of Scotland'.

The aforesaid man, Wallace his name, rallies the Scots;
gathers them like grains, because in French he is 'Valais'.
He gives hot pursuit to the English, to carry on the war,
that Scotland's precious freedom by arms might be restored.
Then England's overthrow was great, of such a kind
as northern lands had never known before.
Even as far as Newcastle, Northumbria was all destroyed,
and thus, their aims achieved, the Scots pressed on for Stainmore.
In that same year of Our Lord the English return again,
I tell you, to do battle with us for Berwick town,
determined on the feast of Cuthbert, in the time of spring.
While Scots looked on, thinking they'd fight on the field,
the English failed to act as they had once agreed,
but all without delay they turned their tails and fled.
When they saw this the Scots in sadness went their way,
but England, backing off, mark their king's shield with shame.
The assembled Scots for these latest gifts give praise,
as those in need give thanks, though the gifts were not complete.
Rising in praise, rejoicing, every house resounds,
but the king takes flight, and in sorrow England groans.

WILLIAM WALLACE'S UNCLE'S PROVERB Latin

Some of Walter Bower's most impassioned writing reflects his nationalist commitment. As a prologue to this short proverb, he puts a speech in the mouth of Wallace in which he exhorts Scottish collaborators and weak-minded nobles in the year 1304: 'Scotland, so desolate! You are far too credulous of lying words, and not ready for the disaster which is on its way. If you were to agree with me, you would not so easily put your neck under a foreign yoke. When I was growing up, I learned from my uncle, a priest, to value this one proverb above all riches, and I have always held it in my mind:

This is the truth I tell you:
of all things freedom's most fine.
Never submit to live, my son,
in the bonds of slavery entwined.

Scotland's Strategy of Guerrilla Warfare
(? c. 1308) Latin

Robert Bruce, whose family had a complicated history of collusion with, as well as resistance to, the English king, ruled Scotland from 1306. But, within weeks of his splendid royal inauguration, he suffered heavy defeats by the English and by the kinsmen of John Comyn, whom Bruce had murdered in February of that year. That winter he was forced to flee, and ended up on Irish soil. On his return to Scotland in 1308, he began a prolonged guerrilla war against the English. The use of marshy ground and the gullies of rivers as part of military strategy also served the Scots well at the pitched battle of Bannockburn in 1314. This description, derived from an unknown source, is from Walter Bower.

Let Scotland's warcraft be this: footsoldiers, mountain and
marshy ground;
and let her woods, her bow and spear serve for barricades.
Let menace lurk in all her narrow places among her
warrior bands,
and let her plains so burn with fire that enemies flee away.
Crying out in the night, let her men be on their guard,
and her enemies in confusion will flee from hunger's sword.
Surely it will be so, as we're guided by Robert, our lord.

On the Death of Edward I (c. 1307) Latin

Walter Bower presents King Edward not only as an oppressor, but as a satanic figure. He compares him to 'the back end of a weather cock, the tail end of all the shit of his devilish race', listing his crimes against humanity. His death is attributed to a remarkable supernatural collaboration: 'The devil threw him down. . . . when he was at the height of his power, the Lord removed him from his throne.' In his account of Edward, the following poem is recorded.

One thousand you will count, three hundred years and
                                      seven more,
on the Translation of ever blessed Thomas the Martyr,
in Burgh by Sands, where end the kingdom's borders,
there Edward fell, by whose evil Scots were slaughtered.

In Holm his brain and entrails lie buried in the earth,
war-monger who lashed the English with his dire scourge.
He trampled underfoot the necks of their haughty men,
corrupted all the world, betrayed the Holy Land.

He invaded the Scots, broke up the realm by fraud,
laid waste our churches, shut up our prelates in prison,
he slew Christ's folk and seized the gold of the tithe.
His sins are well known in all the world.

England will weep when at last it lies in ruin.
Scotland, clap your hands at the death of a greedy king.
Give thanks to God now Robert has been crowned
and guided in virtue's strength by the staff of salvation.
God will make his state on earth a blessed one.

Artúr Dall Mac Gurcaigh
Eoin Mac Suibhne's Voyage to Castle Sween
(c. 1310) Gaelic

This poem belongs to the period of the Wars of Independence which followed on Alexander III's death. During the period, native landowners were displaced and then in turn retook their lands, and the western seaboard was not free from this. The Mac Sweens (Clann Suibhne) had ruled as minor lords in Knapdale for some time before Robert Bruce had them replaced for backing his enemies. The English king, Edward II, wrote to Eoin Mac Suibhne (John Mac Sween), pledging his support if he could wrest back Knapdale, and Castle Sween, from its possessor, John of Menteith. Clann Suibhne remained in the later part of the Middle Ages in Ireland as a famous mercenary clan, and it seems the adventure described here, probably as a battle incitement, was unsuccessful, if it really happened at all.

A fleet's gathering against Castle Sween,
   in Ireland, the venture's well met;
so horsemen may deal with the waves,
   brown barques are cleaned out for them.

Tall men equip the fleet which stays
   its course on the sea's swift expanse;
there's no hand lacks a sleek war-spear
   beside a lovely, polished targe.

With hauberks they are decked out,
   the barques' prows, with branching jewels;
for champions, brown-faced their belts,
   Norsemen and leaders they are.

Gold and ivory inlaid swords deck
   the prow of the brown-sailed barques;
beside a row of bright-tipped spears,
   shields against the ships' long flanks.

Behind shields upon brindled ships,
   juts a crimson gold-jewelled fort;
a clutch of collars and fine helmets
   beside the deadly sharp spars.

Blue spears on the swift barques' shoulders
  as they're loading by the shore,
a strong, sturdy fence of weapons,
  a set of shields on the barques' boards.

Fair tender women on the ships' floors,
  a lofty bed for a refined maid,
chequered rugs are set out for them,
  beds where each may lie alone.

Brindled throws of silk and sendal,
  like rushes strew the ships' floors;
Suibhne's crow with its chosen course,
  a red silk banner above each mast.

With firm gauntlet, with heavy belt,
  down in our skiffs, before setting sail,
the fierce faultless warriors there
  of Ireland's fair tall kindred's plains.

That warrior's like was never heard,
  the heroes' chief who sets them to task;
they had Ireland's golden champions,
  for the slim-fingered, bright, fierce band.

No less to them a ship of the fleet,
  when horses and cows are drowned,
no horse, no cow left, no gifts—
  yet no land's not been sacked by them.

They'd never neglect one of their ships,
  full of strength and firm reliance,
their golden, black-crested masts
  which they raise in the harbour's eddies.

Many a man with sword or breastplate,
  many a fit man, surpassing his leap,
against the mane of the mad, fierce ocean
  hitting the smooth-peaked ships' height.

Who is this who sails the war-fleet
  towards glowery hilled Castle Sween?
A bowstring man who shuns no arrow,
  rugged, notched and shapely spear.

Eoin Mac Suibhne sails the fleet
   across the sea's ridge, stout the chief,
shapely the ships as they're thrown high,
   trying the waves of the fierce sea.

A straight wind they have behind them,
   at Cill Achaidh, at the strand's end;
their speckled sails are billowing,
   foam sprays against the barques' flanks.

Eoin's found a fine anchorage
   in Knapdale's heart, the barques' journey;
shapely, lush-haired, fort-rich eyebrow,
   keen radiant man with masts and warriors.

Let us, at the walls of Alba,
   give welcome to his smooth breast;
handsome, that crimson company;
   for us he drips down fulsome dew.

The streams of Sliabh Monaidh welcome
   Mac Suibhne of Sliabh Mis;
shoals of fish come from the inlets,
   he's dealt his share of the jutting coast.

Branches bend their knees beneath them,
   they welcome our music-rich lord,
fruit of health, each harbour's hazel,
   weighty the welcome they give Eoin.

The learned men of Alba come,
   they welcome the warrior of Mis,
Satirists from the sea of Man
   have bade him welcome in verse.

Usual, their splendid dispute,
   their songs, the tale of Fionn's warriors;
they recognise the rightful giver,
   as befits Eoin's proper status.

Each one sits, in Castle Sween,
   under Cruachan's fierce-speared hawk,
about that encampment, the fair man
   of the plain of Lorg, fresh with herbs.

His two spears which pierce his foe's side,
    like snake poison, his shaft's wound;
the sleek sword, in Guaire's heir's charge—
    by it foreign shoulders are stripped.

I greet Mac Suibhne's rock fortress,
    I see the splendid fort of stones,
a man who'd show their skulls no quarter,
    tall proper ward of swirling cloak.

Splendid ward in a well-knit breastplate
    guarding the brown plated hauberk;
he took Rathlin, low-crested, jagged,
    smooth-topped, white-stoned, steep and sturdy.

The one sword that's best in Europe,
    he's longest, following a rout,
what shield in the world would he not crush,
    fearless lord of Clann Cairm.

Eoin Mac Suibhne, stout of spear,
    with his slim sword, lord's fury
noble, whose shield's a dark-pied shield,
    a welcome lord, harsh the meeting.

The Epitaph of Robert Bruce (1329) Latin

Bower records the epitaph of Robert Bruce, written some years after his death on 7 June, 1329. The poet's praise of the dead king begins with generalisations, identifying him with a long list of both biblical and classical hero figures, but then moves on to particular events in Bruce's life: his life as a guerrilla leader and his victory at Bannockburn ('the king is put to flight'); his victory over Edward II at Byland in Yorkshire in 1322; the peace agreement concluded at Bishopthorpe on 30 May, 1323 or the Treaty of Edinburgh in 1328 (the 'solemn truce'), and the collapse of the peace plan in 1332–33 ('peace suffers a reverse').

Robert Bruce, the nation's virtue, lies in the earth;
bold and righteous prince of joy, in all his ways most sure.
A Paris he was in shapeliness, a Hector renowned for his sword,
royal rose of soldiery, a Socrates, Maro or Cato in his words.

Begotten of Priam, like Achilles the leader of Greeks,
praiseworthy as Ajax, many-talented like Ulysses,
beloved as the Macedonian, like Arthur a jewel among men,
a leader of the peoples, a Maccabeus for intelligence.

Upright like Aeneas, like Pompey's his total command,
gentle as Saint Andrew, like Jonathan his might was admired.
This Saturn gives nobility to the Cretan shores, while rain
which crossed the Aegean flees, and summer flowers again.

He was a Julius Caesar, in hope he was like Simeon,
outstanding king like Charles, with the wisdom of a Solomon.
A law-giver like Gaius, leader in the power of Dido's love,
a Jason at heart, honest as Sejus, spirited spring of Helicon.

His was the strength of Samson and the blood of Bartholomew,
firm his faith like Simon's, a casket of Sabaean incense.
Always gracious in his gifts, born of royal ancestors
under Juno's Jupiter, he was the very bright daystar.

Lamenting the loss of the royal rights of Scots-born men,
postponing idle pleasures, he left his old sweet life for a
                                                    bitter regimen.
Cold he suffered, and for sleep he lay in dens of wild beasts,
while for his food he did not refuse the fruit of acorn-laden trees.

For the protection of his rights he placed his only hope in Christ,
hiding himself in the thorny bush, drinking water, never wines.
With his strong comrades in the assault, he seemed a fierce
                                                    wild boar,
and thus he earned his royal throne, wore down the
                                                    enemy's spear.

At this man's warrior-thrust a host of evil-doers falls;
on the iron-armoured backs of men his wounds are cruel.
He sharpens the weapons of war, sword raging at a host
                                                    of knights:
this one falls, that one dies, and their king is put to flight.

In good order the king of Scots brings his standard forth,
fighting mightily he bears it through a thick-packed host.
To boundless praise he triumphs mightily over the foe,
and sent him homewards, the English king, as our new lyric goes.

When he is made lord of Byland, joyful victory is prepared,
the host in flight is ravaged, and the slaughter multiplied.
A solemn truce is covenanted, but the peace agreed is false.
After the death of the reverend king, peace suffers a reverse.

O what grief among the people! Alas, our grief is doubled.
Every eye is given to weeping while disorder multiplies.
He who in the royal roll was counted flower of kings,
now in a muddy little place is laid as food for worms.

He himself was a shining light before the darkness of our eyes,
the glory which gave fragrant variance to the buds of flowers,
a mirror spread before the people, a rose, a moral guide,
sating men's hearts with sweetness, he was their holy food.

This outstanding king was like a bracelet on our arms,
a precious ring or a jewel in the ear of noble men,
a twisted torque which folk may wear around their throats—
now he lies below, stripped of towering glory's robes.

What is worldly reward or honour? Where is the glory of things?
What worth has the kingdom's throne, or the lovely savour
                                                    of beauty?
What worth have all our talents? – I speak the truth, for sure –
at the end of a man's days, high office has meaning no more.

Scotland, weep piously; for all you love draw deep sighs
in your native voice, and call to mind that glorious king.
Pray the Ruler of the Heavens, pray the Sun of Justice,
to grant him all good things, joy there in Paradise.

FRAGMENTS OF VERSE ON RULERS IN THE ISLES
(c. 14th century) Gaelic

These fragments are from a tract on metrical faults of the late 14th century, the same which contains the verse on David son of Mael Coluim translated above. It is difficult to identify with certainty the individuals described in these pieces, but they certainly seem to come from the work of poets working for the ruling families of the Hebrides, the descendants of Somerled.

Mac Ruaidhrí
Mac Ruaidhrí, king of the islands,
  with bright cheek,
lovely your head above your collar,
  it's your nature.

Aenghus Mac Ruaidhrí
Myself and Mac Ruaidhrí will travel
  and we will arrive in Kells;
Aenghus gave no learning
  to Ó Domhnaill, good hired hand.

Donnchadh
Great the tale, Donnchadh's passing,
  in Ireland and Alba;
the women of both Gael and stranger
  would keen him for the alliance.

Unhelpful
They did not help Arran's folk,
the clan of great Man's smith.

Fearchar Ó Maíl Chiaráin
The Blackthorn Brooch (14th century?) Gaelic

This poet is likely to be the one lamented by his father in the following poem; at any rate he is likely to be related to him in some way. We cannot be sure when he lived, though it could well be as early as the 14th century. If so, this is an early example, and certainly the earliest Scottish one, of the type of love poem, intricate and clever, termed in Classical Irish *dánta grádha*.

In the cloak on this fair breast
this blackthorn brooch would not be,
   if there were, sweet red-lipped Mór,
   any gold brooch in Ireland.

Not right to put in this cloak
aught but a noble white-bronze brooch,
   or a wondrous worked-gold brooch,
   my sweet-worded, red-lipped Mór.

Lush your hair, round amber's aspect –
to put that in your cloak, gold-flecked,
   steady arch who cheats no one,
   not fit's a brooch of blackthorn.

Let none be put, my heart's nut,
in your pied, yellow-striped cloak,
   red cheek who would take a pledge,
   but a brooch which Goibhniu made.

Scarlet cheek which I loved:
throughout the years, until now,
   pure grasp, scarce would your green cloak
   be seen with no golden brooch.

Ó MAÍL CHIARÁIN
Lament for Fearchar Ó Maíl Chiaráin
(14th century?) Gaelic

This father's lament for his son is one of the masterpieces of medieval Gaelic poetry. We do not know the poet's first name, only that he was the father of a son called Fearchar (perhaps the author of the preceding poem), who left Scotland for a poetry tour in Ireland and was killed there. If the Lí referred to in the poem in connection with Fearchar is, as seems likely, Beinn Lí on Skye, then the family may have been from there. All this we know only from the internal evidence of the poem. It is possible that the poem dates from later than the 14th century.

Great lack has come upon me,
  the beacon's body-blow has bent me.
My child's been snatched from my aid,
  my right hand's been struck from me.

Hid, the light of his freckled cheeks,
  constant its grief in my heart;
alas, my son is no more,
  bright branch, once beneath my cloak.

My body is without guide,
  my soul is in the grave;
I've no hope for my one son,
  fresh soil's thin cloak on his cheek.

His mother's wail across the great sea –
  all are listless in her house –
the sound of her keen lament for Ó Maíl
  is the blackbird's cry seeking her young.

It has made blood of my heart.
  Since that day, I am laid low.
Though he has a house of clay,
  longer is my day than his.

My comrade crossed the great sea,
  and I from the shore to my house:
foolish, that delay of mine,
  parting from his fair freckled cheek.

I reached Ireland, walled by waves—
  sluggish my tryst cross the sea—
sad my visit to the fair place:
  I thought my soul would be there.

I was mad not to go with my dear
  across the red-hued sea of glens.
Now he's gone there'll be no joy,
  I was wrong not to guard my chick.

Fresh-haired Fearchar lives no more,
  he'd have charmed women on his way.
My gift-giving man has gone,
  he herds no cattle to my house.

No one comes from east or west
  to my house with horse or gold;
every poet chances on me
  but the great bright young tender one.

You folk who felled the bright branch
  and let his blood on the blade,
the man made you no satire or slight:
  not yours, to wound his white side.

Far from his fine corpse, his friends;
  folk do not stop to talk of him.
Hair, fair-yellow, furrowed and curled,
  far from him those who'd tend him.

Ó Maíl Chiaráin, my fresh fruit,
  my lime-washed sun-house, my branch of nuts.
There's a sleepless crowd in my house,
  the women and men who were his.

Not music, once the news had spread,
  the lament each one made for him.
My house was in a wretched way:
  one bewails him, another faints.

His mother's weeping was great
  till her strength and colour waned;
spent was her flesh, lamenting him:
  it's bad that she was not barren.

My son is my own death,
    a torment, the branch in the tomb;
his death will bring me to the grave,
    dreadful that it's from me he grew.

Though all those good men were keen,
    any stranger was a trifle to them.
His avenging, he got it not:
    the kings of Irishmen failed.

Beer stems not my sorrow's power;
    my eyes are darkened and blind.
My chest is a grid of bare bones,
    heavy now and filled with sighs.

With music, my grief does not ebb;
    it is not likely to leave me.
No woman soothes my pain, no feast,
    nor the sound of kings' great horns.

It has weakened all our youths,
    they hear no cuckoo, our clan.
His fresh face and his smooth sole
    under others' soil, folk find sad.

Many the wounds from his love
    through my body, front and back;
pains are darkening my cheeks,
    a cold jab of grief through my chest.

My fine son's side is here
    sharing with brown beetles one slab.
A beetle will jab its head in my flesh:
    sadder to me, the side it's pierced.

My son's journey west across the sea
    lay, a grave-slab on my heart.
You'd have got wealth without selling poems;
    sad, son, that you took up verse.

Foreigners slew my fine son,
    my dear, the sweet soft-palmed sprig;
son, though I might have no herds,
    it's sad that we don't own your grave.

Dear the foot, not heavy its step,
   dear the sole, like berries' flower;
dear the slim leg and white palm,
   alike, Fearchar's hand and foot.

Alas, a bad journey this,
   my shifting from place to place:
now stretched out upon his grave,
   now, his grave against my breast.

No one's sermons can sink in
   for the sleek white sweet-voiced branch.
'Everyone grieves for their sons':
   what use for any to tell me?

It seems my sense is no use,
   with me, grief-struck on his track;
like pale froth on a cold ford,
   I'm a sad shade, listless, sapped.

Grief for Ó Maíl Chiaráin's in my frame,
   I'm sent astray by his death.
Though I've not died from it on his grave,
   why should clay not cover my flesh?

For God's sake notice me, King!
   From keening, my head will lose its eyes.
Do my tears move you, God?
   Look at me, without son or wife.

The fine lad's slaying is a loss,
   his earth-bound stone, a loss to me.
Wrong has come from the death he got;
   his leaving was grievous to me.

Fearchar's death wastes my eyes;
   I'm like a smith without tongs.
It took from me livestock and land;
   sad that he's struck to the ground.

The Lord's made a damaging raid,
   he's sprung at me from every side:
childless, the Lord has made me,
   he did not take only half.

314

God has not granted my due,
  though a young kindred, my clan.
I'm the branch that's lost its nut,
  I have no grandson, no son.

Reciting his death-song: a dreadful day.
  May it profit him who got it.
Sad that evil's my prize for it:
  it took eye, ear and hand from me.

Going to his grave every day
  has blackened my heart and my flesh;
though Fearchar's grave may grow green,
  I will cut it every time.

I threw a shoe over a house,
  speaking the bright-red brown-haired one's name;
a man ran across to see
  if it had landed top under sole.

Quickly you took him from me,
  the son you gave me, God.
Since he I speak of is gone,
  I defy you now, God.

My son was new-fledged and young,
  fairer than any mother's son;
to buy heaven for a drink—
  the drink-giving cow's in my house.

My heart's foaming in my breast,
  keen and tearful is my seat.
His strange face has gouged my eyes.
  My tears for him are heart's juice.

Many the streams down my face;
  woe that I'm not snatched by death.
I am the tree who has shed its fruit,
  my crop, never fully grown.

House that's around the fair corpse,
  grave, you take my bravery from me.
Bothy where he'd make his poems,
  alas that I see you from here.

Childless now, it seems so long,
  tormented, among the graves.
No children will my wife bear:
  we will be trees without roots.

Each time I weep for Li's branch,
  crying, it seems that I ask:
that woman who stopped him not,
  God, did she have a son?

Alas, this mourning is false:
  it shames me that I don't die from it.
Weak is my body and heart:
  it's wrong that it does not kill me.

This poet, grass growing through him,
  my heart, the deceitless mouth:
fine branch, without wish or joy,
  green earth's thin cloak on the bough.

I weep for him every day;
  nothing occupies me now.
His elegy maddened me,
  God, it's a chore for my soul.

God got no permission from me
  for the deed: he took, as he made.
I don't thank the King who gave him:
  he stole from me the one he gave.

POETRY FROM THE INCHCOLM ANTIPHONER
(partly 14th century) Latin

A 14th-century manuscript in Edinburgh University Library contains a number of poems, some of which date from around the time when the manuscript was made, while the age of others is hard to assess and may be a good deal earlier. The *Inchcolm Antiphoner*, named after the island monastery in the Forth which is dedicated to St Columba, *Innis Choluim*, contains prayers and musical settings for the feast of the patron saint, as well as some for the recently established feast of *Corpus Christi*. The Columban material draws on familiar images of the saint as protector of Scotland, a guarantor of kingship and sea-miracle specialist, alongside the more usual saintly characteristics of miracles, personal holiness and sound doctrine.

Hymn

Dawn shines red-gold, daylight's herald
stirs us up in joy from sleep,
glad to keep this famous feast
of venerable Columba.

Humble he was, gentle and kind,
a man of joyful face, and worthy of honour,
a man of noble birth, steadfast demeanour,
chaste his body and his mind.

Columba's merits and the wonders he worked,
his prophetic deeds, his famous miracles—
of all these no one can fully know how
to write in script or speak in words.

Leaving behind his beloved Irish home,
by Christ's grace he came to Britain.
Through him, the king of Britain's race
received life's proper new beginning.

Our nation's father, excellent pastor,
grant us, Columba, hope of forgiveness,
and from the stain of all our sins
cleanse us, holy Columba.

May you bring us forgiveness of sin,
wash clean the guilty, endow the land,

and us your servants and all catholic folk
commend to the glorious King.

Praise perpetual may there be, glory always
to the Father, the Son, and the Holy Paraclete,
to the one and only Lord who rules over all,
for ever, for all ages.
                                        Amen.

Magnificat Antiphon
God's confessor, O precious dove,
help the faithful who stand by you,
and never allow them to lack God's help
who fly to your protection.

Magnificat Antiphon
Hail! our splendour and our patron,
hail, O righteous radiance,
teacher of right doctrine,
good shepherd and vessel of grace.
O Columba, dove-like one
of happy memory,
make us forever
heirs of your glory.

Benedictus Antiphon
Father Columba, splendour of our ways,
receive your servants' offerings.
Save the choir which sings your praise
from the assaults of Englishmen
and from the taunts of foes.

Memorial of St Columba
Mouth of the dumb,
light of the blind,
foot of the lame,
to the fallen stretch out your hand.
Strengthen the senseless,
restore the mad.
O Columba, hope of Scots,
by your merits' mediation
make us companions
of the blessed angels.
        Alleluia.

Responsory

O Columba, our glorious leader,
cleanse our minds, lest the noxious deceiver
harm your servants by the sea's danger,
    that around you they may gladly sing.
For you, above all others, it is right that you should hear
voices raised in joy. To this place bend your ear,
    that around you may they gladly sing.

A Prayer of Gratitude for the Men of Bute
(c. 1334) Latin

Devotion to Saint Brendan in that part of the country earned the Bute folk the
name of 'Brandans'. When a group of nearly unarmed Brandans were
ambushed by the men of the sheriff, Sir Alan de Lyle, they picked up stones
and defended themselves so successfully that they even killed the sheriff,
whose head was then presented to their lord, Robert Stewart. This poem on
the Brandans of Bute was written around 1334. It is one of the poems recorded
in Walter Bower's *Scotichronicon*.

These Brandans, O King of Heaven, I beg you to preserve,
by whom are embellished the deeds recorded here.

Beseech that saint, I pray, whom you do humbly serve,
that he protect and direct you, and bide with you forever.

A POEM ON THE CAUSE OF THE PLAGUE OF 1349
(c. 1349) Latin

'In 1349 there was a great plague and mortality of the folk of the kingdom of Scotland', writes Walter Bower in the subsequent century, adding that it killed nearly a third of the population, which was certainly true in some areas. This was the Black Death, a horrifying epidemic that had spread across Europe in the previous two years. Many people thought, as Bower did, that the plague was a consequence of sin.

It is for our sin that widespread ruin now enters in.
The evil we do – alas! that the world should love it so.
Death will run wild, for our ancient crimes, round the world.
Near out of my mind you'd think me, if I told you again:
Death runs his dire course – death everywhere, throughout
                                                    the earth.

NOTES

Prayer for Protection (Parce Domine)
Source: Bernard and Atkinson (1898), vol. i, 22–23.

Mugint also appears in *Lives* of various Irish saints: the *Life of Frigidianus of Lucca*, in Colgan, *Acta Sanctorum Hiberniae* (1645) Mar. 18. and cf. Wilson (1964). He was apparently a monk of Whithorn. Though he has no *Life* of his own, he appears in the *Lives* of other saints. For a discussion of these appearances, and his possible identity with other characters, see Bernard and Atkinson (1898), vol. ii, 112–113.

The Gododdin (A-text)
Source: Williams (1938); Jackson (1969); Jarman (1988).

N.B. This translation was completed before the publication of John T. Koch's recent edition, though some limited use was made of his earlier notes in Koch (1995).

The numbers of the stanzas here are those of the stanzas in the actual manuscript, which has only once, alas, been followed before as a means of describing the verses, in Jackson (1969). Stanzas 1–39 correspond to those under Roman numerals in Williams. For the subsequent stanzas, the numbers in Williams have been noted, e.g. CA LXVI. Where stanzas in the A-text correspond in any way to the B-text, these have been noted with reference to the translation in this volume, e.g. B 18.

Four stanzas in the A-text are obvious interpolations and therefore excluded from the translation. CA XLVII is a stanza belonging to the Llywarch Hen cycle and has not been translated for this volume. CA LV is a reciter's prologue; CA LLXXIX concerns a battle that took place some years after Catraeth; CA LXXXVIII is a poem for a small boy; translations of these follow *The Gododdin* in the present collection.

4. There is a play on the hero's name Gwefrfawr, 'rich in amber'. The stanza, like some others, is incomplete. Ysgyrran's son may be Mynyddawg.
9. The hero of this stanza is named elsewhere as Llifiau (A 22) and Llif (B 11), referred to in the latter as coming from 'beyond Bannawg' and therefore a Pict.

10. In this stanza, as in others, the hero is not named, presumably because some lines of the original poem were lost in transmission.

16. The stanza plays on the hero's name, Blaen, meaning 'foremost', 'first'.

20. B 10.

21. This stanza may well have belonged originally to the chain of stanzas 8–11, but it is not impossible that the opening line of those stanzas was later repeated. The three men are presumably those named in stanza 18.

22. B 11.

23. B 9.

25. It was customary for the ruler to distribute gifts on New Year's Day.

26. B 16.

34. The hero's name in the last line may be 'Wid', which could be Pictish.

37. This stanza is §57 in the A-text, where it is conspicuously out of place. I have followed Williams and Jarman in restoring it to the chain begun with stanza 34. This seemed a necessary step, whereas moving stanza 21 to the chain of 8–11 would have been more doubtful.

38. B 28.

39. B 29. Stanza 53 in the A-text (CA XXXIX B) repeats this stanza, except that the first line is replaced by a variation of the opening lines of the stanzas following 53: 'Ready warriors rose for combat / To Catraeth, swift spirited war-host.' Since this appears to be a scribal error, I have excluded that stanza from this translation.

40. CA XLII, B 28.

41. CA XLIII, B 3.

42. CA XLIV, B 4.

43. CA XLV, B 23, 33.

44. CA XLVI.

45. CA XLVIII. This stanza and the following, with their references to the poet's having been imprisoned and rescued, may be later interpolations from a saga about Aneirin. In any case, the line 'I, not I, Aneirin' (*mi na vi aneirin*) is puzzling. If the stanza is from a saga, then the later poet may be noting his use of dramatic monologue; if it is in the original poem, Aneirin may be distinguishing between his ordinary warrior self and his role as poet. Since the verb 'sang' (*ceint*), here as elsewhere, can refer either to composing or reciting the

poem, it is also possible that the line was interpolated by a later reciter.

46. CA XLIX.
47. CA L.
48. CA LI, B 1, 22.
49. CA LII.
50. CA LIII. This stanza may be an interpolation from another poem, since it would seem from the final lines to be unrelated to the material of *The Gododdin*. These lines are interpreted in Williams as referring to the Deirans being driven into hiding; the present translation follows Jarman and Jackson.
51. CA LIV, B 5.
52. CA LVI.
53. CA LVII.
54. CA LVIII.
55. CA LIX.
56. CA LX.
57. CA LXI, B 18.
58. CA LXII.
59. CA LXIII, B 12, 13, 14, 34.
60. CA LXIV, B 38.
61. CA LXV.
62. CA LXVI, B 37.
63. CA LXVII, B 40.
64. CA LXVIII. Williams, Jackson and Jarman accept *merch eudaf hir* as the reading, and speculate on whether this could refer to Mynyddawg's wife. The present translation is based on the conjecture that *merch* was a scribal error for *meirch*, which admittedly does not do much to clarify what seems to be only part of an original stanza. The wearing of purple may suggest Roman imperial lineage.
65. CA LXIX, B 27.
66. CA LXX, B 31.
67. CA LXXI, B 30.
68. CA LXXII.
69. CA LXXIII.
70. CA LXXIV.
71. CA LXXV, B 35.
72. CA LXXVI.
73. CA LXXVII.
74. CA LXXVIII.
75. CA LXXX.

76. CA LXXXI.
77. CA LXXXII.
78. CA LXXXIII.
79. CA LXXXIV.
80. CA LXXXV.
81. CA LXXXVI.
82. CA LXXXVII, B 2.
83. CA LXXXIX. The A-text scribe ended his copying of the poem with this stanza, leaving the remainder of the page and the following page blank, an indication that he was aware his text was incomplete. The later B-text scribe began copying a different and earlier text of the poem at the end of the A-text.

The Gododdin (B-text)
Source: Williams (1938); Jackson (1969); Jarman (1988)

The number of each stanza in Williams has been noted, e.g. CA LXIII D. Where stanzas in the B-text correspond in any way to the A-text, these have been noted with reference to the translation in the present volume, e.g. A 59.

The opening two stanzas in the B-text are clearly additions to the original poem and have therefore been excluded from the translation. The first deals with a later battle; the second is a reciter's prologue; translations of both follow *The Gododdin* in the present collection.

1. CA LI C, A 48. See also B 22 and the note.
2. CA LXXXVII B, A 82.
3. CA XLIII B, A 41.
4. CA XLIV B, A 42.
5. CA LIV B, A 51.
6. CA XC.
7. CA XCI.
8. CA XCII.
9. CA XXIII B, A 23.
10. CA XX B, A 20.
11. CA XXII B, A 22. See also A 9 for another stanza on this hero.
12. CA LXIII D, A 59.
13. CA LXIII B, A 59. This stanza seems to be a truncated version of B 12 except for the final line naming a different warrior, rather than one stanza in a chain using the same opening lines. See also B 34.

14. CA LXIII C, A 59. The first two lines of this stanza have been excluded as a probable interpolation, since the original presumably repeated the opening line of stanzas 12 and 13. Jackson translates the omitted lines as: 'The bright flood, the grey wolf, the terrible following water.'
15. CA XCIII.
16. CA XXVI B, A 26.
17. CA XCIV.
18. CA LXI B, A 57.
19. CA XCV.
20. CA XCVI.
21. CA XCVII.
22. CA LI B, A 48. This appears to be another version of B 1 rather than a different stanza repeating the opening and closing lines. In both cases the text is extremely corrupt.
23. CA XLV B, A 43.
24. CA XCVIII.
25. CA XCIX.
26. CA C.
27. CA LXIX B, A 65. The final line is missing but has been presumed from A 65.
28. CA XL, A 40.
29. CA XLI.
30. CA LXXI B, A 67.
31. CA LXX B, A 66.
32. CA CI.
33. CA XLV C, A 43. See B 23, with which this stanza presumably once formed a chain, if it is not another version of it.
34. CA LXIII E, A 59. See B 12 and 13
35. CA LXXV B, A 71.
36. CA CII. The stanza contains the earliest reference to Arthur as a British hero, although it has been argued that the line referring to him is a later interpolation.
37. CA LXVI B, A 62.
38. CA LXIV B, A 60.
39. CA CIII. Third Fearsome One: there is a traditional triad concerning *Tri Engiriol*, the 'Three Fearsome [or Violent, or Terrible] Ones of Britain'. See Bromwich (1961), 196.
40. CA LXVII B, A 63. The B-text breaks off in the middle of the last word of the second line of this stanza. Three vellum folios, i.e. six pages, were cut out at the end of the manuscript, so that it is uncertain how much is missing from the B-text.

Prologue(s) to The Gododdin
Source: Williams (1938), LV A & B; Jarman (1988) 1

Dwywai's son: Aneirin.

The Battle of Gwen Ystrad
Source: Williams (1968) II.

Since Catraeth in this poem is under Urien's rule, one must perhaps envisage Urien's overlordship of the region around Catterick. We know Catterick was occupied by Germanic people by the mid sixth century, but that fact is not incompatible with British overlordship. Who the enemy of the battle of Gwen Ystrad is is uncertain.

Idon's lavish wine: the river was red with blood.

In Praise of Urien
Source: Williams (1968) III.

Urien is praised in this poem both as a defender of the Britons against the English and as a kind of high king, powerful enough to control the neighbouring British rulers.

The Court of Urien
Source: Williams (1968) IV.

The War-Band's Return
Source: Williams (1968) V.

Sir Ifor Williams suggested that the poem is best read as a dramatic monologue in which the poet's fears for his ruler's life are interrupted by Urien's safe return. The cattle-raid is against another British kingdom, Manaw, which lay in the region around modern-day Falkirk, in central Scotland. Its name is still preserved in place-names such as Slamannan and Clackmannan.

Not one sneeze or two: the idea that numbers of sneezes purported good or ill fortune was common in the early Middle Ages, in Ireland, Wales and Europe as well. As an Irish poem puts it, expressing a Christian opposition to such divination, 'That someone should sneeze in an assembly does not stop me from setting out on a journey.' (Greene and O'Connor (1967) 162–63).

The Battle of Argoed Llwyfain
Source: Williams (1968) VI.

The battle was with Angles from Bernicia and Deira, led by 'Fflamddwyn', whose name ('flame-bringer') may refer to his burning of British settlements or may be a translation of his Anglo-Saxon name. Owain is one of Urien's sons, presumably the eldest; he is called 'bane of the East' because the Anglo-Saxons were 'easterners' in their continental origins and their occupation of British territory.

In Praise of Rheged
Source: Williams (1968) VII, 1–29, 42–57.

This may originally have been two, or even three, poems. The middle section has been omitted as being unrelated and in any case hopelessly obscure and corrupt. The first section or incomplete poem apparently dealt with the rise of Rheged under Ulph and Urien, after a disastrous period of decline, the last with a particular battle.

It is unclear whether Ulph is Urien's ally, his war-leader, or perhaps even a name for Urien himself. The name may be from the Latin name *Ulpius*, or might just possibly be Anglo-Saxon. If the latter, it could be a Welsh version of the Anglo-Saxons' nickname for Urien, 'the Wolf', just as one of the Bernician kings was called by the Welsh *Fflamddwyn* 'flame-bringer', and another *Fflessawr* 'twister'.

The Spoils of Taliesin
Source: Williams (1968) VIII.

The original poem probably ends or breaks off at line 30, 'Like a treasure-rich sea is Urien', since what follows seems to be another poem, not necessarily by Taliesin, despite the line referring to his spoils. This is the only poem dealing with Urien that does not end with the refrain.

Plea for Reconciliation
Source: Williams (1968) IX.

The cause of Urien's displeasure is not known, though the poem refers at one point to mocking Urien's age. Sir Ifor Williams suggested that he may have been offended by Taliesin's visits to

328

other courts and praise of other rulers, perhaps his two eulogies of Gwallawg. However, travel to other courts was common in the Middle Ages. In later Welsh poetic tradition, this type of reconciliation poem became something of a conceit, a way of poets entering the patronage of a new lord, and that may be all that is involved here.

Elegy for Owain ab Urien
Source: Williams (1968) X.

It would seem from this poem that Owain survived his father Urien, for whom no elegy survives. For the reference to Fflamddwyn, see Taliesin's earlier poem on the battle of Argoed Llwyfain.

In Praise of Gwallawg
Source: Williams (1968) XI.

Elegy for Gwallawg
Source: Williams (1968) XII.

The middle section, ll. 28–41, containing corrupt fragments of a different and probably unrelated poem, has been omitted. The final section may be part of a different poem to Gwallawg, since it does not seem to be in the elegiac mode of the first section.

A lord says not 'No': A proper ruler does not simply dismiss a suppliant's request.

Dinogad's Coat
Source: Williams (1938) LXXXVIII; Jarman (1988), 103.

Derwennydd Falls: recent research by Geraint Gruffydd has shown that this is almost certainly Lodore Force, at Derwentwater in Cumbria. Since this area was under Anglian occupation by the 680s, this song was probably composed before then. See Gruffydd (1990).

The High Creator (Altus Prosator)
Source: C. Blume (1908) 275–83.

See Clancy and Márkus (1995) 39–68, for Latin text, translation, and extensive discussion of the background and theological character of the poem, together with some of the sources used by the poet.

Helper of Workers (Adiutor Laborantium)
Source: British Library Cotton Manuscript Galba A, xiv.

See Clancy and Márkus (1995) 72–80, for original Latin text, commentary and discussion; Muir (1988) 40–41.

The use of the word *homunculus*, 'little man', in line 16 is interesting. It is rare in texts prior to this one, and is used occasionally by Adomnán. And Adomnán's own name can also be translated as 'little man', reading *Adom* as the Hebrew for 'man' and *-án* as a diminutive Gaelic suffix. Indeed the *Sanas Cormaic* does gloss Adomnán's name thus: *homunculus*. Is this a clue as to the authorship or to the place of origin?

In the manuscript there is a slight lacuna in the last few lines.

Prayer for Protection from Lightning (Noli Pater)
Source: Bernard and Atkinson (1897) i, 88; Clancy and Márkus (1995) 84–95.

Elegy for Colum Cille
Sources: Clancy and Márkus (1995) 96–128; W. Stokes (1899).

In Praise of Colum Cille
Sources: Clancy and Márkus (1995) 129–43; F. Kelly (1973).

For full commentary, see Clancy and Márkus (1995).

The final verse is in a slightly different metre and may be a later addition.

Last Verses in Praise of Colum Cille
Sources: Clancy and Márkus (1995) 146–51; F. Kelly (1975).

Gaelic elegiac verses
1. Sources: AU, AT 622; Greene and O'Connor (1967) 108–9.
2. Sources: AT, CS 625; Anderson (1926) i. 147–48.

The annals record that Mongán, son of the king of Dál nAraide and also overking of Ulster, was killed with a stone by Artúr son of Bicoir, a Briton (or a Pict). The poem is attributed to a later king of Ulster, Becc Bairche (†718), but there is no evidence for or against his authorship. He died in religious pilgrimage.

The Battle of Strathcarron
Source: Williams (1938), LXXIX A & B; Jarman (1988), 102.

Nwython's grandson: Ywain, son of Beli, son of Nwython.

The Battle of Dunnichen
Source: Radner (1978) 54.

Breo: the final line is uncertain, but rhyme, and other sources indicate that we should posit an unknown place-name in eastern Scotland here.

Elegy for Bruide, son of Bile (Bridei, son of Beli †693)
Sources: Herbert and Ó Riain (1988) 58; Clancy and Márkus (1995) 166–67.

Prayer to Colum Cille
Sources: Clancy and Márkus (1995) 164–76.

Iona
Source: Herbert and Ó Riain (1988) 60–61.

On Cú Chuimne
Source: AU, s.a. 747.

On Garbán Mide
Source: O'Donovan (1868) 81; Meyer (1912) 53.

Hymn for the Virgin Mary (Cantemus in Omne Die)
Source: Bernard and Atkinson (1897) i, 33–34; Clancy and Márkus (1995) 179–92 for Latin text and detailed commentary.

On Almsgiving
Source: Wasserschleben (1885) 38–39. Commentary, Márkus (1998).
   Most of the poem also appears in a slightly later collection of homilies now known as the *Catechesis Celtica*.

Probable biblical sources include: for line 2, 2 Cor. 9:10; line 3, Tobit 4:11; 12: 9; line 7, Luke 11: 41; line 16, Acts 10: 4; line 19, we suspect an echo of Matthew 6:2: 'When you give alms, do not have it trumpeted before you, for this is what the hypocrites do. Your almsgiving must be in secret, and your Father who sees all that is done in secret will reward you.' The last line cites Ecclesiasticus 3: 33.

The Dream of the Road

1. The Ruthwell Cross Crucifixion Poem
Sources: Swanton (1970); Howlett (1976); Ó Carragáin (1987–88).

I have used some of David Howlett's suggestions to fill in the lacunae, indicated in brackets, but others seemed too uncertain.

2. The Dream of the Rood
Sources: Pope (1981); Swanton (1970); Dickins and Ross (1934); Bennett (1984) 26–31; Crossley-Holland (1984) 200–204; Kennedy (1952) 93–97.

The Miracles of St Nynia the Bishop
Source: Strecker 943–61, with some emendations noted by Winifred McQueen (1960). There is only one manuscript of the poem, an 11th-century volume, *Codex Bambergensis*, BII, 10.

See McQueen (1961); Broun (1991); MacQuarrie (1997) 50–73; Hill (1997) for reflections on the Nynia dossier.

Tudvael (or variously Thevahel, Tuduehal, Tuduvallus, Tudwal). We cannot ascertain who this king was. The story is probably told as an illustration and dreadful warning of what happens to kings who oppose Nynia (or his successor bishops of Whithorn). It is possible that, when this story was composed, the dreadful warning was aimed at a particular royal house which traced its ancestry to a king of this name. If there is a historical basis to the story, King Tudwal of Strathclyde is a likely candidate. He flourished in the mid sixth century and was the father of Rydderch Hael, the British king who was, according to Adomnán (*VC*, i, 15), a friend of St Columba. Túathal Maelgarb, a progenitor of the southern Uí Néill (†544) has also been posited.

Hymn for Saint Nynia the Bishop
Source: Strecker (1923).
See also McQueen (1990) 10–11 and passim.

Gaelic Verses on Kings of the Picts
1. *On Óengus (son of Fergus)*
Source: Thurneysen (1891) 33; Meyer (1919) 6–7.
2. *On the death of Cinaed son of Ailpín*
Source: Radner (1978) 112–13; Meyer (1919) 47.

Gaelic Satirical Poems
1. *On Gille-Phádraig*
Source: Thurneysen (1891) 104.
2. *On Eithne, daughter of Domhnall*
Source: Thurneysen (1891) 72; Meyer (1919) 20; Greene and O'Connor (1967) 202–204.

Turf-Einar is praised for killing some pirates
Source: Finnur Jónsson A I, p. 177; *Orkneyinga Saga* v. 1, p. 11.

In the saga, Einar is said to have been sent to the Orkneys by his father Rognvald to clear out the Vikings, who were using them as a base for raiding Norway.

Avenging his father
Source: Finnur Jónsson A I, pp. 31–2;
Orkneyinga Saga, p. 12, v. 2; 15, v. 5; 14, v. 4; 15–16, v. 6; 13, v. 3.

Earl Rognvald was, according to tradition, Harald Fairhair's right-hand man in the unification of Norway.

Poetry of Orm Barreyjarskjald
Source: Finnur Jónsson A I, p. 143.

Hafgerdingadrapa
Source: Finnur Jónsson A I, p. 177.

The Death-Song for Eirik Bloodaxe (Eiríksmal)
Source: Finnur Jónsson A I, pp. 174–75.

the grey wolf: Fenrir, who will destroy Odin and Valhall at the end of the world. *edge-thunder:* 'battle'.
five kings: perhaps five kings Eirik was reputed to have slain during his career; or, less likely, five kings slain alongside Eirik at Stainmore.

The Fall of Rheged
Source: Rowland (1990), pp. 419–28; Williams (1935, 1970).

8. In the manuscript, Dunawd is named again to start the second stanza. I have followed Rowland's suggestion that this was a scribal error and that Unhwch should be named here instead.
11. In the manuscript, the last line of the third stanza is missing. The line in the translation is conjectural, based on consistency with the picture of warriors petitioning the leader for gifts in the preceding stanza.

In Praise of Colum Cille
Source: Meyer (1915) 340.

high heaven's noble seal: the word is *ardrón*, a high or noble seal, the animal seal. This could be a pun on Mugrón's name.

Christ's Cross
Source: Murphy (1956) 32–5, §14.

The Litany of the Trinity
Sources: Plummer (1925) 78–85; Meyer (1894) 42–4.

Herfid's Song on the Battle of Clontarf
Source: Finnur Jónsson A I, pp. 428–29; Einar Ól. Sveinsson (1954) 459–60.

Darradarljod
Source: Finnur Jónsson A I, pp. 419–21; Einar Ól. Sveinsson (1954) 454–58.

Randver's fate: Randver was the son of Jormunrekk, king of the Goths (the historical Ermanaric, †376) who, according to legend, was hanged by his father after having been falsely accused of sleeping with his stepmother by a wicked counsellor.

On Olaf Haraldsson, King of Norway
Source: Finnur Jónsson A I, pp. 295–96; *Orkneyinga Saga* v. 7, p. 41.

In Praise of Rognvald Brusason (Rognvaldsdrapa)
Source: Finnur Jónsson A I, p. 332.

An Elegy for Earl Thorfinn the Mighty (Thorfinnsdrapa)
Source: Finnur Jónsson A I, pp. 343–48; *Orkneyinga Saga*, 52 v.
15; 43 v. 8; 46 v. 9; 47 v. 10; 48 v. 11; 50 v. 12; 50–51 v. 16; 51–52 v.
14; 58 v. 18; 59 v. 19; 61 v. 20; 61–62 v. 21; 62 v. 22, 122 v. 33; 83 v.
28; 68–69 v. 25; 69 v. 26; 81 v. 27; 83 v. 29.

Vatnsfjord, probably Waterford, whose king Rognvald Rognvalds-
son was executed by Sigtrygg Silk-beard of Dublin in 1035,
probably following a successful military venture. It should be
noted that Sigtrygg was an ally of Thorfinn's father Sigurd at
Clontarf. Rognvald's kinsman Echmarcach held part of Galloway.

the English remember: Thorfinn attacked England 1040–42.

an ill fortune: Arnor bemoans the falling out between Thorfinn
and his nephew Rognvald Brusason.

In Praise of Kalf Arnason
Source: Finnur Jónsson A I, p. 396; *Orkneyinga Saga* v. 24, pp.
67–68.

Finn's kinsman: Thorfinn is called Finn's kinsman on account of
his marriage to Ingibjorg Finnsdottir, Kalf's niece.

Advice to Mael Coluim from Mac Duib
Source: *Scotichronicon*, volume 3, eds. J. & W. MacQueen and
D.E.R. Watt, Aberdeen, 1995, pp. 14–16 (Book V, ch. 6).

The Birth of Áedán mac Gabráin
Source: O'Brien (1952).

with no geis: a *geis* was a sort of omen or taboo, the breaking of
which spelled doom for hero or ruler.

Prayer in St Margaret's Gospel Book
Source: Forbes-Leith (1896) 87–8, from the manuscript in Ox-
ford, Bodleian Library, Lat. lit. F.5 (*S.C.* 29744).

A Verse on David son of Mael Coluim
Source: Bergin (1955) 269; T.O. Clancy (forthcoming).

Mael Coluim's son: This is David, son of Mael Coluim III, who
would later become King of Scots (1124–53).

Prayer to Saint Columba
Source: Reeves (1857) xxix; from MS. London, BL Cotton Tiberius, D.iii.

Arran
Source: O'Rahilly (1927) §40, 59–60; Jackson (1971) §19, 70–71, 308.

Columba's Island Paradise
Source: O'Rahilly (1927) §42.

'*Back towards Ireland*': this is a classic traditional 'nickname' for Columba, since he is meant to have abandoned Ireland forever. It is used as a riddling allusion to the speaker in a number of poems attributed to Columba.

THE POETRY OF EARL ROGNVALD KALI
Source: Finnur Jónsson A I, pp. 505–11 and *Orkneyinga Saga*: 1. 130 v. 34; 2. 131 v. 35; 3. 133 v. 36; 4. 163 v. 38; 5. 165 v. 39; 6. 184 v. 43; 7. 195–96 v. 44; 8. 196 v. 45; 9. 197 v. 46; 10. 198 v. 47; 11. 198 v. 48; 12. 200 v. 49; 13. 202 v. 51; 14. 203 v. 53; 15. 210 v. 55; 16. 211 v. 56; 17. 215 v. 59; 18. 217 v. 60; 19. 217 v. 61; 20. 219 v. 63; 21. 219–20 v. 64; 22. 221 v. 66; 23. 221–22 v. 67; 24. 226 v. 68; 25. 226–27 v. 69; 26. 227. v. 70; 27. 231 v. 75; 28. 232 v. 77; 29. 233 v. 78; 30. 234 v. 79; 31. 235 v. 80; 32. 238 v. 81.
See also Bibire (1988).

HALL THORARINSSON
Source: Finnur Jónsson A I, pp. 528; *Orkneyinga Saga* p. 183, v. 42.

EIRIK
Source: Finnur Jónsson A I, pp. 528–29; *Orkneyinga Saga* pp. 179–80, v. 41.

ODDI LITLI GLUMSSON
Source: Finnur Jónsson A I, pp. 529–30; *Orkneyinga Saga* 203 v. 52; 212 v. 58; 220 v. 65; 230 v. 73; 231 v. 74.

ARMOD
Source: Finnur Jónsson A I, pp. 530–31; *Orkneyinga Saga* 1. 201–2 v. 50; 2. 208–9 v. 54; 3. 212 v. 57; 229 v. 71.

THORBJORN SVARTI
Source: Finnur Jónsson A I, p. 531; *Orkneyinga Saga* 229 v. 72.

SIGMUND ONGUL
Source: Finnur Jónsson A I, p. 532; *Orkneyinga Saga* 1. 217–8. v. 62; 2. 232 v. 76.

BOTOLF BEGLA
Source: Finnur Jónsson A I, p. 532; *Orkneyinga Saga* 258 v. 82.

Conflict in Orkney
Source: Finnur Jónsson A I, p. 594; *Orkneyinga Saga* p. 166, v. 40.

The Maeshowe Verse
Source and Commentary: Barnes (1994) 144–58.

Gauk son of Trandil: a character by this name is mentioned in the Icelandic *Njal's Saga* (ch. 26), which says that he was killed by his foster-brother Asgrim Ellida-Grimsson, an ancestor of the Icelander Thorhall Asgrimsson, who was in Orkney in the mid-12th century.

in the south country: referring to the south of Iceland.

Song on the death of Somerled
Source: Text in Skene (1871) 449–51; discussion, translation and context in Anderson (1922) ii, 252–8.

Galienses (line 3): Anderson translates these as Hebrideans, 'perhaps the men of *Innse-Gall*', but they are really just *gall*, 'foreign'. The Hebrides got this name through their occupation by Norse types. *Galienses* here means foreigners and, if the annals are right, they are Dublin Norse rather than Hebrideans.

On the abuse of saints, see Geary (1983) 123–40. See also the story in Broderick (1991) f.38r.f, dated 1154, which is also associated with Somerled, though he comes out of this encounter rather better than he does later in Glasgow.

Kentigern: otherwise 'Mungo', founding bishop (and hence patron saint) of Glasgow in the late sixth and early seventh centuries, when it was part of the British kingdom of Dumbarton.

There is an anonymous and fragmentary *Life* of the saint written at the instigation of bishop Herbert himself by a 'clerk of St Kentigern', and another fuller *Life* written by Jocelin of Furness later in the 12th century.

Krakumal
Source: Finnur Jónsson (1912–15) AI 641–9, BI 649–56.
Commentary: Anne Heinrichs (1992); de Vries (1964–7) II 37–41.

in the Hebrides themselves: some scholars think this expression indicates the poem was composed in the Western Isles.

The Song of the Jomsvikings
Source: Finnur Jónsson (1912–15), AII 1–10, BII 1–10.
Commentary: Kock (1923–44); de Vries (1964–67), II 33–7; Fidjestøl (1992); Finlay (1995); Holtsmark (1937); Lindow (1981); Jón Stefánsson (1907) 43–7.

In Praise of Raghnall, King of Man and the Isles
Source: Ó Cuív (1957).

the sidh of Emhain, Emhain Abhlach: The entire poem plays with the otherworld quality of a site on the Isle of Man, some sort of barrow or mound with supernatural associations, a *sidh*. The name used for Man here, Emhain Abhlach, is redolent of some of the names for the Gaelic otherworld promised land, and Man is depicted under Raghnall as achieving something of the status of Paradise. Where the mound described was situated is not clear, though it could well have been at the site of the Tynwald, which may have been an inauguration site as well as one of assembly.

What god from beside the Boyne: the implication is that Raghnall has otherworldly ancestry, by suggesting that Óengus, the Irish god believed to have dwelt in Brugh na Boinne, the tumulus of Newgrange, was his real father.

many the doorways: the poet suggests that, as an otherworldly place, Raghnall's Emhain could be reached through caves at some of the ritual sites of Ireland, such as Knowth, or Ferns.

fian-men: young, landless warriors who lived by raid and mercenary activity.
Swan, Black Swan: evidently the name of Raghnall's ship.

Columba's Legacy
Source: Meyer (1918), and see AU s.a. 1204.

On Cathal Crobhdherg, King of Connacht
Source: Quiggin (1912).

The poem is the epitome of Gaelic praise poetry, and relies on the classic Gaelic idea that the just king, who enforces judgment and law wisely, will make the land fertile and prosperous.

Redhand: this is the meaning of Cathal's epithet 'Crobhdherg'.
Níall's dark knee: this is presumably a reference to Níall Glundúbh ('black knee'), king of Uí Néill 896–919, and briefly the most important king in Ireland.

From Scotland, for Cathal Crobhdherg
Source: Ó Cuív (1969–70).

A Vision of Donnchadh Cairbrech, King of Thomond
Sources: McGeown and Murphy (1953); Murphy (1944) 93–7.

Donnchadh Cairbrech's Harp
Sources: Walsh (1933) 113–15; O'Curry (1873) vol. 3, 270–73.

Tree, music-tree: the Gaelic word *crann* can have many meanings, including 'tree', 'wood' and 'harp'. The poet plays on this notion in the final verse, suggesting that though he's entitled by birth to all the woods of Scotland, he prefers the Irish wood of the harp.

For Alún, Mormhaer of Lennox
Sources: McKenna (1939) vol. 1, 173–4; (1940) vol. 2, 102–3; Skene (1880) vol. 3, 454–55, 117–119.

To Amhlaíbh of the Lennox
Sources: Ó Cuív (1968).

Donnchadh Cairbrech's Knife
Sources: Bergin (1970) no. 52: 192–93, 303; Ó Cuív (1969–70) 105, 108–9.

Tonsuring Poem
Source: O'Rahilly (1927) II, no. 6: 179–80, 224–26; Ó Cuív (1961) 66.

On the rituals and philosophy of pilgrim crusaders, see Powell (1986) 51–66.

Upon Tonsuring
Source: McKenna (1939) 1, 174–76, (1940) 2, 103.

Heading for Damietta
Sources: Murphy (1953), 71–4; Macquarrie (1985) 34–46; Powell (1986) 137–57.

From Monte Gargano
Sources: Murphy (1953) 74–9; Macquarrie (1985) 38–9; Powell (1986) 137–74; Brundage (1962) 219.

On Returning from the Mediterranean
Sources: Mackintosh (1819) 101; Thomson (1960–68) 280.

Returning from the Mediterranean, to Murchadh na nEach Ó Briain.
Source: Bergin (1970) no. 24, 108–12, 261–63.

Elegy on Máel Mhedha, his wife
Source: Bergin (1970) no. 22, 101–3, 257–58.

A Poem to the Virgin Mary
Source: Bergin (1970) §21.

Given the poet's renunciation of women and wealth and horses towards the end of the poem, we may guess that this poem dates from after his wife's death.

A Poem of Renunciation
Source: Gillies (1979–80) 81–6.

Poem when Dying
Source: Gillies (1990) 156–72.

Verses on the Death of Alan of Galloway
Source: *Scotichronicon*, vol. 5, 148.

SNAEKOLL GUNNASON
Source: Mundt (1977) 110.

On the Death of Alexander II, King of the Scots
Source: *Scotichronicon*, vol. 5, 192.

Epitaph on the Tomb of Geoffrey, Bishop of Dunkeld
Source: *Scotichronicon*, vol. 5, 192.

Poem to Aenghus Mór Mac Domhnaill, King of the Isles
Source: Bergin (1970) §45.

Hymn for St Magnus, Earl of Orkney
Source: Kolsrud and Reiss (1913) 38–40. The manuscript also contains a two-part musical arrangement, almost all in thirds, which is reproduced by Kolsrud and Reiss. See also Anderson (1922) vol ii, 160–162; Beveridge (1941); De Geer (1988).

Song for the Wedding of Margaret of Scotland and Eirik, King of Norway
Source: Kolsrud and Reiss 41–2, who also reproduce the music which accompanies the poem in the original manuscript, with an edition of the same music in modern notation. The MS is in Uppsala University Library, MS Upsalensis C 233.
See also Beveridge (1941) 1–12; De Geer (1988) 241–63.

Scotland after Alexander
Sources: Amours (1907) 144–45. And see Amours (1914) 92 on the song itself. MacDiarmaid (1946) 1.

Christ, borne in virgynyte: a variant early manuscript has 'The frute falzeit on everilk tre', an interesting echo of the imagery of lordship in Gaelic poetry of the same period.

On the Battle of Stirling Bridge
Source: *Scotichronicon*, vol. 6, p. 90.

In the second line, the poet plays with the name 'Wallace' and the French *valais*, perhaps referring to the fishing implement so called in French.

William Wallace's Uncle's Proverb
Source: *Scotichronicon*, vol. 6, p. 298.

Scotland's Strategy of Guerrilla Warfare
Source: *Scotichronicon*, vol. 6, p. 320.

On the Death of Edward I
Source: *Scotichronicon*, vol. 6, p. 332.

Eoin Mac Suibhne's Voyage to Castle Sween
Source: Meek (1998). See also Watson (1937) 6–13, 257–59;
Cameron (1892) vol. 1, 102–3; McLauchlan (1862) 116–19;
Thomson (1989) 27–30.

The Epitaph of Robert Bruce
Source: *Scotichronicon*, vol. 7, pp. 46–50.

Fragments of Verse on Rulers in the Isles
Source: Bergin (1955) §§56, 59, 85, 101.

The Blackthorn Brooch
Source: O'Rahilly (1926) 18, §14.

Lament for Fearchar Ó Mail Chiaráin
Source: Breatnach (1941–42).

I threw a shoe over a house: a means of divination attested in
Scotland. It was bad fortune for the subject for the shoe to land
sole upwards.

to buy heaven for a drink: the meaning of this couplet is unfortu-
nately opaque.

Poetry from the Inchcolm Antiphoner
Source: Edinburgh University Library MS 211. iv. The individual
pieces appear here in the order in which they appear in the
manuscript in its present collation.

The hymn (*Aurora Rutilat*) also appears in the Aberdeen
Breviary, which has been used to make two corrections to earlier
readings: *Britanniae* for *Britanniam* (fourth verse, line 4) and
omnium added to the fifth verse, line 3.

Differing from earlier translations, the fourth stanza here seems
to us to refer to the baptism of the 'King of Britain', for that is the
rite of 'inauguration of life', not his royal ordination.

Isobel Woods (1987, 21–37) dated the relevant portion of this
manuscript to the 14th century, but suggested that the material
for Columba's feast may be considerably older. Dr Woods's
own work on this manuscript was interrupted by her recent and
untimely death, though not before her work resulted in a

recording of a performance of the Columban music from the Inchcolm Antiphoner by *Capella Nova* under Alan Taverner in 1992 [CD GAU 129]. Her sleeve notes for this recording are of interest.

John Purser (1992), 37 ff., illustrates the musical settings of these poems. Some of his speculations about their 'Celtic' religious character are a little bizarre, though he admits they are 'open to much revision'.

A Prayer of Gratitude for the Men of Bute
Source: *Scotichronicon*, vol. 7, p. 104.

A Poem on the Cause of the Plague of 1349
Source: *Scotichronicon*, vol. 7, p. 272.

PRONUNCIATION GUIDES

Welsh

The Welsh names are represented here in modern orthography. For a detailed description of Welsh pronunciation, refer to any introductory grammar. It is hoped that the following notes will be of help in approximating the pronunciation of the names in the poems.

Welsh words are generally stressed on the penultimate syllable: Taliésin, Anéirin, Cátraeth.

Consonants

In general, these are of the same value as English ones, with the following exceptions:

c: always /k/ as in 'coal', never the sound in 'circle'.
ch: as in Scottish 'loch'.
dd: as the '-th-' in English 'breathe'.
f: /v/ as in English 'of'.
ff: as in 'off'.
g: always the sound in 'gimmick', never the sound in 'giro'.
ll: no English equivalent: place the tongue on the ridge of the mouth as for the sound 'd', then blow open-mouthed around the tongue through one side.
ph: as in 'philosophy'.
r: a strongly trilled 'r'.
rh: a trilled 'r' with following aspiration.
s: always the sound in 'sense', never the sound in 'is'.
th: always as in English 'maths', never as in 'weather'.

Vowels

Always pure vowel sounds. They can be long or short, determined by the context of the sound in the word.

a: long, the sound in 'father'; short, the sound in 'fat'.
e: long, the sound in 'neighbour'; short, the sound in 'net'.

344

i: long, the sound in 'fiend'; short, the sound in 'fit'.
o: long, the sound in 'moan'; short, the sound in 'mop'.
u: long, the sound in 'mean'; short, the sound in 'mint'.
y: clear, the sound in 'me'; obscure, the '-i-' in 'panic'.

Diphthongs

The main vowel is the first one, but they are pronounced quickly together:

ae, ai, au: as in Scots 'bite'.
aw: as in English 'cow'.
ei, eu: generally as English 'eye'.
ew: quick combination of 'eh' and 'oo'.
iw, uw, yw: as in English 'dew'.
oe, oi: as in English 'oil'.
ow: as in English 'owe'.
yw: obscure *y*, followed by 'oo'.
wy: quick combination of 'oo' and 'ee'.

Gaelic

The Gaelic names here have been written with two different types of orthography. For the period before c.1200, we have used Old Gaelic spelling conventions; for the period after, we have used a rough version of early modern Gaelic spelling conventions. This mainly affects the consonants. The pronunciation guide given here is very simplified.

Gaelic words are usually stressed on the first syllable: Córmac, Múireadhach, Tóirrdhelbach.

Consonants

The pronunciation of consonants differs depending on whether they are in initial position or are within or at the end of a word. At the beginning of a word, consonants generally have similar values to those in English. They change within words, and this is marked in the post-1200 spellings more clearly. Only where pronunciation is markedly different from English have we indicated it:

pre-1200	post-1200	pronunciation
-b-, -b	-bh-, -bh	/v/ as in 'given', 'have'.
c, -cc	c, -c-	always as in 'cat', never the sound in 'circle'.
-c-, -c	-g-, -g	/g/ as in 'piggy', 'pig'.
d + i, e	d + i, e	'dj', as in Scots 'dew'.
-d-, -d	-dh-, -dh	as the '-th-' in English 'breathe'.
fh-	fh-	not pronounced.
g, -gg	g	always the 'g' as in 'give', never the sound in 'gin'.
-g-, -g	-gh-, -gh	a voiced 'g' at the back of the throat.
-m-, -m	-mh-, -mh	/v/ in 'savour', 'save'.
-p-, -p	-b-, -b	/b/ as in 'cabbie', 'cab'.
s-, -s-, -s	s-, -s-, -s	before a, o or u, or after when final: as English 'save', never the sound in 'as' before e or i, or after when final: as English 'sh'.
t + i, e	t + i, e	as English 'ch' in 'chew'.
-t-, -t	-d-, -d	/d/ as in 'ladder', 'lad'.

346

Vowels

These are pronounced in a similar fashion to the clear vowels of many European languages. In addition, vowels can be added in two ways.

First, an *i* added to *a*, *o* or *u* can be used simply to make the following consonant 'slender': so the *a* in *ai-* has no different sound, but it changes the quality of the following consonant, as in *art* vs. *airt*. Similarly, an *a* or *u* added to *e* or *i* broadens the following vowel.

Second, there are actual diphthongs: áe, óe, oí, uí, etc.

a, ai: as in 'hat'.
á, ái: as in 'halve'.
e, ea: as in 'bet'.
é, éa: as in 'bait'.
i: as in 'pin', or 'peek'.
í: as in 'clear'.
o, oi: as in 'mop'.
ó, ói: as in 'bought'.
u, ui: as in 'cook'.
ú, úi: as in 'cool'.

Diphthongs

áe, aí: as in 'aisle'.
óe, oí: as in 'oil'.
uí: as in 'leave'.

GLOSSARY OF PLACE-NAMES

Aber: unidentified place in southern Scotland.

Aber Lleu: site of the battle at which Urien was slain; Ross Low, opposite Lindisfarne in Northumbria, has been suggested, since it was traditionally while besieging Lindisfarne that Urien was slain.

Acre: a town and fort in Palestine, taken and retaken by Crusaders, and held as a central part of the Crusader kingdom.

Áedh ónt Sliabh: the territory of the Clann Áedha an tSléibhe, in Co. Longford.

Aeron: The region around the River Ayr.

Aeron Eiddyned: an unidentified region of northern England or southern Scotland.

Agdir: the southernmost region of western Norway.

Airghialla: loosely allied kindreds in north-eastern Ireland, from whom the kings of the isles claimed descent.

Alasund: possibly Ålesund, Norway.

Alba: Originally meaning all of Britain, this Gaelic name had, from 900 on, the restricted meaning of the kingdom between the Forth and the Spey ruled by the descendants of Cinaed mac Ailpín. Later, it sometimes had the extended meaning of all the territory ruled by the kings of the Scots.

Anglesey: the large island off the coast of northern Wales, and one of the Welsh agricultural heartlands.

Aran: island(s) off the west coast of Ireland, in Co. Galway.

Arddunyon: unknown; somewhere in southern Scotland or northern England.

Ard nan Each: unidentified location of the property of Muireadhach Albanach in the Lennox.

Arfynydd: meaning 'the region against the mountains', an unidentified region within the kingdom of Rheged.

Argoed Llwyfain: site of battle, variously identified, at locations in northern England and elsewhere.

Arran: island in the Firth of Clyde.

Áth Gabla: perhaps the ford in Co. Meath, not far from Knowth, but perhaps a place in Scotland.

Balloch (Bealach): castle in Dunbartonshire, on the Leven and at the foot of Loch Lomond; the main seat of *mormhaers* (earls) of Lennox.

Banbha: poetic name for Ireland.

Bann: river in Co. Derry.

Bannawg: the barrier of high land, corresponding roughly to the Kilsyth and Gargunnock Hills, where the Bannock Burn rises. It probably formed the southern boundary of Pictland in the west.

Bardafjord: a place of unknown location.

Bergen: a town in Norway.

Berwick-on -Tweed: town on the English–Scottish border, disputed during the wars of independence in the period after 1286.

Bóraimhe: fort on bank of the Shannon, Co. Clare, symbolic of kingship of the kings of Thomond.

Boyne: river in east-central Ireland.

Brecheinawg: here, it is probably the region around Brechin, in Angus, though it is also a region in south-eastern Wales.

Brennych: the English kingdom of Bernicia, established during the sixth century, which became the northern portion of Northumbria.

Breo: unidentified place in eastern Scotland.

Bre Trwyn: probably 'the brae of Trwyn', the latter being Troon, on the Ayrshire coast. Its brae may be the Dundonald hills which overlook the peninsula.

Brewyn: the former Roman fort at Bremenium, near High Rochester, in Redesdale.

Brugh: Brugh na Boinne, the passage grave at Newgrange, Co. Meath, thought to be an otherworld site.

Burgh by Sands: town in southern Cumbria.

Burren: a region in Co. Clare.

Byland: in Yorkshire

Byzantium: anciently Constantinople, the modern city of Istanbul.

Caer Garadawg: unidentified fort, possibly within southern British territory.

Caer Glud: 'the fort of the Clyde', possibly Dumbarton Rock.

Cairpre: see Clann Chairpri.

Caithness: northernmost county of mainland Scotland.

Carn Fraích: inauguration site of later kings of Connacht.

Cashel: stronghold and royal centre of the kings of Munster.

Castle Sween: on Loch Sween in Knapdale, Argyll.

Catraeth: Catterick, in northern Yorkshire.

Ceis: Keshcorann, Co. Galway.

Ceis Cairrgi: unidentified.

Cennanus: Kells, Co. Meath, in Ireland.

Cill Achaidh: unidentified.

Clann Áedha: (?) a branch of the Uí Néill, in either Co. Fermanagh or in Co. Longford (for the latter, cf. Áedh ónt Sliabh).

Clann Aenghusa: a branch of the Uí Néill in Co. Tyrone, near Clogher.

Clann Bhloid: the Uí Briain kings of Thomond.

Clann Chairm: unidentified.

Clann Chairpri: cf. Cenél Cairbri of Carbury, Co. Sligo, a northern branch of Uí Néill. Drumcliff, a Columban monastery, was in their territory.

Clann Chais: the Dál Cais kings of Munster.

Clann Cholmáin: southern branch of the Uí Néill.

Clann Chonaill: northern branch of the Uí Néill, rulers of Tír Conaill (Co. Donegal).

Clann Chonghail: unidentified ancestors of the earls of Lennox.

Clann Fherghusa: branch of the Cenél Eoghain, in Inishowen.

Clann Gofraidh: unidentified ancestors of the earl of Lennox (possibly related to the kings of the Isles and Man).

Clann Loingsigh: a family in Tír Conaill.

Clann Luighdhech: a branch of Cenél Conaill, near Kilmacrenan in Co. Donegal.

Clann Muiredhaigh: the ruling family of Connacht.

Clann Somhairlidh: the descendants of Somairlidh (Somerled) mac Gille-Brighde (†1164), king of Argyll and the Isles.

Clann Táil: a people in Co. Clare.

Cliú: district in Co. Limerick.

Clontarf: near Dublin, site of a battle in 1014.

Cnoc an Scáil: nickname for Tara.

Cnoc Brenainn: Brandon Hill in Co. Kerry.

Cnoc Muaidh: Knockmoy, Co. Galway.

Cnoc Ó Colmáin: unidentified.

Cnoghdha: Knowth, Co. Meath, traditionally an entrance to the otherworld.

Coed Beidd: lit., 'boars' wood'; this may be connected with Beith, in northern Ayrshire, though Bathgate in West Lothian contains the same elements.

Coire Bhrecáin: whirlpool off Rathlin Island.

Coire Dá Ruadh: a whirlpool in the strait between Ireland and Scotland.

Coll: island in the Hebrides.

Colptha: the lower stretches of the River Boyne.

Connachta: the people of Connacht.

Conn's Part: the northern half of Ireland.

Corann, Ces Corainn: Keshcorann, Co. Sligo, a site symbolic of

350

the kingship of the kings of Connacht.

Corco Mruadh: Corcomroe, in Co. Clare.

Crete: an island in the Mediterranean.

Cruachan, Cruachan Aí: symbolic royal site of Connacht in Ireland.

Cúil Cnámha: in Co. Sligo.

Cuile: unidentified site in the northern part of Ireland.

Cuillech: unidentified site in the northern part of Ireland.

Cyrrwys: unidentified territory or people in northern Britain.

Dál nAraide: a kingdom in north-east Ireland.

Damietta: town and stronghold in Egypt, contested in the Fifth Crusade, c.1218–20.

Deerness: a promontory on the east of the Mainland of Orkney.

Deifr: the English kingdom of Deira, which became the southern portion of Northumbria.

Derwennydd Falls: Lodore Force, which flows into Derwentwater in Cumbria.

Dina: a river of unknown location.

Din Dywyd: unidentified fort in northern Britain.

Dolls: an island off the Norwegian coast.

Druim Cáin: another name for Tara.

Drws Llech: lit., 'the gap of the slab', probably the fort of Dunawd ap Pabo. This could perhaps be Leck Castle, in the Lune Valley, southern Cumbria.

Dubglenn: ? al. Glenn Dorcha, now Glendorragha, Co. Mayo.

Dubréiglés: the early chapel in Derry associated with Columba.

Dún Baloir: on Tory island.

Dún Cuil[l]eann: (usually Dún Caillenn), Dunkeld, Columban foundation in Perthshire, and later bishopric.

Dún dá Lethglas: Downpatrick, bishopric in Ulster.

Dún Inbir: in Scotland, perhaps Guardbridge?

Dunkeld: cf. Dún Cuilleann.

Édar: Beinn Édair, the Hill or Howth, on the east coast of Ireland near Dublin.

Efrawg: York.

Eidyn: Din Eidyn, Edinburgh, the main fortress of the Gododdin.

Eirch: unidentified region in northern Britain.

Elfed: Elmet, the region east of the Pennines, including Leeds.

Emhain, Emhain Abhlach: otherworld island; another name for the Isle of Man.

Enach: ? Annaghdown, bishopric in Connacht.

Enach: probably Annagh More in Co. Wexford.

Englanes: unknown.

351

Erc's region: a poetic name for Dál Riata, named for Erc, ancestor of the kindreds of Dál Riata.

Erris: in Co. Mayo.

Ess-dara: waterfall in Co. Sligo.

Ess-Ruaidh: Assaroe, falls on river Erne in Co. Donegal, fabled in song and legend.

Eyrasund: the channel between Denmark and Sweden (modern Øresund).

Fál: poetic name for Ireland.

Fern: a cave, traditionally an entrance to the otherworld.

Fódla: poetic name for Ireland.

Forghas: the River Fergus, Co. Clare, which flows into the Shannon.

Forth: the River and Firth of Forth, in eastern Scotland.

Frémhonn: Frewin, Co. Westmeath.

Gabhair: tributary of the Boyne.

Gabhrán: Gowran, Co. Kilkenny.

Gafran: a region in northern Britain, possibly the Gowrie, along the northern shore of the Firth of Tay.

Gáiléoin: a people of Leinster.

Gautland: a district in Sweden (modern Götland).

Gearr-abhand: 'short river', supposedly a name for the River Leven in Dunbartonshire; also a name of a river in Munster.

Goddeu: unidentified region of the kingdom of Rheged.

Gododdin: a territory in south-eastern Scotland. The name was also used for the tribe that inhabited it, and subsequently as the title for the poem.

Grimsby: a town in eastern England.

Gulberwick: a bay on the east coast of the Mainland of Shetland.

Gwanannon: a region on the border of Gododdin.

Gwensteri: possibly the region around the River Winster, in southern Cumbria.

Gwen Ystrad: unknown strath in northern Britain. The Eden valley has been suggested, with some plausibility.

Gwyddawl: unidentified place in northern Britain.

Gwynedd: a kingdom in north-western Wales.

Hjadningavag: a place of unknown location.

Hjorungavag: a bay in north-west Norway, possibly Liavågen in Sunnmøre.

Humber: a river and estuary on the east coast of England.

Idon: probably the river Eden, in northern Cumbria.

Imbolar: perhaps a suburb of Byzantium.

Imdhán: perhaps in Co. Limerick.

Inber: Inbhir Mór, Arklow, Co. Wexford.

Inchcolm: island monastery in the Firth of Forth, dedicated to Columba.

Inndyris Island: a place of unknown location.

Innse Gall: 'the islands of the foreigners', from perhaps the ninth century, a Gaelic term for the Hebrides.

Innse Líag: unidentified.

Innse Modh: islands in Clew Bay, Co. Mayo.

Iva: a river of unknown location.

Jadar: Jæren, the south-west coast of Norway.

Jom: an island in the Baltic, base of the Jomsvikings, possibly modern Wolin, Poland.

Jordan: the river in the Holy Land.

Kerrera: island in the Firth of Lorne, off Oban.

Knapdale: the Argyll mainland north of Kintyre.

Leven: the River Leven in Dunbartonshire.

Lewis: island in the Outer Hebrides.

Lí: perhaps Beinn Lí, on Skye.

Liathmhuine: district in Munster.

Liffey: river which flows through Dublin; symbolic of sovereignty of kings of Leinster.

Limerick: town and trading port on the River Shannon, founded by Vikings and key holding of the later kings of Thomond.

Lindiseyr: a place of unknown location.

Linn Féic: on the River Boyne.

Llan Lleenawg: unidentified place linked with Lleenawg, the father of Gwallawg.

Lloegr: 'England'. The origin and etymology of the word, which continued into ordinary modern Welsh, are uncertain.

Llwyfenydd: a region within the kingdom of Rheged, perhaps its core. Probably retained in the river Lyvennet, in Cumbria.

Loch Cé: in Co. Roscommon.

Loch Con: in Co. Mayo.

Loch Foyle: loch between Co. Derry and Donegal.

Lochlann: Scandinavia or Norway.

Loch Long: loch in Argyll.

Loch Riach: Loughrea, Co. Galway.

Lorg: Moylurg, Co. Roscommon.

Maen Gwyngwn: unidentified location, explained as 'the stone of the Venicones', a tribe located in the Roman period in eastern Scotland.

Magh Fód: Moyode, Co. Galway.

Magh Málann: plain in Co. Roscommon.

Man: the Isle of Man in the Irish Sea.

Manaw: a region or kingdom in central Scotland, bounded by Clackmannan in the north and the Slamannan hills to the south; the region around Falkirk.

Manawyd: ? see *Manaw*.

Mathreu: unidentified site of battle in northern Britain.

Melrose: monastery in Roxburghshire.

Merin Iuddew: the Firth of Forth.

Mis: Sliabh Mis, either Co. Antrim or Co. Kerry.

Moer: a province of Norway, between Trondelag and the West-land.

Mon: Anglesey.

Monad: a site of royalty for kings in Scotland; various, but perhaps sometimes for Rigmonad, the king's muir, in Fife, from which St Andrews formerly took its name (Cennrígmonaid). See Sliabh Monaidh.

Monte Gargano: mountain on the Adriatic coast of Italy.

Moy: the River Moy, Co. Mayo.

Mugh's Half: Munster.

Mull: island in the Hebrides.

Mull, the: the Mull of Kintyre.

Narbonne: a city in Provence.

Newcastle-upon-Tyne: city in north-eastern England.

Nineveh: the city in the biblical book of Jonah, which averted God's anger and saved itself from destruction by repenting, man and beast alike, in sackcloth and ashes.

Oireacht or *Reilig Oirechtach*: a graveyard in Airecht Úa Cathain, Co. Derry? (and so? Domhnach Caoide/Teampall Uí Buidhe, named for Cóeti, bp. of Iona).

Oykel: a river in northern Scotland, emptying into the Dornoch Firth, and forming the southern boundary of Sutherland.

Penawg: the name implies a region of high land; it must be somewhere in the vicinity of the site of Urien's death. See *Aber Lleu*.

Pencoed: unidentified site of a battle in northern Britain.

Pen-prys: unidentified place in northern Britain, but perhaps related to Dumfries.

Pentir: the Kintyre peninsula on the western coast of Scotland.

Pentland Firth: the stretch of sea between Orkney and the main-land of Scotland.

Perth Manaw: lit., 'the copse of Manaw', unidentified, but see *Manaw*.

Powys: unidentified region in northern Britain; also the name of a

354

kingdom in north-eastern Wales.

Prydain: Ynys Prydain: The Island of Britain.

Prydyn: Pictland.

Prysg Catleu: unidentified site of a battle in northern Britain.

Ranworld: world of the sea-goddess Ran, the sea.

Rathlin: island off the coast of Co. Antrim.

Raudabjorg: an unidentified place, perhaps Roberry in South Walls, Orkney.

Reilig Martain: a cemetery in Derry.

Reilig Odhráin: the cemetery in Iona.

Rheged: the kingdom ruled by Urien in northern Britain, centring on Cumbria; its exact extent is unknown.

Rhos Terra: unidentified place in northern Britain, possibly connected with Glenderaterra in Cumbria.

Rhufoniawg: a region of Gwynedd.

Rhyd Alclud: the medieval ford of the Clyde at the Dumbuck barrier, just east of Al Clud, Dumbarton Rock.

Riadán: a place in Leinster.

Ros Cré: Roscrea in Co. Tipperary.

Rum: island in the southern Hebrides, site of church or hermitage of St Beccán of Rum.

Sandwick: a farm on the Orkney mainland.

Seghais: upper races of the Boyne, famed for its inspirational hazelnuts.

Síl Cellaigh: the ruling clan of Uí Mhaine in Connacht.

Síl Colla: the Airgialla of Ireland, from whom the kings of the Isles claimed descent.

Síl Gofraidh: perhaps the clan descended from Gofraidh Méarach?

Síl Muireadhaigh: the kings of Connacht.

Skarpasker: a place of unknown location.

Slemain: place in Co. Wexford.

Sliabh Mis: mountains, probably those in Co. Antrim.

Sliabh Monaidh: a poetic name for Scotland.

Sord: Swords, in Co. Dublin.

Stainmore: highland barrier in northern England, the southernmost boundary of the rule of the kings of Cumbria and the overkings of Alba in the period before the 12th century.

Strath Leven: the Vale of Leven in Dunbartonshire.

Tara: in Co. Meath, symbolic royal centre of Ireland.

Tay: the river in eastern Scotland.

Thurso: a town in Caithness, northern Scotland.

Torach: Tory island, a Columban monastery.

Torfness: site of a battle, south of the Moray Firth; possibly Burghead in Moray.

Tortan: the site of a *bile* or sacred tree, near Ardbreccan in Co. Meath, Ireland.

Tráigh Bhaile: probably the strand at Dundalk, Co. Louth.

Tuam: Co. Galway, symbolic of Connacht kingship.

Uí Chennsalaigh: dynastic rulers of Leinster, based in southern Leinster.

Uí Chuinn: the descendants of Conn Céadchathach.

Ullarakr: a place of unknown location.

Valhall: the 'hall of the slain', where heroes are taken by valkyries to feast and fight until the end of the world.

Vatnsfjord: probably Waterford, in Ireland.

Vikaskeid: a place of unknown location.

Wallsend: a town in Northumberland.

Waterford: trading-port and viking town in south-eastern Ireland.

Yrechwydd: one of the core regions of the kingdom of Rheged.

GLOSSARY OF PERSONAL NAMES

Ábhartach: legendary Irish character, said to be a magician.

Abhdhán son of Ibhdhán: Ibhdhan was a leprechaun, according to a late Irish tale, who possessed shoes which kept one afloat.

Adomnán: ninth abbot of Iona (697–704).

Áed: Áed mac Ainmirech, king of Tara, and of the Uí Néill, †598.

Aedán mac Gabráin: king of Dál Riata, †c. 608.

Agnar: son of Ragnar Lodbrok.

Ailill: grandfather of Corc of Cashel, and ancestor of the ruling families of Munster.

Aki Palna-Tokason: a Jomsviking, father of Vagn Akason.

Alan, son of Roland, Lord of Galloway, Constable of Scotland (†1234).

Alexander I, son of Mael Coluim, King of Scots (1107–24).

Alexander II, King of Scots, †1249.

Alexander III: King of Scots, †1286.

Almha: grandfather of Fionn mac Cumhaill.

Alún, Ailín: possibly the Alwyn mac Arcill who was also perhaps *rannaire*, or dispenser, for David I, and signatory to many of his charters. His daughter was probably married to Muireadhach, father of Alún Mór, mormhaer of Lennox.

Alún mac Muireadhaigh: the first mormhaer (earl) of Lennox mentioned in charters, probably died c. 1200.

Amhlaíbh: Amhlaíbh Mór, son of Alún, son of Alún Mór, mormhaer of Lennox. Amhlaíbh was progenitor of the Lennox MacAulays.

Amhlaibh: from Norse Olaf, a noble of the western isles.

Amhlaibh: Olaf, king of Man, †1153.

Arbhlatha: unidentified, but probably the mother of Mael Domhnaigh, earl of Lennox (and therefore the wife of Alún Mór, first earl of Lennox).

Armod: a Norwegian chieftain.

Art: ancestor of Columba, Art son of Conn Cétchathach.

Arthur: the late-fifth-century war-leader against the Anglo-Saxons, who became a British legend.

Asa: a Shetland girl.

Asgrim Ellida-Grimsson: a tenth-century Icelander.

Aslak: a Jomsviking.

Aslaug: second wife of Ragnar Lodbrok.

Ati: a legendary sea-king.

Audun: one of Earl Rognvald Kali's companions on pilgrimage.

Austri: a mythological dwarf who holds up the sky. There were four, one for each of the corners of the world – Austri is the east.

Báithín: Columba's cousin and successor as abbot of Iona (†600).

Baldr: a god, the son of Odin, who was killed and departed to Hel.

Basil: St Basil the Great of Caesarea (†379), an influential church doctor and monastic pioneer.

Berchán: St Berchán, legendary Irish prophet.

Bíl: a goddess.

Bjarki: a legendary hero.

Bodhbh Derg: an otherworld figure who lived in Munster.

Bornholm: an island in the Baltic.

Bragi: the Norse god of poetry.

Bran ab Ymellyrn: a ruler among the northern Britons.

Brandub mac Echach: king of Uí Chennsalaigh and of Leinster, †605–608.

Brian Bórama mac Cennétig, king of Munster and, for a time, of Ireland; ancestor of Uí Briain kings of Munster, †1014.

Bruide mac Bili: also Bridei son of Beli, king of the Picts (†693) and victor of the battle of Dunnichen, 685.

Brusi Sigurdsson: an earl of Orkney, brother to Thorfinn the Mighty.

Bui Vesetason: known as 'the Stout'; a Jomsviking, brother of Sigurd and maternal uncle of Vagn Akason.

Cairbre Lifechair: ancestor of the Uí Néill kings of Tara.

Cas: ancestor of the kings of Thomond.

Cassian: John Cassian, influential fifth-century writer on monasticism.

Cathaír: Columba's ancestor on his mother's side, ancestor of the kings of Leinster.

Cathal Crobhdherg Ó Conchobair: king of Connacht, †1224.

Cermad: an Irish god, son of the Daghdha.

Cinaed son of Ailpín: king of the Picts, and founder of the Gaelic dynasty which ruled over the kingdom of Alba from the ninth century on.

Clytwyn: unidentified warrior, perhaps a retainer of Gwallawg.

Coel: a semi-legendary early-fifth-century ruler of northern Britain, progenitor of the Cynferching, the dynasty to which Urien and Owein belonged.

Coirpre: Columba's ancestor on his mother's side.

Columba/Columcille: scion of the Cenél Conaill of Co. Donegal; priest and abbot; founder of the monastery of Iona (†597).

358

Conaing son of Áedán: son of Áedán son of Gabrán, king of Dál Riata, drowned in 622.

Cona(l)l: ancestor of Columba, Conall Gulbain, son of Níall Noígiallach.

Conall: perhaps Conall mac Comgaill, king of Dál Riata (†574) who traditionally granted Iona to Columba.

Conall Cernach: legendary Irish hero of the Ulster cycle.

Conchobhar: king of the Ulstermen in the Ulster cycle of tales.

Conn, Conn Céadchathach: 'Con of the hundred battles', ancestor of the Uí Néill, and eponym of Conn's half, a name from the northern half of Ireland.

Corc of Cashel, Conall Corc: ancestor of the main ruling families of medieval Munster, legendary founder of the power centre of Cashel. Legendary ancestor of the earls of Lennox.

Cormac: Cormac mac Airt, legendary king of Tara, and ancestor of the Uí Néill.

Crédh: legendary ancestress of the kings of Connacht.

Cú Chulainn: legendary Irish hero of the Ulster cycle of tales.

Cú Roí: legendary and otherworldly king of Munster.

Cuthbert: saint and bishop of Lindisfarne (†687).

Cynfarch: father of Urien, progenitor of the Cynferching dynasty of rulers of Rheged and elsewhere.

Darrad: possibly an Odin-name.

Da-Thí: legendary king of Tara.

David: King of Scots, ruling 1124–53, the son of Mael Coluim III, 'Cenn Mór'.

Domhnall: Domhnall Mór O Briain, father of Donnchadh Cairbrech, †1194.

Domhnall: grandson of Somerled and father of Aenghus Mór, king of the Isles, died mid-13th century.

Dorrud: an Icelander living in Caithness (but cf. Darrad).

Draupnir: a mythological golden ring stolen from the dwarf Andvari and cursed by him.

Dubh Saighlenn: perhaps a legendary cow; cf. *Glas Ghaibhnenn*, and note that Manannán, according to one tradition, possessed two legendary cows.

Duí Galach: Dauí, early king of Tara and ancestor of the Connacht kings.

Dunawd ap Pabo: Dunawd Byrr, ruler of northern Britain who died c. 595.

Dwywai: mother of Aneirin.

Dvalin, a dwarf.

Dyfnwal Frych: Domnall Brecc, king of Dál Riata (†642).

Edward I, king of England (†1307).

Efrddyl: Urien's sister; it has been suggested that she was traditionally perhaps involved in the background to the battle in which Urien was slain.

Egil: a viking.

Eginyr: warrior connected with Urien Rheged.

Einar: names of various men, including Earl Turf-Einar of Orkney.

Einherjar: the divine heroes, assembled by Odin in Valhall to defend it at the end of the world.

Eirik: King of Norway (ruled 1280–99).

Eirik: king Eirik Bloodaxe of Norway, Orkney and York, †954.

Eirik Hakonarson: son of Hakon Sigurdsson.

Eithne: Columba's mother.

Elias: a canon of the Glasgow Cathedral chapter.

Elijah: Old Testament prophet.

Elizabeth: mother of John the Baptist.

Ella: king of Northumbria (858–65).

Elno Hen: ruler/warrior in the kingdoms of the northern Britons.

Elphin: one of Urien's sons.

Endil: a mythical sea-king.

Eochu mac Muiredaigh: sixth-century king of the Uí Chennsalaigh and of Leinster.

Eoin mac Suibhne: John MacSween of Knapdale, fl. c.1310.

Erling: one of Earl Rognvald Kali's companions on pilgrimage.

Ermingerd: ruling countess of Narbonne in Provence in the mid 12th century.

Esther: in the Old Testament, the daughter of the Israelite Abihail, who pleased the Persian king Ahasuerus so much that he married her.

Eynæfi: a mythical sea-king.

Eystein: a Viking.

Fáelán mac Siláin: sixth-century king of the Uí Chennsalaigh and of Leinster.

Fearadhach Finn: legendary king of Scotland.

Fedelm: the wife of Eochu mac Muiredaigh.

Fedelmid: Columba's father.

Feidlimid: perhaps great-grandfather of Eochu mac Muiredaigh.

Ferghus: legendary ancestor of Raghnall, king of Man.

Fifa: name of a ship.

Finn: a Norwegian nobleman.

Fionn mac Cumhaill: legendary Irish hero of the Fionn cycle of tales.

Fjolnir: a by-name for Odin.

Flann: probably Flann Sina, king of Tara, †916.

Frey: a Viking.

Freyr: a god.

Frodi: a legendary king of Denmark, said to have brought peace and prosperity in the time of Augustus and Christ.

Gabrán: king of Dál Riata and ancestor of the Cenél nGabráin.

Garbán: probably Garbán Mide, king of Clann Cholmáin, †702.

Gauk Trandilsson: a tenth-century Icelander.

Gaut: an Odin-name.

Gautar: inhabitant of Gautland (cf. also Gaut).

Geirmund: a Norwegian chieftain.

Geoffrey: Galfridus, Bishop of Dunkeld († 1249).

Gilli, Earl of the Hebrides: early 11th century, based on Coll.

Glas Ghaibhnenn: legendary cow, with prodigious amounts of milk, presumably once thought of as belonging to Goibhniu.

Godebawg: Coel Hen Godebawg, a ruler of northern Britain in the early fifth century, and ancestor of the rulers of Rheged.

Gofraidh: son of Olaf/Amhlaíbh, and king of Man, †1187.

Gofraidh Méarach: also Gofraidh Crobh-bhán, king of Man, †1095.

Goibhniu: a legendary craftsman of the Irish, perhaps originally a god of smithcraft.

Gondul: a valkyrie.

Grimnir: an Odin-name.

Guaire: Guaire Aidne, king of Connacht, †664, famous for his generosity.

Gunn: a valkyrie.

Gwallawg: king of an unidentified region of northern Britain, possibly in southern Scotland.

Gwrangawn: unidentified British warrior.

Gwrion: unidentified British warrior.

Gwyddien: warrior connected with Urien Rheged, perhaps his war-leader.

Hakon Paulsson: joint Earl of Orkney with his cousin Magnus, whom he killed c. 1117.

Hakon Sigurdsson: Earl of Norway, 965/70–95.

Halfdan: a son of King Harald Fairhair of Norway.

Hamdir: a legendary warrior.

Harald: King Harald Fairhair of Norway.

Harald: Strut-Harald, an earl in Denmark, father of Sigvaldi and Thorkell.

Harald Gormsson: known as 'Bluetooth', king of Denmark c. 958 – c. 987.

Havard: a Jomsviking.

Hedin: a legendary warrior.

Heflir: a mythical sea-king.

Heiti: a legendary sea-king, ancestor of the earls of Moer.

Helsings: inhabitants of Hälsingland, Sweden.

Herbert: formerly a monk of Kelso, and bishop of Glasgow, 1147–64.

Herian: Odin.

Herrod: a Viking.

Herthjof: a Viking.

Hild: a valkyrie.

Hjadnings: legendary warriors, followers of Hedin (but see also Glossary of Place-names).

Hjalp: name of a ship.

Hjorthrimul: a valkyrie.

Hlin: a goddess.

Hlodvir: father of Sigurd the Stout, Earl of Orkney, who died in 1014. His name is related to French Louis.

Hogni: a legendary warrior.

Hrolf: Hrolf the Ganger, first Duke of Normandy, Court of Anjou (abd. c. 927).

Hrollaug: a Norwegian, one of the four chief settlers of Iceland, he settled in the south of the island.

Hugin: one of Odin's ravens.

Ímhar: from Norse Ívarr, a noble of the western isles.

Ingibjorg: daughter of Thorketil Leira.

Joachim: the father of Mary, the mother of God.

John the Baptist: forerunner of Christ.

Kalf: a Norwegian nobleman.

Kali: the baptismal name of Earl Rognvald Kali of Orkney.

Karl: Karl Hundason, allegedly king of the Scots.

Kentigern: otherwise 'Mungo', founding bishop (and hence patron saint) of Glasgow.

Kugi: an Orcadian or Hebridean.

Laeghaire: probably Laeghaire mac Néill, fifth-century king of Ireland.

Laurence: St Laurence.

Leah: daughter of Laban in the Book of Genesis, married to Jacob. Because Jacob treated her badly, God compensated her by giving her sons.

Leven (Lemhain): legendary daughter of Scottish king, eponym of the River Leven in Dunbartonshire and ancestress of the mormhaers of Lennox.

Lir mac Midhir: presumably Lir, the Irish sea-god, whose son Manannán, was associated with the Isle of Man. Traditionally, he was not the son of Midhir.

Llofan Llaw Ddifro: a nickname meaning something like 'little hand exile-hand', a name the speaker of the cycle on the Fall of Rheged seems to use of himself.

Lodbrok: see Ragnar Lodbrok.

Lokk (usu. Hlokk): a valkyrie.

Lugh: Irish god and hero.

Lughaidh son of Ailill: father of Corc of Cashel.

Mabon: here, either a person (perhaps the Mabon son of Iddno who was Urien's cousin), or perhaps standing for a place, e.g. Gwlad Mabon, 'Mabon's land'.

Macbethad: king of Scots (died 1057).

MacDuib: Macduff, the Earl of Fife in the mid-11th century.

Mac Lughach: fictional grandson of Fionn mac Cumhaill.

Maelbheirn: unidentified enemy of Raghnall, king of Man.

Mael Coluim: Mael Coluim III, son of Donnchad, King of Scots (1058–94).

Mael Coluim Ceann Mór: Malcolm III, king of Scots (died 1093).

Magnus Erlendsson: murdered by his cousin Hakon, with whom he was joint Earl of Orkney, c. 1117.

Maine son of Corc: son of Corc of Cashel and Leven.

Manannán mac Lir: Irish god of the sea.

Marbhán: legendary half-brother of Guaire Aidne, king of Connacht (†664).

Margaret: daughter of Alexander III, and wife of Eirik of Norway (†1283).

Mark: a cleric of Glasgow cathedral in 1164.

Marstan: an unidentified Irish king.

Martin: Martin of Tours, former soldier, founder of a monastery near Poitiers, and later bishop of Tours (†397).

Medhbh: legendary queen of Connacht.

Midhir: mythical Irish figure.

Mo Chummae: a name for St Columba.

Mongán mac Fiachna: son of the king of Dál nAraide, †625; became a legendary figure in Irish story.

Mór: an Irish woman.

Morgant: a king of the northern Britons, mentioned as a contemporary of Urien, and the instigator of his downfall.

Muireadhach: Muireadhach Albanach Ó Dálaigh, poet in Ireland and Scotland c. 1200–28.

Mynyddawg Mwynfawr: Mynyddawg the Opulent, ruler of Gododdin.

Neire: legendary Irish prophet.

Niall: Niall Noígiallach, king of Tara in the fifth century, and ancestor of Uí Néill dynasties.

Njord: a god particularly favoured in the Norwegian Westland.

Nudd Hael: ruler of warrior of the northern Britons.

Nwython: ruler of Dumbarton and/or Pictland in the early seventh century.

Ó Briain: a member of the clan of the kings of Thomond; Donnchadh Cairbrech Ó Briain.

Ó Conchobair: a member of the ruling family of Connacht; Cathal Crobhdherg.

Ó Dálaigh: a member of the Uí Dálaigh family of poets.

Odin: the chief of the Norse gods.

Ó Duibhne: Diarmaid, legendary Irish hero of the Fionn cycle of tales.

Óengus son of Fergus: king of the Picts and conqueror of Dál Riata, †761.

Oisín: Fionn mac Cumhaill's son.

Olaf: King Olaf Haraldsson, St Olaf, of Norway.

Orn: a Viking.

Oscar: grandson of Fionn mac Cumhaill, legendary Irish hero.

Oswiu: king of Northumbria (†670); his son: Ecgfrith, †685.

Owain ap Beli: ruler of Dumbarton, c.642, victor of the battle of Strathcarron.

Owain ab Urien: probably ruler of Rheged after Urien's death.

Pasgent: one of Urien's sons.

Paul: an earl of Orkney.

Pehtgils: a boy, presumably English, who was the beneficiary of a healing miracle of Ninian, and became a monk in Whithorn in the eighth century.

Plecgils: the beneficiary of a vision-miracle by Nynia, his story was known in Carolingian Gaul, and cited by Paschasius Radbertus.

Pyll: unknown northern British warrior involved in the battle of Aber Lleu.

Rachel: daughter of Laban in the Book of Genesis, and sister of Leah. She was also married to Jacob, and was his favourite.

Ræfil: a legendary sea-king.

Rafn: a Viking.

Ragna: an Orcadian lady.

Ragnar Lodbrok: a ninth-century Viking hero.

364

Randver: legendary son of the king of the Goths, who was hanged by his father.

Rhun: a northern British warrior, perhaps Urien's son.

Rind: a goddess or giantess.

Robert Bruce: King of Scots, †1329.

Rognvald: a Viking.

Rognvald: the name of three earls:

(1) Earl Rognvald of Moer (early tenth century), from whom the Orcadian dynasty was descended.

(2) Earl Rognvald Brusason of Orkney, defeated and killed by Earl Thorfinn.

(3) Earl Rognvald Kali of Orkney, poet and crusader (†1158).

Sadhbh: ancestress of the Connacht kings.

Sadhbh: mother of Raghnall, king of Man.

Sanngrid: a valkyrie.

Scurfy: a legendary Viking, occupier of Orkney.

Senyllt: One of 'The Three Generous Men of the Island of Britain' in one text of the medieval Welsh triads. See Bromwich (1961, 1978), 5, 508.

Sibylla: queen and wife of Alexander I (1122).

Sif: a goddess.

Sigmund: a legendary hero.

Sigtrygg: King of Dublin in the early 11th century.

Sigurd: Earl Sigurd II the Stout, of Orkney, †1014.

Sigurd Vesetason: a Jomsviking, brother of Bui and maternal uncle of Vagn Akason.

Sigvaldi Strut-Haraldsson: a Jomsviking, brother of Thorkel the Tall.

Simeon: a devout man who was in the Temple when Jesus was presented, and held the infant in his arms (Luke 2: 25–35).

Simeon: poet, early 12th century.

Sinfjotli: a legendary hero, son of Sigmund.

Skogul: a valkyrie.

Solmund: a Norwegian nobleman.

Solomon: a companion of Bishop Herbert's, here called a knight. He may have been the Solomon who, according to Anderson (1922), vol ii, 257, succeeded Ealdred as dean of the church of Glasgow.

Somerled: son of Gille-Brighde, King of the Isles and Argyll (1153–64), and founder of the dynasty from whom the later Lords of the Isles descended.

Susanna: in the Book of Daniel, an honest and faithful woman unjustly accused of adultery and saved by Daniel's quick-witted interrogation of her accusers.

Svein: Svein Asleifarson, an Orcadian nobleman and Viking, who held land at Gairsay. Active c. 1135–c. 1171.

Svidrir: an Odin-name.

Svipul: a valkyrie.

Svolnir: an Odin-name.

Thomas à Becket: martyr, †1170.

Thora: first wife of Ragnar Lodbrok.

Thord Kolbeinsson: an Icelander.

Thorfinn: Earl Thorfinn the Mighty of Orkney.

Thorgerd Holgi's Bride: Hakon's tutelary goddess.

Thorhall Asgrimsson: a 12th-century Icelander, resident in Orkney.

Thorir: Earl Thorir of Moer, the brother of Turf-Einar; he stayed in Norway and inherited his father's earldom.

Thorkell: Strut-Haraldsson, known as 'the Tall', a Jomsviking, brother of Sigvaldi.

Thorketil: known as Leira ('mud-flats'), a Norwegian chieftain, father of Ingibjorg.

Thorleif Thorkelsson: an Icelander fighting for Hakon Sigurdsson.

Thuvahel (or variously Tuduehal, Tudvael, Tuduvallus, Tudwal): a king who, according to legend, opposed Nynia and got his come-uppance. Possibly Tudwal of Strathclyde, father of Rydderch Hael; or Túathal Maelgarb of Ireland (†544).

Toirrdhelbhach: Toirrdhelbhach Úa Conchobair, king of Connacht, †1156, father of Cathal Crobhdherg.

Torcuill: from Norse Thorkell, a noble of the western isles.

Treebeard: a Viking.

Tuathal Teachtmhar: legendary king of Tara.

Turf-Einar: traditionally, the second Earl of Orkney.

Úa Cais: a member of the Uí Briain kings of Thomond; Donnchadh Cairbrech.

Ull: a god-name.

Ulph: a warrior connected with Urien Rheged: his war-leader, or perhaps another name for Urien.

Unhwch: a warrior associated with Dunawd Fyrr and Urien Rheged.

Urien: king of Rheged in the later sixth century.

Vagn Akason: a Jomsviking, son of Aki Palna Tokason.

Valthjof: a Viking.

Veseti: a chieftain of Bornholm, father of Bui and maternal grandfather of Vagn Akason.

Vigfus Viga-Glumsson: an Icelander fighting for Hakon Sigurdsson.

Volnir: a Viking.

William: commissioner of manuscript of the *Life of Columba* in the early 12th century?

William Wallace: leader of struggle for Scottish independence in the period from 1297 on; Guardian of Scotland; executed August, 1305.

Ygg: a name for Odin.

Ymir: the primeval giant.

Zechariah: father of John the Baptist.

BIBLIOGRAPHY

Abbreviations

AT = *Annals of Tighernach*, edited by W. Stokes, *Revue Celtique* 17-18 (1896-97).
AU = *Annals of Ulster*, edited by Seán mac Airt, Dublin, 1983.
CS = *Chronicon Scotorum*, W. Hennessy, London, 1866.
VC = *Vita Columbae* by Adomnán; see Anderson and Anderson (1961).

Amours, F. J. (1914) *The Original Chronicle of Andrew of Wyntoun*, vol. 1 (Scottish Text Society 63, Edinburgh).
Amours, F. J. (1907) *The Original Chronicle of Andrew of Wyntoun*, vol. 5 (Scottish Text Society 56, Edinburgh).
Anderson, A. O. and Anderson, M.O. (1961) *Adomnán's Life of Columba*, Oxford, (rev. ed. 1991).
Anderson, A. O. (1922) *Early Sources of Scottish History*, 2 vols. (reprinted Stamford, 1990).
Barnes, Michael (1984) 'Norn', *Scripta Islandica* 35, 23-42.
Barnes, Michael (1993) 'Norse in the British Isles' in Anthony Faulkes and Richard Perkins, edd., *Viking Revaluations*, London, 65-84.
Barnes, Michael P. (1994) *The Runic Inscriptions of Maeshowe, Orkney*, Uppsala.
Barnes, Michael P. (1998) *The Norn Language of Orkney and Shetland*, Lerwick.
Bennett, J. A. W. (1984) *Poetry of the Passion: Studies in Twelve Centuries of English Verse*, Oxford.
Bergin, O. (1955) 'Irish Grammatical Tracts V. Metrical Faults: NLI MS. 3 (Phillipps 7022)', *Ériu* 17, 259-93.
Bergin, Osborn (1970) *Irish Bardic Poetry*, Dublin.
Bernard, J. H. and Atkinson, R. (edd.) (1898) *The Irish Liber Hymnorum*, Henry Bradshaw Society, xiii & xiv, 2 vols., London.
Beveridge, J. (1941) 'Two Scottish Thirteenth-century Songs with Original Melodies', *RSCHS* 7, 1-11.
Bibire, Paul (1988) 'The poetry of Earl Rǫgnvaldr's court', in Barbara E. Crawford, ed., *St Magnus Cathedral and Orkney's Twelfth-century Renaissance*, Aberdeen, 208-40.
Blume, Clemens (1908) *Analecta Hymnica*, vol. 51.

Breatnach, R.A. (1941–2) 'Marbhna Fhearchoir Í Mháoil Chíaráin', *Éigse* 3, 165–85.

Broderick, G. (1991) *Cronica Regum Mannie et Insularum*, Douglas.

Bromwich, Rachel (1961, 1978) *Trioedd Ynys Prydein*, Caerdydd.

Bromwich, Rachel & Jones, R. Brinley (edd.) (1978) *Astudiaethau ar yr Hengerdd/ Studies in Old Welsh Poetry*, Cardiff.

Broun, D. (1991) 'The Literary Record of St Nynia: Fact and Fiction?', *Innes Review*, XLII, no. 2 (1991) 143–50.

Brundage, James (1962) *The Crusades: A Documentary Survey*, Milwaukee.

Calder, George (1917) *Auraicept na n-Éces*, Dublin.

Cameron, A. (1892) *Reliquiae Celticae* vol. 1, Inverness.

Clancy, Joseph P. (1965) *Medieval Welsh Lyrics*, London.

Clancy, Joseph P. (1970) *The Earliest Welsh Poetry*, London.

Clancy, T. O. and Márkus, G. (1995) *Iona: The Earliest Poetry of a Celtic Monastery*, Edinburgh.

Clancy, T. O. (forthcoming) 'A Gaelic polemic quatrain from the reign of Alexander I, c. 1113'.

Colgan, *Acta Sanctorum Hiberniae* (1645) Mar. 18.

Crossley-Holland, Kevin (1984) *The Anglo-Saxon World: An Anthology*, Oxford.

De Geer, Ingrid (1988) 'Music and the Twelfth-century Orkney Earldom: A Cultural Crossroads in Musicological Perspective', in B.E. Crawford (ed.) *St Magnus Cathedral and Orkney's Twelfth-century Renaissance*, Aberdeen, pp. 241–63.

de Vries, Jan (1964–67) *Altnordische Literaturgschichte*. Berlin.

Dickins, Bruce Ross, and Alan S. C. (1934), *The Dream of the Rood*, London.

Einar Ol. Sveinsson, ed. (1954) *Brennu-Njáls Saga*, Reykjavik.

Fell, Christine (1993) 'Norse studies: then, now and hereafter', in Anthony Faulkes & Richard Perkins, edd., *Viking Revaluations*, London, 85–99.

Fidjestøl, Bjarne (1992) 'Bjarni Kolbeinsson' in Pulsiano and Wolf (1992) 48.

Finlay, Alison (1995) 'Skalds, troubadours and sagas', *Saga-Book* XXIV/2–3, 105–53.

Finnur Jónsson, *Den norsk-islandske skjaldedigtning*, Copenhagen, 1912–15.

Forbes-Leith, W. (ed.) (1896) *The Life of St Margaret Queen of Scotland, by Turgot Bishop of St Andrews*, Edinburgh.

Ford, Patrick K. (1974) *The Poetry of Llywarch Hen*, Berkeley.

Geary, Patrick (1983) 'Humiliation of Saints' in Stephen Wilson,

369

ed., *Saints and their Cults: Studies in Religious Sociology, Folklore and History*, Cambridge, 123–40.

Gillies, William (1979–80) 'A religious poem ascribed to Muireadhach Ó Dálaigh', *Studia Celtica* 14/15, 81–6.

Gillies, William (1987) 'Gaelic: the classical tradition' in R. D. S. Jack, ed., *The History of Scottish Literature, vol. 1: Medieval and Renaissance*, Aberdeen.

Gillies, William (1990) 'A death-bed poem ascribed to Muireadhach Albanach', *Celtica* 21, 156–72.

Greene, David & Frank O'Connor (1967) *A Golden Treasury of Irish Poetry* AD 600–1200, London.

Gruffydd, R. Geraint (1990) 'where was *Rhaedr Derwennydd* (*Cann Aneirin*, Line 1114)?; in A. T. E. Matonis and D. F. Melia, edd., *Celtic Language, Celtic Culture: A Festschrift for Eric P. Hamp*, California.

Heinrichs, Anne (1992) 'Krákumál' in Pulsiano and Wolf (1992), 368–9.

Herbert, M. and Ó Riain, P. (1988) *Betha Adamnáin: The Life of a Adamnán*, Dublin.

Hill, Peter (1997) *Whithorn and St Ninian: The Excavation of a Monastic Town 1984–91*, Stroud.

Holtsmark, Anne (1937) 'Bjarne Kolbeinsson og hans forfatterskap', *Edda* 37, 1–17.

Howlett, David (1976) 'A reconstruction of the Ruthwell crucifixion poem', *Studia Neophilologia* 48, 54–8.

Jackson, Kenneth H. (1969) *The Gododdin: The Oldest Scottish Poem*, Edinburgh.

Jackson, Kenneth H. (1971) *A Celtic Miscellany*, Harmondsworth.

Jarman, A. O. H. (1988) *Aneirin: Y Gododdin*, Llandysul.

Jarman, A. O. H. and Hughes, Glyn (1992) *A Guide to Welsh Literature, vol. 1*, Cardiff.

Jômsvikinga Saga. The Saga of the Jomsvikings, N. F. Blake, ed., London, 1962.

Jón Stefánsson (1907) 'Biarne Kolbeinsson, the skald, bishop of Orkney, 1188–1223', *Orkney and Shetland Old-Lore Miscellany I/1*, 43–7.

Jónas Kristjánsson (1988) *Eddas and Sagas*, Reykjavík.

Kelly, F. (1973) 'A poem in praise of Columb Cille', *Ériu* 24, 1–34.

Kelly, F. (1975) 'Tiughraind Bhécáin', *Ériu* 26, 66–98.

Kennedy, Charles W. (1952) *Early English Christian Poetry*, London.

Koch, John T. (1995) with J. Carey, *The Celtic Heroic Age: Literary*

Sources for Ancient Celtic Europe and Early Ireland and Wales, Malden, Massachusetts.

Kock, Ernst A. (1923–44) *Notationes norrœnæ: anteckningar till Edda och skaldediktning*. Lund.

Kolsrud, O. and Reiss, G (1913) *Tvo Norrøne Latinske Kvæde med Melodiar utgjevne fraa Codex Upsalensis C233*, Cristiania.

Lindow, John (1981) 'Narrative and the nature of skaldic poetry', *Arkiv för nordisk filologi* 92, 94–121.

MacDiarmaid, Hugh (1946) *A Golden Treasury of Scottish Poetry*, London.

Mackintosh, Donald (1819) *Collection of Gaelic Proverbs*, Edinburgh.

Macquarrie, Alan (1985) *Scotland and the Crusades*, Edinburgh.

Macquarrie, Alan (1997) *The Saints of Scotland: Essays in Scottish Church History, AD 450–1093*, Edinburgh.

MacQueen, J. (1961) *St Nynia* (2nd edn., 1990).

MacQueen, W. (1960) 'Miracula Nynie Episcopi', *Transactions of the Dumfriesshire and Galloway Natural History and Antiquarian Society*, vol. xxxviii.

Márkus, Gilbert (1998) 'Almsgiving: the heart of the spiritual life', *Spirituality* 18, 158–64.

McGeown, Hugh and Gerard Murphy (1953) 'Giolla Brighde-Albanach's vision of Donnchadh Cairbrech', *Éigse* 7, 80–3.

McKenna, Lambert (1939) *Aithdhioghluim Dána* vol. 1; (1940) vol. 2.

McLauchlan, T. (1862) *The Dean of Lismore's Book*, Edinburgh.

McTurk, Rory (1991) *Studies in Ragnars saga loðbrókar and its Major Scandinavian Analogues*, Oxford.

Meek, Donald E. (1998) ' "Norsemen and Noble Stewards": the MacSween poem in the Book of the Dean of Lismore', *Cambrian Medieval Celtic Studies* 34, 1–49.

Meyer, Kuno (1894) *Hibernica Minora*, Oxford.

Meyer, K. (1912) 'Sanas Cormaic', *Anecdota from Irish Manuscripts* IV, Halle/ Dublin.

Meyer, K. (1915) 'Mitteilungen aus irische Handschriften', *ZCP* 10.

Meyer, Kuno (1918) 'Mitteilungen aus irischen Handschriften', *ZCP* 12, 392–5.

Meyer, K. (1919) *Bruchstücke der älteren Lyrik Irlands*, Berlin.

Muir, B. J. (1988) *A Pre-Conquest English Prayer-Book*, Woodbridge.

Mundt, M. ed. (1977) *Hákonar saga Hákonarsonar*, Oslo.

Murphy, Gerard (1944) 'Giolla Brighde's Vision of Rolf Mac-Mahon', *Éigse* 4, 93–7.

Murphy, Gerard (1953) 'Two Irish poems written from the Mediterranean in the thirteenth century', *Éigse* 7, 71–9.

Murphy, G. (1956) *Early Irish Lyrics*, Oxford.

Murphy, G. (1961) *Early Irish Metrics*, Dublin.

Njal's Saga, tr. Magnus Magnusson and Hermann Pálsson, Harmondsworth, 1960.

Ó Carragáin, Éamonn (1987–8), 'The Ruthwell crucifixion poem in its iconographic and liturgical contexts', *Peritia* 6–7, 1–71.

Ó Cuív, Brian (1957) 'A Poem in praise of Raghnall, king of Man', *Éigse* 8, 283–301.

Ó Cuív, Brian (1961) 'Eachtra Mhuireadhaigh Í Dhálaigh', *Studia Hibernica* 1, 56–69.

Ó Cuív, Brain (1968) 'A poem attributed to Muireadhach Ó Dálaigh', in J. Carney & D. Greene, edd., *Celtic Studies: essays in memory of Angus Matheson, 1912–1962*, London, 92–8.

Ó Cuív, Brian (1969–70A) 'A pilgrim's poem', *Éigse* 13, 105–9.

Ó Cuív, Brian (1969–70B) 'A poem for Cathal Croibhdhearg Ó Conchubhair', *Éigse* 13, 195–202.

O'Brien, M.A. (1952), 'A Middle-Irish poem on the birth of Áedán mac Gabráin and Brandub mac Echach', *Ériu* 16, 157–70.

O'Curry, Eugene (1873) *Manners and Customs of the Ancient Irish*, vol. 3.

O'Donovan, J. (1868) *Cormac's Glossary (with notes and indices by W. Stokes)*, Calcutta.

O'Rahilly, T. F. (1927) *Measgra Dánta* I & II, Cork.

O'Rahilly, T. F. (1926) *Dánta Grádha*, Cork.

Orkneyinga Saga, edited by Finnbogi Guðmundsson (Reykjavik, 1965).

Orkneyinga Saga: the History of the Earls of Orkney, trans. Hermann Palsson and Paul Edwards, (Harmondsworth, 1988).

Pennar, Meirion (tr.) (1988) *Taliesin Poems*, Lampeter.

Percy, Thomas (1763) *Five Pieces of Runic Poetry Translated from the Islandic Language*, London.

Plummer, Charles (1925) *Irish Litanies*, London.

Pope, John C. (1981) *Seven Old English Poems*, New York, 2nd edn.

Powell, James M. (1986) *Anatomy of a Crusade, 1213–1221*, Philadelphia.

Pulsiano, Phillip and Wolf, Kirsten, edd. with Paul Acker and Donald K. Fry (1992), *Medieval Scandinavia: An Encyclopedia*, Hamden, Connecticut.

Purser, John (1992) *Scotland's Music: A History of the Traditional and Classical Music of Scotland from Early Times to the Present Day*, Edinburgh.

Quiggin, E. C. (1912) 'A poem by Gilbride Macnamee in Praise of Cathal O'Conor', in O. Bergin and C. Marstrander, edd., *Miscellany presented to Kuno Meyer*, 167–9.

Radner, J. (1978) *The Fragmentary Annals of Ireland*, Dublin.

Reeves, William (1857) *The Life of Saint Columba written by Adomnán*, Dublin.

Roberts, Brynley F., ed. (1988) *Early Welsh Poetry: Studies in the Book of Aneirin*, Aberystwyth.

Rowland, Jenny (1990) *Early Welsh Saga Poetry: A Study and Edition of the Englynion*, Cambridge.

Sammes, Aylett (1676) *Britannia Antiqua Illustrata*, London.

Scotichronicon, vol. 5, edited by Simon Taylor and D. E. R. Watt with Brian Scott (Aberdeen, 1990).

Scotichronicon, vol. 6, edited by Norman Shead, Wendy Stevenson, D. E. R. Watt with Alan Borthwick, R. E. Latham, J. R. S. Philips and Martin S. Smith (Aberdeen, 1991).

Scotichronicon, vol. 7, edited by A. B. Scott and D. E. R. Watt with Ulrike Morét and Norman F. Shead (Aberdeen, 1996).

Skene, W. F. (1871), *Johannis de Fordun: Chronica Gentis Scotorum*, Edinburgh.

Skene, W. F. (1880) *Celtic Scotland*, vol. 3.

Stokes, W. (1899) 'The Bodleian *Amra Choluimb Chille*', *Revue Celtique* 20, 31–55, 132–83, 248–89, 400–37.

Strecker, K. (1923) *Monumenta Germanica Historica: Poetae Latini Aevi Carolini*, IV, Berlin.

Swanton, Michael (1970) *The Dream of the Rood*, Manchester/New York.

Thomas, Gwyn (1976) *Y Traddodiad Barddol*, Caerdydd.

Thomson, D. S. (1960–8) 'The MacMhuirich Bardic Family', *Transactions of the Gaelic Society of Inverness* 43, 276–304.

Thomson, D. S. (1989) *An Introduction to Gaelic Poetry*, 2nd edn, Edinburgh.

Thurneysen, Rudolf (1891) 'Mittelirische Verslehren', *Irische Texte* 3.1, 1–182, Leipzig.

Walsh, Paul (1933) *Gleanings from Irish Manuscripts*, 2nd edn., Dublin.

Wasserschleben, Hermann (1885) *Die irische Kanonensammlung*, Leipzig.

Watson, W. J. (1937) *Scottish Verse from the Book of the Dean of Lismore* (Scottish Gaelic Texts Society 1), Edinburgh.

Williams, Ifor & Williams, J. E. Caerwyn (edd.) (1968) *The Poems of Taliesin,* Dublin.

Williams, Ifor (1935, 1970) *Canu Llywarch Hen,* Caerdydd.

Williams, Ifor (1938, 1970) *Canu Aneirin,* Caerdydd.

Williams, J. E. Caerwyn and Ford, Patrick K. (1992) *The Irish Literary Tradition,* Cardiff.

Wilson. P. A. (1964) 'St Ninian and Candida Casa: literary evidence from Ireland', *Transactions of the Dumfriesshire and Galloway Natural History and Archaeological Society* (41) 156–85.

Woods, Isobel (1987), ' "Our Awin Scottis Use": Chant Usage in Medieval Scotland', *Journal of the Royal Musical Association* 112, 21–37.